15.95

THERE ARE TWO ERRORS IN THE THE TITLE OF THIS BOOK

broadview press

THERE ARE TWO ERRORS IN THE THE TITLE OF THIS BOOK

a sourcebook of philosophical
puzzles, problems, and paradoxes

Robert M. Martin

broadview press

Cataloguing in Publication Data

Martin, Robert M.
   There are two errors in the the title of this book: a sourcebook of philosophical puzzles, problems, and paradoxes

ISBN 0-921149-98-0

1. Paradoxes. 2. Puzzles. I. Title.

BC199.P2M37 1992   165   C92-094870-7

copyright © 1992, Broadview Press

design and typesetting by Fredrik Graver

Broadview Press gratefully acknowledges the support of the Canada Council, the Ontario Arts Council, and the Ontario Publishing Centre

broadview press   or   broadview press
P.O. Box 1243   269 Portage Rd.
Peterborough, Ont.   Lewiston, NY
K9J 7H6   Canada   14092   USA

printed in Canada

Table of Contents

To Thea and Sheldon

ACKNOWLEDGEMENTS

The items in this book have three sources:

(1) Some were invented by me

(2) Others were thought up by other philosophers

(3) Some are part of the folklore of the philosophy profession, or of the general tradition of jokes and puzzles.

I have tried to acknowledge in footnotes the inventors or promulgators of items in the second category. But sometimes the creations of individuals wind up in the third category: they are passed from philosopher to philosopher, and their origin becomes obscure. I hope I will be forgiven, then, for occasional omission of a crediting footnote.

For their ideas and encouragement I offer my grateful thanks to my friends and colleagues Victoria McGeer, Duncan MacIntosh, Sheldon Wein, Roland Puccetti, Richmond Campbell, Ed Mares, Nathan Brett, and Terry Tomkow; also to George J. Martin, and to the participants in the Sunday Forum, Heritage Village, Southbury, Connecticut. I also thank Charles Curry for pointing out a mistake (not in the title!) in the first printing.

These days it seems that publishers consider for publication only manuscripts that are almost exactly like dozens of books already selling well. Don LePan of Broadview Press is an exception to this rule. I offer him my gratitude, both for his courage in publishing this odd work and for his helpfulness while it was in preparation.

ABOUT THIS BOOK

Philosophical writing is always ponderous, pompous, tedious, technical, obscure, and grimly serious, right? Wrong.

Actually, philosophy is fun. It's interesting. It answers questions you've always wondered about and raises questions you've never thought of. It tickles your imagination and your funny-bone, and expands your mind. This book is designed to prove all that to you.

Philosophy starts when something goes wrong. Sometimes perfectly ordinary things seem inexplicable when you start to think about them. Sometimes perfectly reasonable assumptions lead, by perfectly acceptable reasoning, to bizarre and unbelievable conclusions. Sometimes ordinary ideas are put together in a new way, and something surprising emerges. So this book is full of puzzles—that's where philosophy begins.

But that's not where it ends. Some students get the mistaken and discouraging idea that the subject contains only unanswerable questions, and wonder what the point is. This idea is wrong. We'll look at the beginnings, at least, of some very good, surprising, interesting answers.

> You'll notice that some paragraphs in this book are written in this contrasting type-style. In these parts answers are given to questions just raised. When you see a passage in this type-style coming up, that's a good place to stop reading for a while and try to figure out answers yourself. Then when you read these passages, you can see whether your answers match what's given. Don't worry if, from time to time, you come up with a different answer from the one given: sometimes there are many ways to answer a question. Try to see why the answer given is plausible. Is it better than yours?

Some solutions philosophers have proposed are much too complicated to be included in here, of course. You'll notice, from time to time, sections labelled "For Further Reading," which tell you where to look for further discussion of the issues.

In many cases, however, philosophical debate still rages about questions that have been around for a long time. That's what makes the introductory study of philosophy different from the introduction to many other subjects, where you learn only what's settled and uncontroversial. And that's one reason why some people enjoy philosophy more than these other subjects: you can join in the debate right from the start.

> *Philosophers love to fool around with ideas. A good deal of chatter around any university philosophy department consists of jokes, anecdotes, and silly intellectual play. Often, however, these bits of fluff have a real philosophical purpose. (Well, sometimes they do.) In this book you'll occasionally come across a passage written in this type-style; this indicates a fluffy bit. Don't ignore it! It's usually not merely for fun. Even when it seems silly or irrelevant, there's something philosophically important about it—something deeper that it illustrates, which merits thought.*

CHAPTER I

DIFFERENCES THAT MAKE NO DIFFERENCE:
The Practical Meaning of Questions
and Answers

1. William James and the Squirrel

Around the beginning of the Twentieth Century, the American pragmatist philosopher William James described this puzzle:

> Some years ago, being with a camping party in the mountains, I returned from a solitary ramble to find every one engaged in a ferocious metaphysical dispute. The corpus of the dispute was a squirrel—a live squirrel supposed to be clinging to one side of a tree-trunk; while over against the tree's opposite side a human being was imagined to stand. This human witness tries to get sight of the squirrel by moving rapidly round the tree, but no matter how fast he goes, the squirrel moves as fast in the opposite direction, and always keeps the tree between himself and the man, so that never a glimpse of him is caught. The resultant metaphysical problem now is this: *Does the man go round the squirrel or not?*... Every one had taken sides, and was obstinate....

Who is right?

> The important point here is not who is right, but what James says about this problem:

>> "Which party is right," I said, "depends on what you *practically mean* by 'going round' the squirrel. If you mean passing from the north of him to the east, then to the south, then to the west, and then to the north of him again, obviously the man does go round him.... But if on the contrary you mean being first in front of him, then on the right of him, then behind him, then on his left, and finally in front again, it is quite as obvious that the man fails to go round him, for by the com-

> ments the squirrel makes, he keeps his belly turned to-
> wards the man all the time....

This is a clever solution, and one that marks a turning point in modern philosophy. James argues that this example demonstrates, in trivial miniature, a method for solving otherwise unsolvable metaphysical disputes, and much of philosophy since then uses this methodology.

The influence of this style has not always been beneficial. Spend some time in a bar where undergraduate philosophy majors hang out, and you might hear a good deal of pompous but useless philosophizing to the following effect: "But what do you really *mean* by 'God'/'justice'/'good'/'freedom'/etc., etc.?" It's easy to see why bystanders get the idea that philosophy has abandoned what they take to be its historical mission—The Search For Wisdom—and is now a trivial search for definitions. And why they think that philosophers would save a lot of time and talk merely by consulting a good dictionary.

But this sort of quibble over words is far from what James—or contemporary philosophers—really do. James's example is misleading: it's merely a trivial verbal dispute that disappears as soon as the ambiguous senses of a phrase are revealed. But solving real philosophical disputes is rarely this simple a matter.

When James calls the squirrel argument a "metaphysical problem," he's being ironic. There are traditional metaphysical problems in philosophy that are not so trivial; and getting clear on exactly what is "practically meant" is often a very subtle matter. But James may be right in thinking that this sort of methodology can help with real philosophical problems.

Consider, for example, the dispute over the justice of capital punishment. Philosophers might want first to try to answer the question, "What's really involved in *justice*?" This question asks about the "practical meaning" of 'justice', and it's an important and difficult question, not solvable merely by looking the word up in a dictionary. We want to know, for example, what tests we should use to judge whether some policy is just or not; so when a dictionary tells us that 'justice' means "moral rightness; equity. Honour; fairness. Fair handling; due reward or treatment,"[1] that's not much help.

---

1   *The American Heritage Dictionary of the English Language* (New York: American Heritage, 1969), p. 711.

The Unanswerable

- What's the opposite of a duck?
- What does Thursday weigh?
- What was Snow White's father's name?
- What time is it right now on the moon?
- How many angels can dance on the head of a pin?

I'll bet you can't answer these questions. Why can't you? The reason is not that there's some information you lack. There's something wrong with each question.

SOME QUESTIONS TO THINK ABOUT: Why are these questions unanswerable? Is it the same reason in each case? Is it that there's nothing "practically meant" by these questions?

Some philosophers have thought that many traditional philosophical questions lack "practical meaning," and they conclude that they're phony questions nobody should waste time thinking about. Medieval philosophers devoted a lot of time to thinking about angels, but perhaps you shouldn't be too quick in dismissing their problem as a phony one before you've studied in depth what they wrote; perhaps for them there was some upshot to this question.

FOR FURTHER READING: The James quote is from "What Pragmatism Means," in *Essays in Pragmatism* (New York: Hafner, 1948), p. 141. The "ordinary language" philosophers, for example J.L. Austin and Gilbert Ryle, often provide subtle, interesting, and surprising analyses of what is "practically meant." Just about any of the many works by Austin or Ryle provides a good example of this methodology in action. A particulary good example is Austin's article "A Plea For Excuses" (originally published as "The Presidential Address to the Aristotelian Society, 1956" in *Proceedings of the Aristotelian Society, 1956-1957*, vol. 57. The article appears in many anthologies, including J.L. Austin, *Philosophical Papers* (Oxford: Clarendon Press, 1961) and V.C. Chappell, ed., *Ordinary Language* (Englewood Cliffs, NJ: Prentice-Hall, 1964).) Chappell's book also contains an article on ordinary language philosophy by Ryle. A.J. Ayer is a good example of a philosopher who rejects many traditional philosophical problems as meaningless. See his *Language, Truth, and Logic* (New York: Dover Publications, n.d.)

2. When Everything Gets Bigger

Could you tell if, one day, everything in the universe suddenly doubled in size?[2]

> Your shoes would suddenly get twice as big, but so would your feet. You would suddenly become ten or twelve feet tall, but your clothes, your room, and your car would also double. Yardsticks would become twice as long. The corner store would be twice as far away, but walking there would take the same time because your legs would be twice as long. Everything would be twice as far away, but you would double in size, so they would look the same distance away as before. There would be no *practical* effect of this change at all. Applying James's method to this case would tell us that there's no practical difference between the idea that everything doubles in size, and the idea that everything stays the same. So a dispute whether everything has just doubled or not is perhaps really no dispute at all. (Is this right?)

Proponents of the "relational" theory of space say that there is no such thing as the absolute size of anything: we ascertain something's size by comparing it to other things. So we shouldn't say that this mass doubling might or might not happen: we should rather say that it makes no sense even to contemplate it.

A similar point can be made about the supposition that everything suddenly speeds up to twice as fast as it used to be, or that everything suddenly moves three feet to the left.

The Right-Handed Universe

Let's apply this sort of approach to another sort of case. Imagine that the universe contained nothing at all except one *right* hand. Now, imagine that the universe contained nothing at all except one *left* hand. Are you imagining two *different* universes?

> All the relations between points in the first universe would be exactly the same as in the second universe. The "relational" theory of space tells us that there is no absolute "handedness" of anything. There wouldn't be any difference between these universes.

But the great nineteenth-century German philosopher Immanuel Kant argued that there *is* a difference between a universe containing only one right hand and a universe containing only one left hand, and so concluded that the relational theory of space must be wrong. But the

2   This famous puzzle is due to the French mathematician Jules Henri Poincaré.

relationist can reply that Kant is wrong: there is no difference between these universes.

3. Mildred's Peculiar Sensations

Look around until you see something green. While you're looking at that green thing, you are having a particular kind of visual experience. Call that kind of experience a GE (for "green experience"). We think that others also get GEs when they look at green things, but suppose that your friend Mildred doesn't. I don't mean that Mildred is blind or colour-blind. I mean that her experiences are systematically different from yours. When she looks at something green, she has the experience you get when you look at something yellow—a YE. Her experiences, we imagine, are systematically transposed, as given by the following table:

OBJECT IS:	RED	ORANGE	YELLOW	GREEN	BLUE	VIOLET
YOU GET:	RE	OE	YE	GE	BE	VE
SHE GETS:	VE	BE	GE	YE	OE	RE

So whenever Mildred looks at a red thing, she gets a VE; whenever she looks at a blue thing, she gets an OE; and so on.[3]

Blind or colour-blind people sometimes act differently from people with normal vision; but Mildred doesn't. She has no trouble identifying green things. You ask her what colour the leaves of that tree are, and she unhesitatingly and correctly replies, "green." She has, of course, learned to associate the word 'green' with her YE, just as you have learned to associate the word 'green' with your GE. She can, at a glance, tell correctly which are the limes and which are the lemons in a pile of mixed citrus fruit. The lemons are the ones that give her a GE when she looks at them, and the limes give her a YE. Just like you, she drives through green lights and prepares to stop when the light turns yellow. In fact, all her behaviour is just like yours. Could you tell that there's something different about her experiences? Could she? Could anyone?

It seems that here we are imagining a difference that makes no difference. Perhaps there really is no difference. What we're imagining here seems In no way distinguishable from the supposition that her experiences are exactly the same as yours.

Some philosophers react to the proposal that Mildred has

3   This example occurs widely in the philosophical literature, and is called the "inverted spectrum."

5

inverted-spectrum sensations by claiming that this proposal is impossible. What is *meant* by 'a green experience' is nothing but the sensation one usually gets when looking at something green, so whatever Mildred gets when looking at limes is by definition a GE. It can't be anything else.

Another Inversion in Mildred

Now try to imagine that Mildred has "inverted experiences" of this sort: whenever you step on her toe, she feels pleasure. Whenever she is cold and tired and lies down in her nice warm bed, she feels pain. But she behaves just like the rest of us: she groans when you step on her toe and pushes you off. She hurries eagerly to get into bed after a cold and hectic day. The only difference is in her inward sensations. Peculiarly, she tries to avoid pleasures and to seek pain. Is this shown to be nonsense by the same sorts of considerations we raised when considering her inverted spectrum of visual sensations?

SOME QUESTIONS TO THINK ABOUT: If you think that it's impossible for Mildred to have inverted sensations, does this show that all that matters, when we try to determine what sensations someone has, is what they say, how they act, and what features of the external world they're interacting with? Suppose you were in Mildred's place. Would you be convinced that you actually felt pain when someone stepped on your toe?

4. A World of Fake Antiques

Philosophers have often imagined things that everyone knows aren't true, and challenged us to prove—or indeed to give any reason at all to think—that they're not true. One example is the Five-Minute Hypothesis (invented by Bertrand Russell[4] in 1921). Here's how this goes:

Imagine that the entire universe was created exactly five minutes ago, complete with all sorts of "signs" of a non-existent past. The soles of your shoes came into existence five minutes ago worn down, looking like they had been walked on for months. That stuff in the bowl in the back of your refrigerator came into existence covered with green fuzzy mould, just as if it had been left there for weeks. You were created five minutes ago complete with all sorts of fake memories of a past that never happened.

4   *The Analysis of Mind* (New York: Macmillan, 1921), pp. 159-160.

We can't prove that the Five-Minute Hypothesis is false by uncovering evidence around us of what happened more than five minutes ago. Finding a newspaper dated yesterday, for example, won't prove anything, because the hypothesis explains this and all such "evidence" of a past: all those things are fake antiques.

Notice that the Five-Minute Hypothesis and our ordinary way of thinking are tied in their relative ability to explain the way things seem now. Both the hypothesis that I really have been wearing those shoes for months, as I seem to remember, and the Five-Minute Hypothesis, explain why the soles of my shoes are worn. We can say: both hypotheses are consistent with all the evidence.

But consistency with all the evidence is not the only criterion we have for the truth of an explanatory hypothesis. Notice that the Five-Minute Hypothesis involves all sorts of unexplained coincidences. The shoes I pseudo-remember wearing are in fact now worn down, so there is a coincidental coherence between this pseudo-memory and the current state of the shoes. Similarly, another pair, that I pseudo-remember leaving in the back of my closet permanently just after I bought them are now, by coincidence, not worn down. Today's newspaper and the radio news both coincidentally report that the same thing happened yesterday. There are innumerable unexplained coincidences such as this involved in the Five-Minute Hypotheses. A hypothesis full of such unexplained coincidences is a bad one.

But why can't the Five-Minutist reply that a fiendishly clever demon has arranged all these coincidences to fool us?

One way of dealing with the Five-Minute Hypothesis is to treat it as another instance of a "difference" that makes no difference. But we can't resist thinking that it would be a *big* difference if this hypothesis were true.

> *The age of the universe was the subject of investigation by the Reverend James Ussher, Archbishop of Armagh. Ussher's* Annals of the Ancient and New Testaments, *a scholarly book published in 1650, reported the results of some careful calculations based on scripture: the universe was created in 4004 B.C. This date was accepted by the Church of England as authoritative and was printed in the margins of their Authorized Version of the Bible. More detailed computations by Doctor John Lightfoot, vice-chancellor of the University of Cambridge, made the matter more precise: the Creation took place on October 23, 4004 B.C., at 9 a.m. (Lightfoot didn't specify in which time zone it was 9 a.m.)*

> *As science progressed, evidence accumulated that some rocks were millions of years old. How could this be squared with the official view that nothing was more than six thousand years old? The answer given was analogous to the Five-Minute Hypothesis: In 4004 B.C., the world was created complete with rocks that seemed much older. They were fake antiques.*

5. The Brain in the Vat

Here's another example, similar to the Five-Minute Hypothesis. Imagine that you are actually a brain in a vat. That is, a mad scientist removed your brain at birth and installed it in a vat full of nutritive solution to keep it alive. Your brain has been connected by wires to a computer that feeds in incredibly complicated electrical impulses; as a result you have a rich variety of experiences that you take as sensations originating in the external world, but that are in fact all delusions. Like the Five-Minute Hypothesis, this hypothesis is consistent with all your current experience. Do you have any reason at all to think you are not such a brain in a vat?

A possible answer to this question depends on the account of what is involved in thinking about something, which will be discussed later in an item called "Thinking About Vienna" in Chapter XII. If that account is correct, then the only way for a thought to be *about* something is for it to be connected in the right sort of way to that thing. Now suppose that you really are a brain in a vat. All of your experiences, then, would have come from the wires planted in your brain. None of your thoughts would be connected in the right sort of way with the sky, or breakfast, or Vienna, so none of your thoughts would be about any of these things. Neither would your thoughts have the right sorts of connection with your brain, or with the vat it was in; so you wouldn't be able to have thoughts about your brain or its vat. (It's an interesting question whether you'd be able to have thoughts about anything at all.) So if you were in fact a brain in a vat, you couldn't believe that you were a brain in a vat, and you couldn't believe that you weren't.

SOME QUESTIONS TO THINK ABOUT: If this line of reasoning is right, what does it show? Perhaps it shows that the belief that one is a brain in a vat can't be true. If you were a brain in a vat you couldn't believe it.

But does that show that you're not a brain in a vat? Well, if you were, you couldn't believe you were. But it's still possible that you actually are a brain in a vat. If you were, then your beliefs would be about who-knows-what; but never mind. Have we actually proven that you're not a brain in a vat? Can we prove it? If not, then why do you think you aren't?

FOR FURTHER READING: The brain-in-the-vat example, and a version of the answer to this puzzle that we have considered, are found in Hilary Putnam's *Reason, Truth and History* (Cambridge: Cambridge University Press, 1981).

6. It's Practically True

William James's position is that questions about whose answers we seem to disagree are answered (or made to disappear) when we consider the "practical meaning" of what is being argued about. He thought that the real significance of the dispute whether X is true or false was what difference believing X would make to anyone's life. If there is no difference, then the dispute is empty. But where there is a difference, James argued that the test for whether X was true or false involved the evaluation of the practical results of believing X— whether people who believed X would be better off in coping with their surroundings than people who didn't. If they were better off, then there are grounds for believing X. What James has here is a theory of truth: X is true when believing X makes people better off.
Is this theory correct?

> Sometimes this theory gives results that look right. Suppose, for example, that Archibald believes that the Number 4 bus stops on this corner, and Millicent believes it doesn't. It's easy to imagine that the person who is correct is also the person who will be better off when she or he wants to catch the Number 4 bus.

But James had more controversial uses of his theory in mind. In his book *The Varieties of Religious Experience*,[5] he described what he took to be the typical psychological effects of religious conversion and belief. These effects, he claimed, were beneficial for the believer. Since the practical implications of religious belief are beneficial, it follows from his theory of truth that religious beliefs are true.

SOME QUESTIONS TO THINK ABOUT: James's defense of religious belief is, of course, open to debate. For one thing, we could question his claims about the beneficial effects of religious belief. But more importantly, we might wonder whether the fact that a belief is good for people is all there is to a belief's being true. Couldn't some beliefs be

5   New York: Longmans, Green, 1902.

good for people even though false? Couldn't some beliefs be bad for people even though true?

Suppose that a historian discovers what people ate for breakfast in Ancient Rome. It's hard to see how this belief could have any beneficial effect on us. The historian's belief is, then, true but useless. James's theory of truth cannot make sense of this claim; is his theory then mistaken?

FOR FURTHER READING: "Pascal's Wager," examined in Chapter II, in a section of the same name, is another argument for religious belief based on the benefits of that belief. In Chapter VII we'll take another critical look at the idea that the benefits of believing something are grounds for thinking it's true.

Into the Mainstream of Philosophy

In this chapter, as in all the following ones, there are what seems to be a rather random and disorganized bunch of musings, but there is method in this madness. The items in each chapter are, for the most part, connected to one of the major fields of academic philosophical study.

At the end of each chapter is an item titled "Into the Mainstream of Philosophy," where I'll briefly describe the general area of mainstream philosophical study relevant to the chapter at hand, occasionally mentioning the conventional names philosophers use to refer to their major areas of concern and their major positions on these areas. I'll pull together some of the musings into the chapter, to show you how they are systematically connected.

You've already seen some notes on where you might find further reading on the particular problems and positions discussed. In the "Into the Mainstream" items I'll often suggest how to find readings on the general issues raised in the chapter.

A good place to start reading philosophy is in any of the scores of major introductory philosophy anthologies widely available in university bookstores. The articles in anthologies are by a wide variety of philosophers, and are usually grouped by subject matter; you'll find contiguous articles arguing for different positions on the same question. Most anthologies contain articles that are important, deep, revealing, and at the same time understandable to someone not yet immersed in the field.

Well, then, about this first chapter:

We had a glance at James's views. His position, influential not only among American philosophers, is called pragmatism. It goes some way to answering questions about *meaning*—by telling us what the meaning of a question or of a declarative sentence is. It is also the germ of a theory of *truth*, holding that what it is for a sentence to be true is for it to be (putting things roughly) *useful*. The core of his position is that the meaning or truth of anything is to be determined by its connections with real-life experience. This position has had a rather radical effect in some areas. What are we to make of the (supposedly) meaningful—perhaps sometimes even true—things that are said in religion, for example, where talk about God and angels seems quite disconnected from everyday mundane reality? How are we to understand scientific theory? You can't ever experience an electron; so how can you talk about one? (Perhaps, on James's criterion, talk about electrons is "really" just talk about the sort of things we can interact with: light bulbs, electric meters, and so on.) How can historians talk about a past they can't interact with? How (if at all) can psychologists discover anything about the minds of other people, locked privately inside them?

Pragmatism has affinities with another view, popularized originally by a group of Viennese philosophers who came to England and America around the time of World War II: the Vienna Circle. Their view, called logical positivism, emphasized the necessity of sense-experience and practical testability in evaluating the truth, and understanding the meaning, of any statement. Like James's, this view tended at first to have a destructive, or at least a radically re-evaluative, effect on many areas of talk and enquiry.

Philosophy since it began has struggled with "sceptical questions": How do we know that we're not brains in a vat? How about the Five-Minute Hypothesis? What makes us think that there is an external world at all? (Maybe it's all hallucination!) How can you prove that anything is right or wrong? Pragmatism and logical positivism are both sometimes inclined to see these questions as meaningless: since an answer, whatever it may be, would make no difference in our experience, there's something wrong with the question. Not everyone has found this answer satisfying.

CHAPTER II

GOD:

The Philosophy of Religion

1. The Practical Meaning of Religious Talk

Murgatroyd and Millicent come across a patch of land containing flowers and weeds. The following discussion ensues:

Murgatroyd: A gardener must tend this plot.

Millicent: I don't think so. Look, it's full of weeds.

Murgatroyd: The gardener must like those weeds. They are nice, aren't they?

Millicent: Those weeds grow around here all by themselves; anyway, I've talked to people who live around here, and nobody told me anything about seeing any gardener at work.

Murgatroyd: Well, the gardener must have been here when everyone was asleep.

They take turns watching, day and night, but no gardener is seen. Murgatroyd explains this fact by supposing that the gardener must be invisible. They set up an electric alarm system sensitive to heat, and patrol with bloodhounds, but there's no reaction from either. Murgatroyd is still not convinced.

Murgatroyd: The gardener is not only invisible, but undetectable to the alarm system and without an odour the bloodhounds could smell.

Millicent: I'm getting fed up with your argument. Your gardener is supposed to be invisible and completely undetectable to anyone, and is supposed to have planted things the way they would have grown anyway. What makes him different from no gardener at all?

The analogy here is to arguments about God's existence. Believers often admit that there's a natural scientific explanation of the way things are. They also admit that God is undetectable by all the ordinary detection methods.

The question we might ask here is this: How is the assertion that such an undetectable God exists any different from the assertion that there isn't any God? Here's one possible answer:

> There's no real difference in beliefs or expectations about the real world in the religious believer and in the disbeliever. There's just a difference in how they feel about things. If so, then maybe there's no question about who is right and who is wrong.

SOME QUESTIONS TO THINK ABOUT: If this response to the invisible gardener story is right, then religions don't say things that should be judged true or false. What they say is more like poetry: the expression of feelings and attitudes. If you are a religious person, consider whether this squares with your view of religious "truths."

The response given above to the argument between Millicent and Murgatroyd is something like William James's response to the squirrel debate. Do you see the similarity?

FOR FURTHER READING: The parable of the invisible gardener, and the response to the question we've considered, are both found in John Wisdom's article "Gods," in *Proceedings of the Aristotelian Society*, 1944-45, reprinted in *Logic and Language*, ed. Antony Flew (Garden City, NY: Anchor, 1965) and elsewhere. For a three-way discussion of these issues, see Antony Flew, R.M. Hare, and Basil Mitchell, "Theology and Falsification," in *New Essays in Philosophical Theology*, ed. Antony Flew and Alasdair MacIntyre (New York: Macmillan, 1955).

One Hell of a Rainstorm

It says in the Bible that during the Flood, "all the high hills that were under the whole heaven were covered." The mathematician John Allen Paulos has done some calculations. He figures that in order to cover every mountain, there must have been ten to twenty thousand feet of water on the earth's surface, about half a billion cubic miles of water. It rained forty days and forty nights. To produce a flood of that size in those 960 hours, it must have rained, on average, fifteen feet of water per hour. A really heavy and destructive rainstorm in our day can put an inch or two of water on the ground per hour. But fifteen feet of water in an hour, Paulos remarks, is enough to sink an aircraft carrier. How did Noah's little wooden ark, loaded with thousands of animals, stay afloat?[1]

---

1   *Innumeracy: Mathematical Illiteracy and Its Consequences* (New York: Vintage, 1990), pp. 16-17.

Maybe you want to reply that this is just another one of those religious miracles we're not supposed to be able to understand. Or maybe you think that what's said in the Bible is not supposed to be taken literally like this. Perhaps someone who "believes in the Bible" need believe in different *facts* than someone who doesn't.

A QUESTION TO THINK ABOUT: Suppose you agree that the difference between believers in the Bible and non-believers *isn't* a matter of believing different facts. Then what is the difference?

2. God's Difficulties

Most religions believe that God is omnipotent. This means that God can do anything He wants to do. Could God create a stone too heavy for Him to lift?

Let's suppose He can. Then, if He did, He'd have created a stone that He couldn't lift. Since He couldn't lift it, He wouldn't be omnipotent. So let's suppose He can't. But then there is something God can't do, so He isn't omnipotent. Either way, omnipotence is impossible. Maybe omnipotence makes no sense.

The suggestion here is that major religions must be mistaken in thinking that there is an omnipotent God, because omnipotence is logically impossible.

God the Counterfeiter

Another thing God can't do is make a genuine ten dollar bill. God could, presumably, make an atom-for-atom duplicate of a genuine ten dollar bill which would fool everyone, but that bill would be counterfeit. Only bills produced by the government mint are genuine. God could, of course, make the mint produce a genuine bill, but He couldn't make one directly.

Here's another limit to God's omnipotence. The familiar poem says that "only God can make a tree," but perhaps God can't make a tree. According to some biologists, what it takes for something to count as an oak tree, for example, is that it has to have come from another oak tree. Suppose you manufactured something out of chemicals that looked and worked exactly like an oak tree, that even dropped acorns in the fall that grew into things just like it. What you made wouldn't be an oak tree, since it didn't come from an oak tree. Your inability to make an oak tree isn't the result of your lack of ability in biochemistry. No matter how accurate a look-alike you made out of chemicals, it wouldn't *count* as an oak tree, since oak trees are, *by definition*, what comes from other oak trees. So God, with infinite biochemical abilities, couldn't make an oak tree either.

These two peculiar cases have something in common. What it takes to be a genuine ten dollar bill or an oak tree is not merely a matter of what something is made of, or how its parts are put together, or how it works. In both cases, there has to be a *historical* characteristic present—something true about its past.

> *Historical characteristics played a role in a recent newsworthy event. During the riots and looting in Los Angeles, somebody broke into Frederick's of Hollywood, the famous erotic underwear store, and stole Madonna's bra from their Museum of Famous Underwear. Frederick's posted a huge reward for the return of the famous garment, and a few days later, a bra was brought in by someone claiming the reward. It was exactly the brand, model, and size of the one stolen earlier, but it was a phony: it wasn't the one worn by Madonna. It differed from the genuine article only in a historical characteristic. We can wonder: if all its present characteristics were identical with those of the real one, how did the Frederick's staff know it was a phony?*

SOME QUESTIONS TO THINK ABOUT: In order to count as an *antique*, something has to have a historical property: it has to have been made more than a certain number of years ago. Can you think of other categories that require historical properties?

We can distinguish between intrinsic and relational properties. The former are characteristics of a thing that are true of it in itself; the latter are true of it insofar as it is related to something else, or insofar as something happened at another time or place. Two things might be identical in all their intrinsic properties and differ only in their relational properties. A genuine ten dollar bill and a really perfect counterfeit are an example of such a pair. Historical properties are one sort of relational property; another is *ownership*. Imagine that you and I each own brand-new copies of the same book. The books are (almost perfectly) alike in all their intrinsic properties, but they differ in an important relational way: one is owned by me, and the other isn't. Because they're intrinsically indistinguishable, there might be no way for someone to tell which is mine and which is yours just by looking at them— that is, by examining their intrinsic properties. Of course, someone could tell which was mine if I had written my name in it, but then they would differ in a relevant intrinsic property.

This is another relational property: being the tallest mountain on earth. No matter how much you examined Mt. Everest, no matter how much you knew about its intrinsic properties, you couldn't tell whether it was the tallest mountain on earth unless you knew how it was related in size to the other mountains. Can you think of other sorts of relational property?

If you subscribe to a religion including belief in an omnipotent God, what sort of changes would you have to make if you were convinced that God really can't be omnipotent? Would that affect the real substance of your religion in important ways?

But can you think of ways to get around the problems about omnipotence? Here are some suggestions.

> The argument shows that it's logically impossible for anything to be omnipotent. But logical problems don't bother God. God isn't subject to the laws of logic. He can even do the logically impossible.

One problem with this answer is that it's impossible for us to understand the idea of doing the logically impossible. For example, suppose that I said to you, "I have filled a glass with water, but the glass has nevertheless remained empty." First you'd suspect that I was playing with words, or telling an obscure joke. But if I assured you that I was speaking literally, you would doubt what I was saying, not because you think I'm limited in my powers, but rather because the very idea of filling a glass that nevertheless remains empty makes no sense at all. If you allowed that I could do this, you would be attributing to me something that you, and nobody else, could understand.

Some religious people cheerfully admit that religious truths surpass all understanding. But other people aren't comfortable with the idea of saying, or trying to believe, things that make no sense.

Here's another suggestion for a response:

> Let's agree that if He couldn't create a stone too heavy for Him to lift, He wouldn't be omnipotent. If he could create this stone *and did*, then there would be a stone around He couldn't lift, so again He wouldn't be omnipotent. But suppose He *could* create this stone *but didn't*. Where's the problem with His omnipotence now?

A Proof That Everything Is Hunky-Dory

Let's assume that God, as conventional religions conceive of Him, really did create the universe. God, of course, wanted to create the best universe He could, and His omnipotence means that He was capable of doing anything He wanted. So it follows that this is the best of all possible universes. (This view has been called "cosmic Toryism," referring to the smug and complacent attitude of certain members of the British

Conservative Party.) You're wrong if you think that anything could be any better. Does that make you feel good? You should cheer up.

Now that you know that everything is perfect, you'd better be more careful about changing the way things are. When you walk through the woods, you might move a pebble an inch south, messing up God's perfect creation.

God Made Me Do It

The doctrine of God's omnipotence raises similar problems when connected with the idea that we have free will. Does the fact (if it is a fact) that we are free mean that our decisions can't be controlled by outside influences? If so, then there's another limitation on God's power. As in the unliftable stone example, we can put this problem in the form of a dilemma:[2] If God *can* create a person whose actions He can't control, then this person's actions would be a limit to His power—He wouldn't be omnipotent. If He *can't* create such a person, then that's a limit to His power—He wouldn't be omnipotent. Either way, omnipotence is impossible.

We might want to reply to this argument in a way analogous to the reply to the unliftable stone argument: that God *could* create an uncontrollable human but *doesn't*. But this reply won't work here: religions usually hold that God *did* in fact create humans with free will.[3]

3. How There Got to be Only One God

The belief that there is only one God who is genuinely perfect—infinite in power and knowledge—arose a long time ago, and there is little hard historical evidence about how it came about. Here, however, is one hypothesis.

Today's major monotheistic religions, Judaism, Christianity, and Islam, all have their origins in the Middle East: Judaism developed there first, then Christianity arose within the Jewish tradition and separated from it. Later the Muslims (the followers of Islam) branched off from Christianity. Is their common origin in the Middle East just a coincidence? Some people think not.

Most religions are polytheistic, recognizing the existence of a number of limited Gods. Polytheists often see one of the gods as the god of their group, the one who looks specially after their interests. In a sense,

2   In Chapter V I'll talk about what dilemmas are.
3   A similar problem about God's power is discussed much later, in the item called "God Knows What I'll Do."

polytheism reflects and encourages a sort of tolerance and inter-tribe stability. A polytheistic tribe typically accepts the existence not only of their own special god, but also of the gods of the neighbouring tribes.

In the hostile climate and terrain of the ancient Middle East, however, there must have been little tolerance and stability. Water and food were hard to come by. Often these necessities were available only for a short time in one place; when they ran out, the tribe had to move on. So tribes were nomadic, constantly on the move. Stability of territory could not develop, and we can imagine a good deal of inter-tribe conflict and hostility as one tribe encroached on another.

The constant hostility of these tribes did not encourage tolerant recognition of the others' gods. We can imagine that their conflict was reflected by religious competitiveness, with each tribe claiming that its god was bigger, better, stronger than the others'. "My god is stronger than yours!" says the priest of Tribe *A*. "Oh yeah? Well, my god is stronger than one hundred men!" claims the priest of Tribe *B*. "My god is stronger than one thousand men!" retorts the Tribe *A* priest. This continues. At last one tribe comes up with a topper that can't be beaten: "*My* god is *infinitely* strong. He knows *everything* and can do *anything* he wants." A god who is literally infinite in all his attributes must be the *only* real god there is. Thus monotheism.

The infinite god that results is a highly abstract entity, not much like the polytheistic gods, who are seen merely as people writ large. The logical problems we have examined regarding God's infinity are faced only by a highly rarefied and abstract monotheistic theology.

On this view, then, monotheism grows out of and encourages hostility to other religious groups, and encroachment on them. History and current events do seem to show an extraordinary amount of intolerance for other religions among the monotheistic religions, and even between the sects within them. Wars are not uncommon in history, of course, but wars based on religious intolerance seem especially prevalent among and between monotheists. Think of the Crusades, which were religious wars between the Christians and the Muslims; the waves of Christian anti-Semitism; and the present-day hostility and warfare between Middle Eastern Muslims and Jews. Rival sects of Muslims wage war in Lebanon and rival sects of Christians in Northern Ireland. The history of Christianity is marked by expansionism, the attempt to convert the rest of the world to its own unique God, often by force when persuasion fails.

Historians and theologians may cringe at this oversimplification of the history and analysis of religious thought, but perhaps there is a grain of truth to it. In any case, you might consider whether the notion of a unique and infinite god really does reflect and encourage belligerence and intolerance, as this historical hypothesis indicates.

4. Proving the Existence of God

The Miracle on the Expressway

Hugely unlikely events are sometimes seen as miracles by religious believers, and counted as evidence for the existence of God. Bertrand Russell (an unbeliever) offered the following facetious argument along those lines:

The next time you're on an expressway, take note of the number on the license plate of one car at random. Now calculate the probability of seeing exactly that number: given the thousands of cars with different license plate numbers that travel on that expressway, the probability of seeing that one is minuscule. A miracle! God must exist.

A QUESTION TO THINK ABOUT: Nobody is fooled by this reasoning, but it's not easy to explain exactly what has gone wrong. Can you?

God and Wales

Among the more serious attempts to prove God's existence, one sort of argument frequently proposed says that the way the visible natural world is arranged gives us reason to think that it was designed by an intelligent being, on purpose; and this being must be God. The assumption behind this argument is that the visible world wouldn't have gotten to be the way it is all by itself, by ordinary natural processes. (Compare, in this respect, the argument for the invisible gardener, considered above.) This familiar argument has received a great deal of consideration and critical response from philosophers. Here, however, is a novel and interesting version of this argument.

Imagine you are taking a train west from London. You doze off for a while, then wake up and look out the window. Adjacent to the tracks you see a field of flowers in bloom, which spell out in different colours, "British Rail Welcome You To Wales." You believe as a result of seeing this that you are entering Wales.

It's reasonable for you to come to this belief only if you think that somebody planted the flowers to spell out that message on purpose. But if, by an incredible coincidence, a field of wild flowers just happened to spell out that message, you wouldn't be justified in coming to believe that you were entering Wales. Of course, it's also reasonable for you to think that

19

the flowers were arranged that way on purpose by somebody who wanted to give you the message they spelled. The point here is that we wouldn't be justified in taking things as *signs*, as giving us *information*, if we didn't think that they were purposely arranged that way by an intelligent designer to communicate something to us.

Now, note that we often gather information from the *natural* world—from features of the world that we know were not designed and arranged by people. For example, the shape of a particular hill you recognize out the train window would tell you that you're on the outskirts of a certain town. So it must be that even certain features of the natural world—the ones we justifiably get information from—were made on purpose by an intelligent designer. But they weren't designed by people; they must have been designed by another being, one even more clever and powerful than we are. They must have been designed by God.[4]

SOME QUESTIONS TO THINK ABOUT: I don't think this argument works. If you share my reaction, you might try to figure out exactly where it goes wrong. Perhaps you should think about the principle that only what's designed and put there on purpose can give us information. The train story is intended to convince us that this principle is right; are you convinced? Why/why not?

> *Some unusual arguments for God's existence:*
>
> *The Bible has been translated into hundreds of different languages, but God's existence is mentioned in every single translation! Such widespread testimony would be inexplicable unless He exists.*[5]
>
> *"This old world has three times as much water as land but with all of its twisting and turning not a drop sloshes off into space."*[6] *This phenomenon is cited as evidence of God's guiding hand.*

5. Why Believing In God Is a Good Bet

Pascal's Wager, named for its inventor, the French philosopher and mathematician Blaise Pascal (1623-62), is a very peculiar argument in favour of belief in God. Here's how it goes.

---

4   I have heard this argument attributed to Antony Flew.
5   Presented in a paper by one of my students.
6   *Ebony* symposium, "Why I Believe There Is a God" (Vol. 18, November 1962) p. 96. Quoted by B.C. Nerlich in "Popular Arguments for the Existence of God," in *The Encyclopedia of Philosophy*, vol. 19, ed. in chief Paul Edwards (New York: Macmillan, 1967), p. 409.

Many religions suppose that God punishes non-believers with suffering in hell after death, and that He rewards believers with bliss in heaven.

Now, suppose you believed in God. Either God exists or He doesn't. If He does, you'll be granted the huge reward of post-mortem eternal heavenly bliss; if He doesn't, you will be wrong, but there's no great harm in this. You would have made a fairly harmless mistake.

But suppose you don't believe in God. Either God exists or He doesn't. If He does, you'll suffer hell-fire and damnation. If He doesn't, you'll be right, but there's not a great deal of benefit attached to this.

Here's a table that summarizes the potential benefits and dangers of belief and disbelief, given God's existence or non-existence:

	GOD EXISTS	GOD DOESN'T EXIST
YOU BELIEVE	You get huge benefit	You get tiny harm
YOU DON'T BELIEVE	You get huge harm	You get tiny benefit

Should you believe?

You can see that believing gives a potential huge benefit, at the risk of tiny harm. Non-belief gives a potential huge harm, or else a tiny benefit. Even if you happen to think God's existence is hugely unlikely, it's clearly a very good bet for you to believe anyway.

Compare this argument with James's reasoning discussed above; the similarity is that both argue in favour of belief in God on the grounds that it's potentially good for you.

One thing that makes Pascal's reasoning peculiar is that it argues that it's a good idea for you to believe something on the basis of a cost-benefit analysis. It does not give you the normal sort of reason in favour of believing something—namely, reason to think that it's true.

Later on, in the item called "The Power of Positive Thinking" in Chapter VII we'll encounter a related case.

Why Believing in God Is Not A Good Bet

But consider this contrary reasoning of the same type.

There's really very little evidence for the existence of God, and rational people harbour reasonable doubts about it. Surely a just God who values rationality wouldn't punish people for being reasonable. He might even reward them for their careful and independent habits of thought. And he might even punish believers for their credulity—for their sloppiness of mind in going along with the herd, believing what there's so little evidence for.

On the other hand, believing the truth is a good thing, its own reward. If there isn't any God, non-believers are right, and believers wrong. We should all value being right above being wrong.

So the table above is mistaken. Here is the right one:

	GOD EXISTS	GOD DOESN'T EXIST
YOU BELIEVE	Punishment for credulity	Misfortune of being wrong
YOU DON'T BELIEVE	Reward for rationality	Benefit of being right

Should you believe?

Either way, you're better off being a non-believer.

Into the Mainstream of Philosophy

Traditional religious truths have been a cornerstone of the intellectual foundation of philosophy through the centuries—as they have been, of course, in every area of life. But philosophers have always wanted to use their tools of rational, logical enquiry on the accepted dogmas of religion, just as they use them on every other area of thought. Religious believers often thought that these truths might be justified by rational considerations, and there is a long history of attempts to provide logical arguments to prove God's existence—and an equally long history of the critical treatment of these arguments. The history of philosophical theology contains many more arguments than I have introduced here, of course, and more serious ones—most of the arguments I've presented are silly ones, interesting not because they might actually convince someone, but because of the errors they make. An examination of some of the serious arguments for God's existence, and their criticisms, is a good place to start in the study of philosophy of religion—if not to undermine or create belief, at least to give your intellectual skills a workout. It's also interesting to consider the attempts to reconcile the apparent imperfection of the world with God's omnipotence and benevolence. This problem is classically known as the problem of evil.

Until recently, it got you into a lot of trouble to question the official views of religion, or even to suggest that they needed some clear-headed sceptical consideration. Wise-guy sceptics like Bertrand Russell got themselves in big trouble within living memory. Within the past fifty years, conventional religious belief has suffered a considerable decline in the intellectual arena, but philosophy of religion is still a very lively area. The classical arguments for God's existence still provoke interesting debate. But an important new trend involves the attempt to understand religious belief and practice in new ways. You can see how the pragmatists and the logical positivists might merely reject talk about God as meaningless or false; but you can also see how they (and their contemporary successors) might want to think of religious talk and action as a special and unusual sort of thing. Perhaps "statements" of religious "truths" aren't even meant to have the same sort of meaning, function, and testability as ordinary statements about the visible and mundane. Much contemporary philosophy of religion searches for an account of what might be the real meaning of religion.

CHAPTER III

TAKING CHANCES:
Probability Theory

R.A. Sorenson claims to have had a friend who objected to assigning chores by a random lottery, because that's biased in favour of lucky people.[1]

1. Some Probable Facts

Rosencrantz Flips a Coin

In the beginning of Tom Stoppard's play *Rosencrantz and Guildenstern are Dead*,[2] Rosencrantz has idly been flipping a coin, and it has come up heads ninety-two times in a row. He is surprised, and he should be. Runs of two or three heads in a row are not rare, but runs of ninety-two heads in a row are rather unlikely. How unlikely? Well, the odds of this happening are exactly 1 in 4,951,760,157,141,521,099,596,496,896. This is not an easy number to comprehend.

Imagine you were flipping a coin, one flip per second, trying to get a sequence of ninety-two heads in a row. Each "sequence" of flips ends when you get a tail. Half of these sequences would last only one flip— tails the first time—and thus be one second long. But some of these sequences would last longer, when you were lucky enough to get an initial run of heads. Your average sequence would be two flips long, and thus would last only two seconds.

The more sequences you ran, the more likely it would be that larger runs of heads showed up. For example, it would be fairly reasonable to expect at least one run of ten heads in a row for every 512 sequences. That is, the probability that at least one run would contain ten heads in a row would be greater than 50 per cent if you had more than 512 sequences. To make it more likely than not that you'd get a run of ten heads in a row, then, you would have to flip coins for 1,024 seconds,

---

1   In *Blindspots* (Oxford: Clarendon Press, 1988), p. 186.
2   London: Faber & Faber, 1967.

that is, for almost eighteen minutes. How long would you have to flip to make it 50 per cent likely that a run of ninety-two heads would show up? A long time. You'd certainly need help. Suppose you engaged 5.6 billion people—the whole population of the earth—in flipping, day and night, year in, year out, without stop. Then it would be 50 per cent likely that one of us would come up with a run of ninety-two heads if we all flipped coins for 1.7×10^{12} years—that's 1,700,000,000,000 years. That length of time is about 100 times the estimated current age of the universe. It's not worth the effort.

> *Among the explanations Rosencrantz considers for this unusual event is that it's "a spectacular vindication of the principle that each individual coin spun individually is as likely to come down heads as tails and therefore should cause no surprise each individual time it does." This is a philosophical joke, of course.*

Another Surprising Sequence

Now suppose that you flipped a coin ninety-two times and got this sequence (which I've generated using a randomizing program on my computer):

TTHTTHHTTTTHHTTTHHHHTTHTHTHHTTTHHTHTTTHHTTHTTTHTTTHHHHTHTHHHHTHHTT
TTHHTTTTTHTTHTHTHHHTHTHHHHHHTHTHHTTHTH.

Would you be surprised?

> Before you answer, note that the probability of throwing exactly this sequence of heads and tails is exactly equal to the probability of throwing ninety-two heads in a row. Every possible string of ninety-two throws is equally surprising! But we have made the same mistake as Russell was joking about in his license plate "proof" of God's existence (see above, "The Miracle on the Expressway").

You're On A Roll!

Examine that random sequence of coin-flips in the last item carefully. Do you see that sequence about two-thirds of the way through where it goes TTTTHHTTTT? That's two bunches of four tails within ten flips! Tails is really having a hot streak! But the rally fizzles, and Tails goes into a slump. The momentum switches to Heads—about a dozen flips later, Heads gets five in a row. Notice how quickly the momentum usually shifts: several times during this run, TT is followed by HH, or HH by TT.

Does all this talk of streaks and rallies, momentum and slumps, remind you of sportscaster talk? Maybe such things really do exist in sports, but they certainly don't in a random series of coin flips. *None* of these notions is needed to explain what's going on in the random series of flips. It's just random; that's all there is to it. The important thing to remember is that in any long random series, patterns will (just by accident) show up. But these patterns don't need any explanation. (What would need explanation is if they *didn't* show up.)

The next time you're listening to sportscaster prattle, ask yourself whether the "patterns" they're so interested in detecting need all that elaborate explanation they give them, or whether they're just accidental features of a largely random series.

FOR FURTHER READING: For an excellent discussion of the probability of improbable chance events, see Chapter 2 in John Allen Paulos's *Innumeracy: Mathematical Illiteracy and Its Consequences* (New York: Vintage, 1990). Paulos convincingly argues, for example, that DiMaggio's streak of hitting safely in fifty-six consecutive games was not all that unlikely. Given the normal range of batting averages of baseball players, and the number of games that have been played, it's not surprising that just by accident some player has had a streak of this size.

Your Extraordinary Ancestors

The following reasoning embodies a similar mistake about probabilities. See if you can discover where the mistake is.

One hundred years ago, life was tougher and medical science less effective, and a larger percentage of the population died in infancy and childhood. Several hundreds of years back, it was quite common for people to die before they reached puberty; and in general the pre-puberty mortality rate increases the further back one looks.

Now consider that large group of people who are your ancestors: your mother and father, your four grandparents, your eight great-grandparents, and so on. Here's an extraordinary—even miraculous—fact about them: not a *single one* of them died before reaching sexual maturity!

How Many Ancestors Do You Have?

Answering this question depends on how far back we're supposed to go; do those prehuman organisms which evolved into us count as ancestors? It's difficult to date the appearance of humans, not only because we don't know all the facts. Even if we knew all the facts about the history of our pre-human primate ancestors evolution into the first humans, it would be a matter of somewhat arbitrary decision where to count the first humans as showing up, along a scale of gradually changing organisms. The Population Reference Bureau in Washington, D.C., you might like to know, now counts the first humans as showing up in about 200,000, B.C., and calculates that there have been about 100 billion humans, including the 5.3 billion now alive, on earth so far.

We can, however, make some assumptions and calculations. You had two parents, four grandparents, eight great grandparents, sixteen great-great-grandparents, thirty-two great-great-great-grandparents, and so on. Assume that your human ancestors gave birth to the next generation when they were twenty, on average. One hundred years ago, then, gets us five generations back, to the time of your thirty-two great-great-great-grandparents. Two hundred years ago is ten generations back; then you had $2^{10} = 1,024$ ancestors alive. Five hundred years ago, twenty-five generations back, these calculations give you 33,554,432 ancestors. One thousand years ago, there must have been 1,125,899,906,842,624 of them. But this number is *much* larger than the number of humans alive then, which was somewhere around 300 million. It's over ten thousand times the number of humans that have ever existed. Something has gone drastically wrong here, but what?

> The answer is that some of your ancestors themselves share ancestors. That is to say, at a number of places in your family tree there must have been cases in which married ancestors of yours were at least distantly related. Suppose, for example, that your mother and your father shared the same great-great-great-grandparents. This fact alone would cut the number of people in your family tree in half. There must have been a lot of this in everyone's family.

The Miracle of You

If your mother and father had never met, then you would never have been born, right? But *they* would never have existed (nor would you) if *their* parents had never met; and so on back through the number—whatever it is—of your ancestors. An enormous number of fortuitous and improbable meetings and marriages, stretching back into the distant past, were necessary for you to be here today.

Not just that, but each man releases millions of sperms during each ejaculation. Had a different one of your father's sperms fertilized your mother's ovum, a person with a different genetic makeup would have been born—not you, right? So each fertilization of an ovum is the outcome of an enormous lottery. Had any of these been different, in any of your ancestors, you would not be here today.

Now put these two facts together, and calculate how improbable your existence really is. Your being here is so improbable that we can't even conceptualize probabilities that small. It's a miracle! Everyone else's existence is a miracle too! Most of the events in the universe, come to think of it, are also miracles!

This is still another mistake analogous to Russell's "proof."

2. One-third of Two

Take three cards out of a deck: an ace, a king, and a queen. Shuffle them and put them face down on a table. Clearly the probability of picking an ace out of these three at random is ⅓.

But suppose you brush one of the three, at random, off the table; it falls face down on the floor, and you don't turn it over, so you don't know which card fell. Now you pick one of the two remaining cards at random. What is the probability now of picking an ace?

> A surprising number of people either think the probability is ½ or can't answer the question. The real answer is ⅓. People are mislead by the fact that you are picking one card out of *two*.

3. Happy Birthday Dear You-Two

Suppose there are forty people in a room; how likely is it that two (or more) of them share the same birthday?

> Most people would estimate that it is quite improbable, since there are over nine times as many days in the year as there are people in the room; but in fact, it is about 90 per cent likely—that is, likely enough to be a safe bet.
>
> It's easiest to think about the probability that a certain room contains *no* shared birthdays; the probability of at least one shared birthday is one minus that number.
>
> Imagine a party at which guests show up one at a time. When the host is alone in the room, it's of course impossible that there are two in the room sharing a birthday. The first person enters; her birthday may be on any one of the 365 days of the year, and chances are 364 out of 365 (.9973) that her birthday is different from the host's. When the third arrives, the likelihood that there are still no shared birthdays is this number times the probability that the third guest has a different birthday from either of the first two—363/365. Thus it is about .992 likely that there are no sharers among the three. When the fourth arrives, the probability that there are still no shared birthdays is .992 times 362/365 = .984. At the fifth arrival it is .984 times 361/365: .973.
>
> We continue to multiply by gradually smaller numbers as more people arrive. When there are ten people, the probability there is no shared birthday is about 88 per cent; it falls slightly below 50 per cent when the twenty-third guest arrives; it is slightly below 30 per cent when the thirtyeth shows up. When there are forty people in the room, the probability is around 10 per cent that no birthdays are shared, so it is about

90 per cent that there is a shared birthday. If there are fifty guests, the probability of no shared birthdays is a mere 3 per cent.[3]

4. The Trouble With Taxis

Suppose that psychologists have discovered that witnesses to a single-car accident are 80 per cent likely to be able to report the colour of the car correctly. Now, suppose that 95 per cent of the taxis in Moose Jaw are yellow, and the remaining 5 per cent are blue. A taxi dents a light-pole and then speeds away; a witness reports to the police that the taxi was blue. Should the police regard this evidence as trustworthy and think it likely that a blue taxi was the culprit?

Most people would say that since people are 80 per cent trustworthy at reporting, the police should regard this testimony as fairly (80 per cent) reliable. But this is wrong. In fact, the odds are almost five to one that the witness was mistaken, and the taxi was really yellow.

Here's a way to think about this that may make it more plausible. Consider a random bunch of one hundred witnessed taxi accidents in Moose Jaw. Since 95 per cent of the taxis are yellow (and assuming that the colour of the taxi has no bearing on how accident-prone it is), about ninety-five of these accidents will involve yellow taxis, and about five of them blue taxis. Now consider the yellow-taxi accidents and the blue-taxi accidents separately.

Since witnesses are 80 per cent reliable, they will report the colour in the ninety-five yellow taxi accidents correctly in about seventy-six cases; in the remaining nineteen yellow taxi accidents they will report falsely that the colour was blue. And they will report the colour in a blue taxi accident correctly in four of the five cases; in one case, the report will be an incorrect report that it was yellow.

So among these one hundred accidents, there will likely be nineteen cases in which the witness says the taxi was blue and was incorrect; and four cases in which the witness says the taxi was blue and was correct. For a random taxi accident, then, it's more likely that the report of a blue taxi was mistaken. In fact, the probability that it was correct is only four out of twenty-three: 17 per cent.

The mistake in this case arises because most people consider the wrong probability. Eighty per cent is the probability that a witness says "blue" given that the taxi was blue, but the question is about a different probability: that the taxi was blue given that the witness says "blue."[4]

3   Another traditional mathematical surprise reported in Paulos's *Innumeracy*, pp. 35-37.
4   A similar example is given in *Innumeracy*, p. 164-165.

5. Do Coins Obey the Law?

Suppose a coin is flipped five times and comes up heads every time. What would you guess the next flip will be?

> Many people think that it's quite likely that the next flip will be tails—that the coin, in docile obedience to the "law of averages," will try to even out the total. If it's a fair coin, however, the probability that the next flip is heads is ½. (In fact, the first five flips are evidence that the coin is not fair—that it's a trick coin designed to come up heads—so these flips make it more likely that the next flip will come up heads.)
>
> The mistake is such a common one among gamblers that it even has a name: it's called the Gambler's Fallacy, or the Monte Carlo Fallacy. (Many gamblers at Monte Carlo presumably believe that the longer a number has not come up on a roulette wheel, the more likely it is that it will come up, or that if black has come up on many more than half of the last run of rolls, then it's likely that red will come up on more than half of the next run of rolls.)
>
> The coin mistake is based on a correct premise: that as the number of flips of a fair coin increases, the percentage of heads and tails will tend to grow more equal, closer to 50 per cent each. But the way this will happen is not by the coin's preferring tails for a while: a large number of succeeding flips will most likely be about half heads and half tails, and adding this large number of heads and tails will tend to wash out, in the grand total, the early preponderance of heads.

Why it's Not Certain that You'll Be in a Plane Crash

What are the chances that a plane you're travelling on will crash? I don't know the exact figures, but let's suppose that the chances are about one in a million.

Now let's suppose that somebody took a million plane trips. Would the chances that that person would be in a plane crash rise to one in one—that is, would it be certain? Many people would think so. But this is a mistake about probabilities related to the ones we have already seen. Let's see if I can make clear exactly where the mistake lies.

Let's begin with a simpler case. Imagine a cup containing two jelly beans: one red and one green. Suppose you reach in without looking and pick one of them out. What is the probability that the one you picked is red? The answer, of course, is ½.

Now suppose instead that you make two picks out of the cup: what is the probability of picking a red one now? Well, that depends. I haven't given you enough information about the picking procedure for this question to be answered. Perhaps the procedure is this: you pick one jelly bean out; then, holding on to that one (or eating it), you pick a second one—the only one remaining. If that's the procedure, then it's certain that you'll get the red one, because you get both. The probability that you have the red one after the first pick is ½; after the second pick it's ⅔, or 100 per cent. You just do a simple addition of fractions: ½+½.

But perhaps the procedure is this: you pick one jelly bean out and look at it. Then you replace that jelly bean, shake the cup up, and pick again. Now, it should be clear, it's not certain that you'll get the red one on either of the two picks. You might get the green one both times.

Here's the difference between these procedures. In the first procedure, what you get on the first pick affects the probability of picking a red jelly bean on the next pick. If you do get the red one the first time, for example, the probability of picking a red one the second time is of course zero. If you don't get a red one the first time, that means that the only remaining one is red, so the probability of getting a red one the second time is 100 per cent. But in the second procedure (when you replace the first one), the probability of getting a red bean on any pick is ½, and is independent of what happens on any other pick.

Now, the plane-crash problem is like the second jelly bean procedure. That is: the probability of any particular plane's crashing is (we assume) one out of one million, and is unaffected by whether or not another plane has crashed earlier. That's why a simple addition of fractions ($\frac{1}{1,000,000}+\frac{1}{1,000,000}$ etc.) doesn't calculate the probability of a plane crash in several trips, and that's why the probability of a crash in one million trips is not 1 million x $\frac{1}{1,000,000}$ = 1.

A Frequent Flier Bonus

Well, how *do* you figure out the odds of a crash among one million flights? Let's look first at the simpler jelly bean case, second selection procedure.

When previous picks are replaced, there are four different possibilities for the results of two picks:

Pick 1	Pick 2
R	R
R	G
G	R
G	G

Each of these possibilities is equally probable. Now, among these four ways, one has no red jellybeans picked (the last one on the list). That means that the chances of your picking no red jelly beans at all is $\frac{1}{4}$; and the chance of your picking the red jelly bean at least once is 1 minus $\frac{1}{4} = \frac{3}{4}$.

How can we calculate these numbers in general? Note that the chance that any one pick does not get a red jelly bean is $\frac{1}{2}$. The chance that the jelly bean picked on the first pick is non-red *and* the jelly bean picked on the second pick is non-red is $\frac{1}{2} \times \frac{1}{2} = \frac{1}{4}$. So the probability of getting red on at least one pick is 1 minus $\frac{1}{4}$: $\frac{3}{4}$.

Let's apply this to the airplane case. The chance of no crash on any one flight is $\frac{999,999}{1,000,000}$. The chance of no crash during a million flights is this number times itself 1 million times, in other words, this number to the millionth power. In case you don't have the time to work out this arithmetic on your pocket calculator, I have done it for you. The probability of no crash during a million flights is .363; so the probability that there will be at least one crash is .627—about 2 out of 3. So it's more likely than not that at least one of these flights will end in a crash, but at least it's not certain. That's a small frequent flier bonus.

You needn't start worrying about the odds of being in a plane crash getting as high as 2 out of 3, by the way. If you went on ten separate plane trips a day, every day of the year, it would take you 274 years to travel on a million flights.

A QUESTION TO THINK ABOUT: The chances that someone has a bomb in his or her luggage on any particular flight are small, but they're large enough to make some people worry. The chances that any particular flight is carrying *two* people who have bombs in their luggage are very much smaller. (If the probability that there's one person is $\frac{1}{n}$, then the probability that there's two people is $\left(\frac{1}{n}\right)^2$. Do you see why?)

The reasoning so far is correct, but consider the following. Smedley is quite worried that flights he's on will be destroyed by luggage-bombs. But the chances of there being two bombs are so small that he's not concerned about that event. What he does, then, is to carry a bomb in his luggage, designed not to go off, of course. He reasons that in order to be in danger of being killed by a luggage-bomb, someone else must have a bomb on the plane too, but the chances of two bombs on the same plane are so small that he doesn't have to worry. Smedley is making a mistake in his reasoning about probabilities. Can you explain exactly where his mistake lies?[5]

---

5   An old story told again by Paulos in *Innumeracy*, p. 33-34.

Into the Mainstream of Philosophy

Philosophers concern themselves with probability in two ways. One of these is the attempt to provide the rules for calculating probabilities. In this we overlap with what's done in mathematics departments. This is a fairly well developed science, and you can find out its basics in many introductory logic books, to be found in university bookstores. The mathematics of elementary probability theory isn't too complicated, and there are plenty of interesting puzzles even at this level. My chapter has provided a rather unfair sample of the applications of probability theory, in that I have presented a number of cases in which the theory gives results that are unexpected and rather surprising. In ordinary life, we confidently apply probability calculations in all sorts of ordinary ways, with unsurprising results. The academic study of probability rarely conflicts with our ordinary ways of probabilistic thought. Its usual concern is rather to explain our ordinary thought—to provide a systematic and precise theory for it.

The second area of philosophical concern about probability is to explain what it means. Here's a sample question. Suppose a coin is flipped once and is then destroyed. (It's a chocolate coin: you flip it and then eat it.) It comes up heads. Now what does it mean to say that the probability is 50 per cent that the coin comes up heads? A natural way to explain the statement that something is 50 per cent probable is to say that about 50 per cent of a very long series of events will come out that way. But there isn't a very long series of flips of the chocolate coin: there's only one flip. Does it make any sense to talk about probabilities here? A second sort of question is raised indirectly by the Rosencrantz example. Suppose (to make things a little less bizarre) that a coin is flipped five times and comes up heads each time. We nevertheless want to say that the probability of its coming up heads is only 50 per cent, and that the run we got was fairly unlikely. What does this mean? How can we say that the probability of heads was only 50 per cent, despite the fact that we got 100 per cent? What is probability anyway?

CHAPTER IV

MAKING CHOICES:
Decision Theory

1. The One-and-a-Half Million Dollar Life

Suppose you're the city official in charge of traffic control signs. Motorists are complaining about the large number of stop signs around town; traffic could move faster if they were replaced with yield signs. On the other hand, this replacement would make intersections slightly less safe. What sort of reasoning should you go through to consider making the changes?

Let's think about one particular intersection where your engineers have carefully studied the traffic flow. On average, they tell you, seventy vehicles per hour feed from a road onto a highway at this point, containing an average of 2.5 people per vehicle. Replacing the stop sign with a yield sign here will save, on average, ten seconds per car (because the stop sign causes significant traffic backups). On the other hand, this replacement would likely result in an average of about one additional fatality at the intersection per year.

Over the next year, replacing the stop sign with a yield sign will result in a total saving of 255,500 hours for motorists and passengers. Is saving this time worth the price of one life? In an article published by the Transportation Research Control Board in Washington, D.C., called "Guidelines for Converting Stop to Yield Control at Intersections"[1] gives suggestions on the matter. It proposes that time saved be calculated at $6.71 per hour. At this rate, the time that would be saved at the intersection over the next year would be worth about $1.7 million. The article also calculates the worth of one human life at $1.5 million, less than the worth of the time saved. So you would replace the stop sign with a yield sign.

Is this reasoning crazy? Many people would say it is. Let's consider the reasons why.

1   National Cooperative Highway Research Program Report 320, October 1989. This is a real article; I am not joking.

It's disgusting to measure loss of life in terms of dollars.

If it makes you fell less crass, you can think of value in terms other than money. Think instead in terms of an arbitrary "value unit." Suppose, then, that a life is worth 1.5 million value units, and an hour saved is worth 6.71 value units. Or you might simply do your calculations on the basis of the assumption that saving one life is equal in worth to preventing the waste of about 225,000 hours. Using either of these assumptions gives the same conclusion.

But there's something deeply twisted in calculating this comparison—never mind how you calculate it. You simply can't weigh the loss of life against other values.

This answer may appeal to you, but consider this: imagine that you're the administrator of a publicly funded hospital, wondering whether to buy some new, fancy equipment. Suppose that equipment, over its life span, could be expected to save ten lives, but over this time the total cost of buying and running this equipment would be $25 million. Is it worth it? To answer this question rationally you *must* somehow assign a dollar-equivalent to saving a life. How else could you answer it? This sort of evaluation sometimes is, and must be, done.

No, this is a wrong way for an administrator to think. Hospitals are supposed to save lives by whatever means they can. If you can possibly get the money, you should buy the equipment, no matter the cost.

Well, suppose that in order to buy that equipment for the hospital, we'd have to cut back drastically on other publicly funded operations. For example, we could get that $25 million by firing half the public school teachers in the area. Would this be worth it? Probably not. The point here is that nothing—not even saving a life—is so important that it's worth doing *no matter what* the cost. You *must* weigh the potential value of a proposal against other values.

But a life saved is of *infinite* value. It's worth *more* than any number of hours saved.

Some people say this, but they can't mean it. Consider the consequences of adopting this position. Putting a stop light at *every* corner would be very costly, not only because of the time it would waste for motorists, but also because of the cost of erecting the lights themselves. But if life has *infinite* value, then even the *smallest* chance of saving a life would be worth *any* expense, so put those stop lights everywhere. This can't be right.

Further consider the fact that if we allow people to drive cars at all, there will be some number of traffic fatalities. If we banned driving altogether there would be tremendous costs, and not only in terms of time. But if a life literally has *infinite* value, then banning cars completely would be worth it. Whenever a bridge or a high-rise building is built, it's likely that accidents will kill a couple of construction workers. So we should never build any bridges or high-rises again. A few people die every year when they choke on fishbones lodged in their throats, so we should ban the sale of fish. Taking a bath probably carries a tiny risk of death—you might drown—so if a life has infinite worth then you shouldn't take baths. You run a slight additional risk of death when you leave the house, so you should stay at home and do nothing for the rest of your life.

But this is absurd. Life has great value, but not *infinite* value.

Well, then what is the value of life? How much time wasted is equal to one life? These are not easy questions to answer, but it seems in order to act rationally we must try.

> *All there is left to do is to discover these [scientific] laws.... Life will be really easy...then. All human acts will be listed in something like logarithm tables, say up to the number 108,000, and transferred to a time-table.... Then...new economic relations will arise, relations ready-made and calculated in advance with mathematical precision, so that all possible questions instantaneously disappear because they receive all possible answers.... Of course, you can't guarantee...that it won't be deadly boring. "What do you say, folks, let's send all this reason to hell, just to get all these logarithm tables out from under our feet and go back to our own stupid ways." A man, always and everywhere, prefers to act the way he feels like acting and not in the way his reason and interest tell him.*[2]

Would you prefer not to think about things rationally? Would you prefer to act in ways that *don't* further your interests?

2. Some Decision Puzzles

The Elusive Wine-Bottle

Suppose you have received the magnificent inheritance of $10 from a late rich uncle. The string attached is that you can invest this money if you like, but you must use the money (or the eventual proceeds from its investment) to buy a bottle of wine. You're glad to have the money,

2   Fyodor Dostoyevsky, *Notes from the Underground*, trans. A.R. MacAndrew (New York: Penguin, 1961), pp. 109-110.

since you love wine and can't afford much. Now, you can buy a medio-cre bottle for the $10 right now, but a perfectly safe investment will give you 10 per cent interest per year; so next year at this time you'll have $11. Even counting in inflation and taxes, let's imagine that the proceeds of your investment will get you a slightly better bottle of wine, so you decide to wait, because you're in no hurry. But next year you can invest that $11 for another year, yielding $12.10 a year from then, which will buy a still better bottle. So you invest again. Do you see a philosophical paradox arising?

> Every year you face the same choice, and every year you're better off investing than spending. So you never buy the bottle. You not only de-prive yourself of the bottle you'd enjoy; you also violate the terms of the will.

A version of this paradox has resulted in a problem for some of my friends. They have wanted to buy a computer for years, but prices for computers have kept coming down, and they keep thinking (correctly) that they should wait a while to get a better deal. So they never buy a computer.

A QUESTION TO THINK ABOUT: What has gone wrong with the reasoning in these two examples?

The Proof That Many People are Crazy or Stupid

There is a pretty persuasive line of reasoning that argues to the conclusion that anyone who ever buys a lottery ticket or gambles in a casino is either crazy or stupid. This is a distressing conclusion, given the huge number of people we're talking about.

When is a choice rational? Answering that question is a tall order, but some philosophers think that progress towards an answer can be made by thinking in terms of the *expected utility* of an action.

The utility of something for you is simply a measure of how much you like it. If you would prefer X to Y, then X has more utility than Y. If you'd trade two Y's for one X, then X has at least twice the utility of Y. In some cases, we might even be able to assign numbers to the utilities someone gives some things. Now we can say that the rational choice among alternatives is the choice that would give that person the greatest utility. If an action has several consequences, its utility is the sum of the utilities of each of the consequences.

But many choices are made when we're not sure what the results will be. Sometimes the outcomes of our action are a complete surprise, pleasant or otherwise. But sometimes we can at least judge the *prob-abilities* of outcomes of our choices. When we know the probability of an outcome, we can calculate its *expected utility* by multiplying its utility times its probability. Suppose, for example, that there's one chance in 1,000 you'll win a lottery, and if you win you'll get $3,000. The expected utility of this outcome is $1/_{1,000}$ x $3,000 = $3.

There's a probability of $^{999}/_{1,000}$ that you'll get nothing. So the expected utility of this outcome is $^{999}/_{1000}$ x $0 = $0. So the total expected utility of all outcomes is $3 + $0 = $3. But suppose it costs $1 to buy a ticket. Then the total expected utility of playing this lottery once is $3 − $1 = $2. If you buy only one lottery ticket once, you're likely to lose, of course. But if you play many times, you can expect to come out ahead in the long run, by $2 per game played. It's a good idea to play this lottery.

But suppose that lottery costs $5 per ticket. The total expected utility of playing this lottery once is now $3 − $5: −$2. This means that in the long run you can expect an average loss of $2 per game played. This is not a rational way to make money. Playing this game is like throwing $2 down the toilet each time.

But the games run by lotteries and casinos *all* work like this second lottery. They *all* offer players an average expected loss on each game. The reason is simple: they are *all* running their gambles to make money; and for them to make money in the long run, players must, on average, lose money.

Now why would anyone play a sucker's game such as this? Here are two possible reasons: (*a*) they're suffering from a psychological problem that forces them to gamble self-destructively; (*b*) they don't understand the logic behind expected utility. Putting the matter very bluntly, they're either crazy or stupid.

But before you get too depressed about the mental health and intelligence of the rest of the human race, consider two things people might say to explain why they play lotteries and gamble in casinos.

(1) "It's fun." What this means in terms of our calculations is that we haven't calculated the overall utility of the second lottery correctly, because we haven't added in the enjoyment of playing. Suppose that the fun is worth, in monetary terms, $3 per game. Even though the average money loss will be $2, the fun-value gain is $3; so everything considered, you'll be ahead, on average, by the equivalent of $1 each game. You will still lose money in the long run, but you will have enough fun playing to make it worth it.

(2) "The five dollars I spend on a ticket means next to nothing to me, but if I won a prize it would be worth a great deal." This again means that we haven't calculated the worth of each game correctly. The calculation multiplies the *utility*—a measure of desirability—times its probability. Now, we have merely stuck in dollar figures here. Using these implies

that $3,000 has six hundred times the value of $5, but this may not be the case. Here, in fact, what the person seems to be saying is that the worth of $3,000 to him or her is *greater* than six hundred times the worth of $5. Suppose, then, that we assign (arbitrarily) a utility of 5 units to $5, and a utility of *10,000* units to $3,000. This makes the calculations quite different: the average payoff is $(\frac{1}{1000} \times 10,000) + (\frac{999}{1000} \times 0) = 10$ units. The cost of playing is 5 units, so we're ahead on average $10 - 5 = 5$ units each game.

Perhaps this restores your faith in humanity's sanity and intelligence. But then again, there's the matter of the popularity of "Wrestlemania."

3. The General Makes Some Bad Choices

Two psychologists, Amos Tversky and Daniel Kahneman, conducted a famous series of experiments on people's decision-making. Here's one of their results.

First they gave a bunch of people Problem 1:

1. Imagine you are a general surrounded by an overwhelming enemy force that will wipe out everyone in your six hundred man army unless you take one of two available escape routes. Your intelligence officers explain that if you take the first route you will save two hundred soldiers, whereas if you take the second route the probability is $\frac{1}{3}$ that all six hundred will make it, but $\frac{2}{3}$ that they'll all die. Which route do you take?

Three out of four people choose the first route, since two hundred lives can definitely be saved that way, whereas the probability is $\frac{2}{3}$ that the second route will result in more deaths.

Maybe this reasoning is okay and maybe it isn't. Notice that on standard decision theory we could calculate the "expected deaths" for the second route as $(\frac{1}{3} \times 0) + (\frac{2}{3} \times 600) = 400$. This is the same as the "expected deaths" for the first route: $(1 \times 400) = 400$. But perhaps (as in the lottery case) something else is going on in here. Maybe people also want to avoid the possibility of everyone dying on the second route.

Anyway, then Tversky and Kahneman gave people problem 2:

2. Imagine again you're a general faced with a decision between two escape routes. If you take the first one, four hundred of your soldiers will die. If you choose the second route,

the probability is ⅓ that none of your soldiers will die, and ⅔ that all six hundred will die. Which route do you take?

Four out of five people now choose the second route, reasoning that the first route will lead to four hundred deaths, while there's at least a probability of ⅓ that everyone will get out okay if they go for the second route.

Can you see what's wrong with the reasoning the majority of people are doing here?

> Look carefully at problems 1 and 2. They describe identical choices! It looks like there isn't any subtle evaluation of alternatives going on here. What's going on here is just a flat-out mistake. People are making irrational decisions, misled by the way the question is phrased.

FOR FURTHER READING: A good selection of reports on Tversky and Kahneman's work is found in D. Kahneman, P. Slovic, and A. Tversky, eds., *Judgement Under Uncertainty: Heuristics and Bias* (Cambridge: Cambridge University Press, 1982).

4. A Good Lottery Strategy

In some lotteries you choose your own number to play. If that number comes up, you win the jackpot. If several people have picked that number, then the jackpot is divided among them. Suppose you can pick any number between 1 and 1,000. Would you be tempted to pick 1? How about 1,000? Would you think it's more likely that 437 would win than 1?

> Assuming this is a fair lottery, the chances of 1, 1,000, 437, or any other number between 1 and 1,000 coming up are all equal: one out of 1,000.

Were you tempted to avoid picking 1 or 1000? Many people are, because these numbers don't look "random" to them—they look "special." People think that it would be an unlikely coincidence for one of these special numbers to come up; they think that numbers such as 119, 437, 602, and 841 are much more likely to come up in a random draw.

Now, given this mistake many lottery players make, and given the rules of this lottery, there's a good strategy for you to use in choosing a number. Can you see what it is?

> What you want to do is to pick a number that nobody else has picked, so that you will get the whole jackpot, instead of having to share it. Given that people are less likely to pick "special" numbers like 1, 1,000, 500, and 666, you should pick one of these. Of course, the strategy of picking a number others will see as "special" doesn't make it more likely that you'll win. Each number stands an equal chance—one out of

1,000—of winning. But it does make it more likely that *if* you win, you'll win big, because you won't have to share the jackpot with many others.

Another way of making it likely that there aren't many others who have picked the same number is to pick the number that won the previous lottery. As we've just seen in the coin-flipping case, people often expect that the "law of averages" makes it especially unlikely that a number will repeat. Thus many of them will reason incorrectly that the number that came up last time is now "special" and won't come up again.

5. How To Go Home a Winner

Here's a sure-fire way to go home a winner at any gambling game.

For simplicity, let's imagine that you're playing this simple game: you put down a bet and flip a coin. If the coin comes up heads, you collect twice your original bet from the casino; if it comes up tails, you lose your bet.

Bet $1 on the first toss. If you win, you get $2; you're ahead, so go home. If you lose, you're down $1; play again, betting $2 on the next game. You have lost $1 on the first game, and bet $2 on the second, so you have spent $3. If you win on this second game, you get $4, so you're $1 ahead. Go home. If you lose, you're down $3. Bet $4 on the next; now you've spent $7. If you win you get $8; so you're a dollar ahead; go home. If you lose, you're down $7; bet $8 on the next game. And so on.

If you keep losing, you'll have to bet $16, $32, $64, and so on, on succeeding games to make sure you'll come out ahead, all told, if you win. But it's absolutely certain that you'll win if you keep at it: you can't keep throwing tails forever! When you win, go home.

Other gambling games aren't this simple; neither are the odds so fair, as we've seen, when you're playing against a casino. But the general strategy can be widely applied: keep betting enough so that if you win, you'll be ahead all told; and quit when you're ahead. It can't fail to work.

Is there a flaw in this reasoning? If not, why doesn't everyone use this strategy, and always go home a winner?

No, there is no flaw in this reasoning. One reason why people don't follow it is that it's difficult to quit while you're ahead. There's a simple psychological explanation for this: the experience of winning is such a strong behaviour-reinforcement that it tends to make people continue to play.

But a more important reason why this strategy isn't widespread is that, to carry it out, you would have to have, in theory, an indefinitely large amount of funds available. Every time you lose in this simple game, you have to double your bet. How long can you keep doing this? If you're lucky you'll win before you run out of money, but this is not guaranteed. So this is a secure strategy only for people with an indefinitely large bankroll, and there aren't any such people.

SOME QUESTIONS TO THINK ABOUT: Imagine you had an indefinitely large bankroll and could keep doubling your bet forever. (How could this be? Well, maybe you're Dictator of Klopstockia, and can order the Klopstockian Mint to print up more money any time you run low.) Would this strategy work then?

Notice that, using this strategy, you'd be ahead just $1 whenever you went home; you might not think this sort of win is worth it. But how about this: whenever you win, using this strategy, you put your $1 in a vault and start playing again, using the same strategy. You could do this forever, right?

Those of you who know a little about economics will be able to answer this question: why won't this strategy work even for the Dictator of Klopstockia?

6. Getting Monty's Goat

Announcer: And now...the game show that mathematicians argue about...Let's Make a Deal. Here's your genial host, Monty Hall! [Applause]

Monty: Hello, good evening, and welcome! Now let's bring up our first contestant. It's...You! Come right up here. Now, you know our rules. Here are three doors, numbered 1, 2 and 3. Behind one of these doors is a beautiful new *Pontiac Gran Hormonismo*!

Audience: Oooh! Aahh!

Monty: Behind the other two is a *worthless goat*!

Audience: [Laughter]

Monty: Now, you're going to chose one of these doors. Then I'm going to open one of the other doors with a goat behind it, and show you the goat. Then I'll offer you this deal: if you stick with the door you've chosen, you can keep what's behind it, plus $100. If instead you choose the remaining unopened door, you can keep what's behind it. Now choose one door.

Audience: Pick 3! No, 1! 2!

You: Um, oh well, I guess I'll pick...3.

Monty: Okay. Now our beautiful Charleen will open door number 2. Inside that door, as you can see, is a worthless goat. You can keep what's behind your door 3 plus $100, or you can make a deal and switch for whatever's behind door 1. While we take our commercial break, you should decide: do you wanna *make a deal*??

While the first commercial is running, you think: I really want that car. I can stick with door 3 or switch to door 1. There's a car behind one of them and a goat behind the other. It's random, fifty-fifty, which door hides the car. But I'll also get $100 if I stick with door 3. So I'll stick.

But the first commercial is immediately followed by a second. While the second commercial is running, you think: It was ⅓ likely that door 3, the one I picked, had the car, and I'd get the goat if I switched. But it was ⅔ likely that door 3, which I picked, had a goat. If it does, then the car must be behind door 1 (since I can see that door 2 has a goat). So if I switch to 1, then I get the car. That means that switching gives me a ⅔ chance of winning the car. Of course, I'll lose the extra $100 if I switch, but it's worth paying that price for a ⅔ chance of getting the car. So I'll switch.

Then while the third commercial is running, you review both lines of reasoning. Both look completely correct, but they come to opposite conclusions. What should you do?

The right answer is given by your second line of reasoning: you should switch. The probability that door 3 has the car is ⅓; so the probability that it doesn't—that it's behind 1 or 2—is ⅔. After Monty opens one of these, which he knows hides a goat, the probability of the other hiding a car is now ⅔. This answer is right, but hard to believe.

A version of this problem has recently caused great public controversy. In September 1990, Marilyn von Savant (listed in the Guinness Book of World Records *for "highest I.Q.") published the puzzle in* Parade *magazine, and answered it with an argument that you should switch. Since then, she estimates she has received ten thousand letters, most, especially those from mathematicians and scientists, scathingly attacking her reasoning. During July 1991, Monty Hall himself ran a little experiment in his Beverly Hills home to see who was right, and announced that his results show that switching is the right strategy. The case is complicated by the fact that, in the original version published by Ms. von Savant, it was not clear whether Monty would offer the switch automatically, whether or not the first door picked was in fact the one with the car.*

FOR FURTHER READING: See John Tierney, "Behind Monty Hall's Doors: Puzzle, Debate and Answer?," *The New York Times*, July 21, 1991.)

7. Voting Problems

Why You Shouldn't Vote

What are the chances that your vote will make a difference in who wins an election? What I mean by "making a difference" is breaking what otherwise would have been a tie, or creating a tie, in the final total. The chances of this happening are minuscule. You are foolish to think that your vote is even remotely likely to create or break a tie, and thus to affect who wins, so no matter how passionately you care about the outcome of an election, it's a waste of time to vote.

This reasoning, so far, sounds impeccable. But, of course, if this is true in your case, it's true for all the other thousands or millions of voters too. Therefore it doesn't make sense for anyone to vote!

This line of reasoning is sometimes known as the Voter's Paradox.

How Not to Choose a Movie

Confusingly, the following is also sometimes known as the Voter's Paradox.

When there's a difference of preference among a group of people, taking a vote will always provide a fair solution by giving the majority's preference. Right? Wrong.

Consider the following example. There are three people, Alice, Bertha, and Carl (abbreviate their names A, B, and C). They want to go to the movies together, and there are three movies in town: "One Night of Bliss," "Two Tickets to Timbuktu," and "Three Babies and a Man" (call these 1, 2, and 3).

A, B, and C discuss the merits of each movie inconclusively. Here are the preferences of each:

- A prefers 1 to both the others, and prefers 2 to 3.
- B prefers 2 to both the others, and prefers 3 to 1.
- C prefers 3 to both the others, and prefers 1 to 2.

They decide to put matters to a vote. First they vote on whether to go to 1 or 2. A votes for 1 (preferring it to any other); C really wants to go to 3, but prefers 1 to 2; so he also votes for 1. B prefers 2 to 1, so she votes for 2. It's two to one in favour of movie 1. That's progress, anyway.

Well, because 2 has been ruled out, they decide to compare 1 and 3 in a vote. A votes for 1; B votes for 3; C votes for 3. Disappointingly for A, it now appears that 3 is the winner.

But A (who likes 3 least) suggests that they test whether 3 is really the best choice, by comparing it to 2. So they take a vote comparing 3 and 2. C votes for 3, but A and B vote for 2. Well, things are getting confusing, so they make a list of what they have discovered, by these perfectly straightforward votes:

- Vote I: 1 is preferable to 2
- Vote II: 3 is preferable to 1
- Vote III: 2 is preferable to 3

This conversation follows:

A: Look, Vote I tells us that 1 is better than 2, so let's go to 1.

C: Yeah, that would be okay if it weren't for Vote II, which chooses 3 over 1. 3 is clearly the winner. Let's go there.

B: No, despite the desirability of 3, Vote III clearly shows that the majority of us prefer 2 to 3. 2 is the grand champion. We go there.

A: I agree that 2 is well liked. But remember that we decided, by a clear majority in Vote I, that 1 is better even than 2.

C: Yeah, that would be okay if it weren't for Vote II, which chooses 3 over 1. 3 is clearly the winner. Let's go there.

B: No, despite the desirability of 3, Vote III clearly shows that the majority of us prefer 2 to 3. 2 is the grand champion. We go there.

And so on.

Several things are interesting about the problem A, B, and C have found themselves in. Their problem is to try to use their individual preferences to establish what might be called the group will. But the preferences that they try to combine into a group will fail to give a good answer, given the two-at-a-time comparative voting method they use. Whatever choice is made, these preferences tell us that another choice is better.

An elementary principle of preference theory is, it seems, transitivity. This principle says that if p is better than q, and if q is better than r, then p is better than r. The first interesting feature of this example is that the preferences that are revealed by Votes I-III violate this principle. 1 is better than 2 (vote I); 2 is better than 3 (vote III); and by transitivity it would follow that 1 is better than 3. But vote II establishes that 3 is better than 1.

The group will of A, B, and C, as manifested by this group of preferences, is unworkable. Perhaps this is because it violates the principle of transitivity. Must all groups of preferences satisfy this principle?

The second interesting fact is that a seemingly straightforward procedure for arriving at the group will resulted in this pickle. Each of the three starts with individual preferences that are perfectly straightforward and individually workable; their individual preferences violate no rules of rational preference. And the procedure they use to form a group will on the basis of their individual preferences also seems perfectly okay; majority vote is, after all, the clearest example we have of an eminently fair and workable way to form a group will based on individual preferences. But here it has run aground, badly.

The group will is an important concept in the thought of many political philosophers, who thought that the measure of the worth of any political system is not to what extent that system furthered any particular person's will, but to what extent it furthered the group will. Problems such as this one lead to wonders about the possibility of understanding the group will as some kind of sum of individual wills. Is there a good way of summing them?

How to Win at Dice

Here is an example involving probabilities with a similar paradoxical conclusion. This one is a bit more complicated.

Suppose that you're going to play a game with four specially marked six-faced dice. Here's how the four dice, A, B, C, and D, have their faces marked:

A	0	0	4	4	4	4
B	3	3	3	3	3	3
C	2	2	2	2	7	7
D	1	1	1	5	5	5

Each time you play, your opponent chooses one of them and then you choose another. Whoever throws the higher number wins.

It seems plausible to think that these dice are not equally good; some are more likely to win than others. If there's one that's most likely to win, then your opponent should pick that one to throw. If she throws this one all the time, then in the long run, she'll come out the winner. If all the dice are equally good, then you're likely to come out even in the long run. If some are tied for best, then she can pick one of the best ones, and the best you can do again is tie. So it seems that your opponent has a strategy that, in the long run, means she's very unlikely to lose. And it seems that the person who has the first choice of the die to throw has the advantage.

But which die is the best one?

> Perhaps you reason: the die with the highest average value on its faces is the best. Calculation shows you that *C* has the highest average value.

This reasoning so far is all wrong. Let's compare what is likely to happen given choices by you and by your opponent.

Suppose your opponent chooses *B*. You can beat her (on average) by choosing *A*. Your opponent always throws 3, but $\frac{4}{6}$ times on average you throw 4. This means that, on average, $\frac{4}{6}$ times you win. In the long run, A will win 2 out of 3 times. So *A* is better than *B*.

Suppose she chooses *C*. You can beat her (on average) by choosing *B* because $\frac{4}{6}$ times *C* throws 2, which is beaten by *B* which always throws 3. So *B* beats *C*, on average, 2 out of 3 times. *B* is better than *C*.

What if she chooses *D*? You beat her again by choosing *C*. Comparing *C* and *D* is more complicated. One half of the time *D* throws 1, so *D* is beaten by *C*, which always throws a higher number. The other half of the time *D* throws 5, which is beaten by *C* $\frac{2}{6}$ times. This means that half of the time (when *D* throws 1) *C* wins; the other half of the time *C* wins $\frac{2}{6}$ times. *C* is better than *D*, because *C* beats *D* 2 out of 3 times on average.

But if she chooses *A*, you can beat her by taking *D*. Half the time *D* throws 5 and wins. The other half of the throws, *D* wins on average $\frac{2}{6}$ times. So on the whole *D* beats *A*, again 2 out of 3 times.

Summarizing:

- *A* is better than *B*
- *B* is better than *C*
- *C* is better than *D*
- *D* is better than *A*

There is no die that is better than all the rest, or tied for best. Just as in the last example, "better than" is not transitive.

What this means is that if you play this game against an opponent who chooses her die first, you can always choose a die that is likely to beat her. So the first person to choose is at a *disadvantage* in the long run. Perfectly correct reasoning about probability shows that the second person to choose a die can always pick one likely to beat the other one.

This correct conclusion is deeply contrary to our feelings about probability and preferability.[3]

This result is exactly like that of the previous example, involving movie choice. Whichever movie you name, I can pick one that two out of three people would prefer.

Rock, Scissors, Paper

Rock, Scissors, Paper is a simpler game with the same structure. You probably know how this works: a different hand-sign stands for each of these three things. Two people produce a hand sign simultaneously. The winner is determined by these rules: Rock beats Scissors, Scissors beats Paper, and Paper beats Rock. It's a fair game when the two people make their signs simultaneously; but imagine that you get your opponent to go first, and then you produce your sign after you've seen what your opponent does. It's easy to see how you could win every time. The interesting thing here, as in the cases of choosing a movie and the dice game just discussed, is that there isn't anything that's better than the rest.

Into the Mainstream of Philosophy

The philosophical topic of this chapter is called decision theory. You can see that it's to some extent an application of probability theory (the topic of the previous chapter) to action in situations of uncertainty. Philosophers share this area of study with economists. As is the case in probability theory, decision theory is mostly an attempt to systematize and clarify the way we all think rationally in everyday situations; and as in the case of the previous chapter, this one provides a rather unrepresentative sample of its theory, insofar as I have produced cases in which theory conflicts surprisingly and sometimes bizarrely with ordinary expectations. The problem is worse in the case of decision theory, however, in that it seems that a larger number of our ordinary procedures and expectations differ from what theory (so far) counts as rational behaviour. The basic theory of rational decision is currently less adequate and more controversial than the theory of probability.

Unfortunately, most introductory philosophy and logic books ignore decision theory altogether. It's a fascinating and important field,

---

3   This example is found in Ian Stewart, *Concepts of Modern Mathematics* (Harmondsworth, England: Penguin, 1975), pp. 248-250, and in Paulos, *Innumeracy*, pp. 134-5, where Paulos attributes its invention to the statistician Bradley Efron.

and its beginnings are not hard to grasp. The best books I can recommend for the beginner are: Part 3 of Ronald N. Giere's *Understanding Scientific Reasoning*, 3rd ed. (Fort Worth: Holt, Rinehart and Winston, 1991), which sets up the basics in a very clear and friendly fashion; and Richard C. Jeffrey's *The Logic of Decision*, 2nd ed. (Chicago: University of Chicago Press, 1983), which starts you at the beginning, and proceeds in a rather brisk and formal fashion to some fairly advanced topics.

CHAPTER V

LOGIC

1. Some Mistakes About Logical Words

Dilemmas

The word 'dilemma' is commonly used loosely to mean a problem or predicament. Careful speakers use the word in its strict sense, restricting it to cases in which the predicament arises from a choice between two equally balanced, and equally undesirable, alternatives. In this sense, then, it is a mistake to say that we face the *dilemma* of a growing number of homeless people, since no choice between two alternatives is indicated.

The "horns of a dilemma" are the two undesirable consequences. This picturesque metaphor sees us as being charged by a horned animal: if we dodge one of its dangerous protuberances we are gored by the other.

Logicians use the word to refer to that variety of argument in which certain assumptions are shown to lead logically to one or the other of two unacceptable consequences. A "destructive dilemma" concludes that those assumptions must be wrong. A "constructive dilemma" is a different sort of argument. Here's one:

- If it rains, the picnic will be cancelled.
- If it doesn't rain, Pete will insist we go to the beach, so the picnic will be cancelled.
- It will either rain or not.
- Therefore the picnic will be cancelled.

The Exception that Doesn't Prove the Rule

Another interesting English usage that derives from a mistake is the cliché, "The exception proves the rule." What could this mean?

One kind of rule is a generalization about how things are: "All birds fly." Penguins are an exception to this "rule"; but this exception doesn't prove the rule—it disproves it.

Another kind of rule is a statement that tells you what to do: "Drivers must stop at red lights." The fact that ambulances and fire trucks are an exception again *disproves* the rule. (Compare another cliché: "Rules are made to be broken.")

What could "The exception proves the rule" mean? Perhaps there's something reasonable embodied in it. Even though exceptions can never *prove* generalizations or rules for action, nevertheless most of our generalizations and rules *tolerate* exceptions. Most of the general "truths" we believe are true only on the whole. Rules for behaviour usually do admit of justified exceptions.

But the origin of this cliché is an interesting mistake. A central meaning of the word 'prove' was once *test* (whence "the proof of the pudding," and "proof" as the measure of alcohol in drinks: the results of comparing it to "proof spirit"—a mixture of alcohol and water kept as a standard for testing). In this sense, the statement makes perfectly good sense. A proposed exception does put a supposed rule to the test; if it's a genuine exception, the rule *fails* the test. In current English we mostly ignore this old sense of 'prove', though the old cliché lives on, now meaning something quite different.

Begging the Question

Another logical term widely misused by careless speakers is 'begging the question'. This is often thought to mean *raising* (or *forcing*) the question. It doesn't. To beg the question is to presuppose the conclusion in one's argument and thus to reason circularly. (Peculiarly, all valid deductive arguments seem to beg the question: see "Why Argue," in Chapter VII.)

I imagine that people began using the phrase improperly because "this begs the question" *seems* to mean that this begs us—asks us earnestly, entreats us—to raise and consider the question.

The phrase actually seems to come from a mistranslation of the Latin phrase medieval logicians used to refer to an argument that assumes its own conclusion: *'petitio principii'*. This is fairly literally translated as "assuming the starting point." But 'petitio' also means "begging" (whence the English word 'petition').

2. Circular Reasoning

The Divine Circle

Here's an example of circular reasoning. Some neatly dressed people who came to my door once actually used this to try to convince me of the existence of God.

Them: The Bible says that God exists.

Me: But what makes you think that everything in the Bible is true?

Them: Well, it's the word of God.

Me: How do you know that?

Them: It says so right there in the Bible.

Me: Sorry, I have something else to do right now.

The Marvellous Suspension Bridge

My seventh-grade civics teacher one day decided to take time off from telling us about the major agricultural and industrial products of every country in the world to describe that wonder of modern engineering, the suspension bridge. The following dialogue ensued:

Mr. V.: The engineering problem is to hold the roadway up in the air. It's held up by a lot of vertical cables attached on top to those big curving horizontal cables.

Us: What holds up those big curving horizontal cables?

Mr. V.: They're held up by those big vertical steel posts.

Us: What holds them up?

Mr. V.: They're attached to the roadway.

Us: Yeah, but what holds up the roadway?

Mr. V.: I already told you. They're held up by those vertical cables.

Us: And what holds up those vertical cables?

Mr. V.: How many times do I have to go through this? The big curving horizontal cables hold them up.

After a few trips around this circle, Mr. V. finally saw the problem. "Well," he concluded, "those big vertical steel posts go down below the roadway, and they're embedded in great big cement blocks that float on the surface of the water."

Mr. V.'s reasoning is circular, but it's not exactly what logicians call "circular reasoning," which is the mistake of using what you're trying to prove in the course of trying to prove it.

3. The Illogic of English

"Or" Confusions

The "logic" of the English language is a mess.

A simple example of this is provided by the logical word 'or'. That word is sometimes used to connect two sentences to make a third; for example, we can connect "Bernadette is in the pub" and "Bernadette is in class" to make "Bernadette is in the pub *or* Bernadette is in class." This sentence is true if Bernadette is in class, not in the pub; and it's true if she's in the pub and not in class. But what if the class is being held in the pub, and *both* parts are true?

But consider this sentence: "It's raining or it's Tuesday." Again we can see that the sentence is true on a rainy Thursday and on a sunny Tuesday, and that it's false on a sunny Thursday. But how about on a rainy Tuesday?

> You might be tempted to say that the sentence is false on a rainy Tuesday. 'Or', it seems, means *one or the other, but not both*. But it's not completely clear that 'or' always means this. Suppose somebody served you coffee, and told you, "You can have sugar or cream." This sentence seems to imply that it's possible that you have sugar and cream. 'Sugar or cream' here means *either one or the other only, or both*.

Logicians distinguish between the *exclusive* and the *inclusive* senses of 'or'. The first allows the truth of one of the two sentences connected by 'or' but not the truth of both. The second allows one of them to be true, *and* it allows both of them to be true.

It's sometimes not clear which sense 'or' has, so English is in this way logically ambiguous. It's important that legal documents be unambiguous, so in legal English one sometimes uses the awkward term 'and/or' to make it clear that the inclusive sense is what's meant. It's possible that other languages do not share this ambiguity. In Latin, there are two words for 'or': '*aut*' and '*vel*'. I have heard it claimed that the first expresses the exclusive 'or' and the second the inclusive. I'm not sure if this is true. I have consulted several fat Latin dictionaries that attempt to explain the several ways in which these two words have different senses. None gives exactly this difference, expressed in clear logical ways, though several rather ambiguously suggest it.

"The" Confusions

This is another example of the logical messiness of English.

What is the logic of phrases of the form "The x..."? Under what conditions would "The tallest mountain in the world is Mount Everest" be true?

> This sentence is true provided that there's exactly one tallest mountain (that is, that two or more aren't tied for tallest), and it's Mount Everest. Here the word 'the' tells us that we're talking about exactly one thing.

But what does "The lion is a dangerous beast" mean? Under what conditions would it be true?

> This sentence does not mean that exactly one lion is dangerous. It means that *all* lions are dangerous. This is not the result of the fact that we're talking about lions, not mountains. "The lion chasing Irving is a dangerous beast" refers to exactly one lion, not to all of them.

What does "In a zoo, the lion is a dangerous beast" mean?

> It's ambiguous. It might mean that the speaker has a particular zoo in mind, and that this zoo contains exactly one lion, and that that lion is dangerous. Or the speaker might mean that all lions in any zoo are dangerous.

This is one of very many reasons why non-English speakers have so much trouble learning English.

The Messy Counterfactual

Verdi was Italian and Bizet was French. They were not countrymen. But what if they were countrymen? Which of the following sentences is true?

- If Verdi and Bizet were countrymen, then Bizet would have been Italian.
- If Verdi and Bizet were countrymen, then Verdi would have been French.

> Notice that they can't *both* be true, because then the Italian Bizet and the French Verdi would *not* have been countrymen. Can they both be false? Is there some third country they both would have belonged to? Or if exactly one of them is true, which one?

We don't really know how to answer these questions.

How about these two:

- If Julius Caesar were commander in Korea, he would have used the A-bomb.

- If Julius Caesar were commander in Korea, he would have used catapults.

    Each of these seems reasonable to say. Both of them can't be true: if Caesar had the A-bomb, he surely wouldn't have used catapults.

Sentences of the form "If *A* were the case, then *B* would be the case" are known by logicians as *counterfactuals*. To determine whether a counterfactual is true, we imagine a "possible world" like the real one, except that *A* is true; the counterfactual is true provided that *B* would be true in that possible world.

Counterfactuals are hard to evaluate for truth when it's not clear exactly what changes we should assume in the possible world we imagine. We know that Caesar used the most powerful weapons available to him. In the possible world we imagine, he is commander in Korea. But should we think of that possible world as one in which only the weapons that Caesar really had were available to him? Or as one in which the weapons that really were available during the Korean War were available to him? You can see from these examples that counterfactuals are not very well behaved logically.[1]

FOR FURTHER READING: A well-known work on the logic of counterfactuals is David Lewis, *Counterfactuals* (Oxford: Blackwell, 1973)

4. The Unspoken Implication

It Never Turns Blue Either

Years ago (so the story goes) a company that sold canned tuna increased its sales tremendously when it began using the advertising slogan "It Never Turns Black in the Can". Millions of consumers chose that brand, visualizing the blackened fishy mess they might encounter if they opened a can of a competing brand. The slogan was misleading: *no* brand of tuna *ever* turned black in the can. But what it *said* was actually *true*. How can a statement lead you to believe something it doesn't actually say?

    It's tempting to think that all that's really meant by a statement has to do with what would make it true. But we often say things intending to communicate more than what's literally implied. Imagine I look at my watch and say to you, "It's one o'clock." What I intend to communicate is more than merely what time it is: I also want to let you know that it's time for you to go. Perhaps it's a good idea to think about the meaning of statements as more than merely what facts make them true or false: we

1   The first example is Kripke's; the second is Quine's.

should also think about what they're actually used to communicate, given certain contexts.

FOR FURTHER READING: John R. Searle's book *Speech Acts* (Cambridge: Cambridge University Press, 1969) is a far-ranging treatment of meaning considered with regard to the *uses* we make of language.

Has the Present King of France Stopped Robbing Banks?

Related matters arise in connection with a famous debate about philosophy of language. Consider the sentence

- The present king of France is bald.

Given that there is no king of France at the moment, is this sentence true or false? Bertrand Russell argued that this sentence strictly implies that there is at present a king of France, so the sentence is false. (But then, the sentence

- The present king of France is hairy.

is also false.) P.F. Strawson, however, argued that the first sentence does not strictly imply that there is a present king of France: it merely *presupposes* it. Because what the sentence presupposes is false, we wouldn't say either that the sentence is true or that it's false. This seems likely: perhaps you'd agree that we couldn't sensibly say that it's true or false. But the idea that some meaningful sentences are neither true nor false is a surprising one that goes against the way we normally think about language, and also against powerful theoretical motivations in the philosophical theory of meaning to think that all meaningful declarative sentences are either true or false.

A better-known example of a related phenomenon is the following. Suppose the prosecuting attorney, while cross-examining the accused man, asks him: "True or false: you have now stopped robbing banks?" Assume the man has never robbed a bank. Can you see why he would have trouble answering this question?

If he answers "True," the implication is that he used to rob banks, but he doesn't now. If he answers "False," the implication is that he used to rob banks and he still does. Strangely, the statement "He has now stopped robbing banks" seems to be neither true nor false.

FOR FURTHER READING: Russell's views on the present King of France were presented in his *Introduction to Mathematical Philosophy* (London: George Allen & Unwin, 1919), pp. 167-180. P.F. Strawson's reply is in his article "On Referring" in *Essays in Conceptual Analysis*, Anthony Flew, ed. (London: Macmillan, 1956), pp. 21-52.

5. Much Ado About Nothing

Over the years, logicians have concocted a bunch of puzzles involving the negative words "nothing," "nobody," and so on. Here are some of these cases:

> "What did you put into that closet?"
> "I put nothing in there."
> "Really? You put *that* in there? It looks empty to me!"

> Hamburger is better than nothing.
> Nothing is better than steak.
> Therefore hamburger is better than steak.

> No cat has two tails.
> Every cat has one more tail than no cat.
> Therefore every cat has three tails.

> The sun and the nearest star Alpha Centuri are separated by empty space.
> Empty space is nothing.
> Therefore nothing separates the sun and Alpha Centuri.
> If nothing separates two things, they're right next to each other.
> Therefore the sun and Alpha Centuri are right next to each other.

These examples fool nobody. ("Really? He's fooled by them?") What's of interest here is what these mistakes show about the language. In grammar class I was taught to chant, "A noun is a name of a person, place, or thing." But clearly the noun 'nothing' is not the name of a person or place or thing. Some of the blunders in these examples seem to result from mistakenly treating it as the name of a thing.

SOME QUESTIONS TO THINK ABOUT: How, after all, do ordinary nouns work? Nouns aren't always names. 'Unicorn' isn't the name of anything. (Even proper names aren't always names: 'Santa Claus' doesn't name anything either.)

And exactly what is the difference in the way these negative nouns work?

> *"Take some more tea," the March Hare said to Alice, very earnestly.*
> *"I've had nothing yet," Alice replied in an offended tone: "so I can't take more."*

"You mean you can't take less," said the Hatter: "it's very easy to take more than nothing."[2]

Into the Mainstream of Philosophy

Logic is the attempt to provide a theory of what makes a good argument good. Two factors can make an argument bad: if the assumptions it starts from are false, or if it reasons from these assumptions in the wrong way. In general, it's not a matter of logic whether the assumptions of an argument are true or false; more precisely, then, logic is the theory of how to reason from assumptions in the right way.

Much of the work of logicians concentrates on systematizing and making precise—discovering the rules of—the perfectly ordinary, uncontroversial, unsurprising reasoning of the sort we do every day. But the surprise here is that our everyday reasoning is interestingly complex—easy to do, but hard to explain systematically.

There are two sorts of logic you'll come across. Sometimes logicians do informal logic. "Informal" here doesn't mean "casual"—it means that they talk through their ideas in ordinary English. The contrast is with formal logic, often called "symbolic logic," which resembles technical science or mathematics: it uses special symbols (which are, however, carefully defined in English). In this area, logic merges with some of what mathematicians study (though people with mathophobia need not fear the elementary parts of formal logic).

Here's a tiny and elementary bit of symbolic logic. Let's use the symbol 'v' to mean inclusive *or* (see "The Illogic of English," above). Then the logic formula 'A v B' stands for the sentence we get when we connect the two sentences symbolized by 'A' and 'B' with 'or'. The symbol '~' stands for 'not'. '~(A v B) negates the whole sentence 'A v B'—the parentheses show that the '~' negates the whole sentence, rather than just the 'A'. (In the sentence '~A v B', just the A is negated.) Now consider these two sentences, '~(A v B)' and '~A v B'. Suppose that the truth value of A is True (i.e., that 'A' is true) and that the truth value of 'B' is also True. Can you see why the truth value of '~(A v B)' is False, but the truth value of '~A v B' is True? Let '&' stand for 'and'. Can you see why whatever the truth values of 'A' and 'B' are, the truth values of '~(A v B)' and '~A & ~B' are the same?

2   Lewis Carroll, *Alice's Adventures in Wonderland*, chapter 7. In *The Annotated Alice*, annotated by Martin Gardner (New York: Bramhall House, 1960), p. 101.

There are scores of textbooks in symbolic logic widely available. There is some difference in the symbols they use, but any of them can provide you with an idea of how one begins in symbolic logic.

CHAPTER VI

MORE LOGIC:
Surprises and Paradoxes

1. Impossible Surprises

The Surprise Quiz that Never Happens

Your logic teacher announces, "There will be a surprise quiz given during one of the next three class-meetings." That annoying A-student in your class requests that your teacher define 'surprise'. The teacher obliges: "A surprise quiz is a quiz whose date you can't figure out in advance. You won't know it's coming until I actually give it to you."

After a moment's thought, the student announces that it can be proven that such a quiz is impossible. Can you figure out the student's reasoning?

> Will the quiz be given during the third meeting of class? If it were, then the quiz wouldn't have taken place during either of the first two classes. At the end of the second class, we'd know that the quiz must happen during the third class, so we would be able to figure out the date of the quiz in advance. So a quiz during the third class wouldn't be a surprise. Therefore, the surprise quiz can't happen during the third class.
>
> So will it happen during the second? We already know that it can't happen during the third class. At the quizless end of the first class, we'd be able to figure out that there must be a quiz during the second class. Thus a quiz during the second class wouldn't be a surprise. So it follows that the quiz couldn't take place during the second class either.
>
> The only remaining possibility is the first class; but we know this, so that wouldn't be a surprise either. It follows that a surprise quiz is impossible.

Obviously this conclusion is mistaken; a surprise quiz is, of course, possible.

A QUESTION TO THINK ABOUT: What has gone wrong in the apparently impeccable reasoning that has led to this conclusion? (I don't think you'll come up with a good answer to this, but it's worth thinking about anyway.)

FOR FURTHER READING: The famous logician and philosopher W.V.O. Quine presents what he thinks has gone wrong in this reasoning in his article "On a Supposed Antimony," printed in his collection of articles, *The Ways of Paradox and Other Essays* (New York: Random House, 1966); this is a slightly amended version of his article "On a So-Called Paradox" in *Mind* 62 (January 1953).

The Surprising Meatloaf

The last example purports to show the impossibility of a surprise; this one, the necessity of a surprise.

Every year on her husband Marvin's birthday, Irene rushed home from the philosophy class she taught to cook him a dinner with a surprising menu. One year it was a Chinese banquet in which each dish had an interesting name. Here's the menu:

Hairy Melon Soup
Jade Trees Hidden in the Dragon Tongue
Grandmother Pockmark's Bean Curd
Ants Climb a Tree
Red Around Two Flowers
Drunken Chicken
Strange-Taste Chicken
Peking Dust

Another year it was "Flambé Dinner" in which each dish was served aflame. On a third occasion, an appalling concoction appeared; the surprise was that all the ingredients rhymed (ham, clam, jam, yam, Spam, and lamb).

But one year, Marvin sat down to a birthday dinner of leftover meatloaf, mashed potatoes, and canned peas.

Marvin was a little upset, and thought he ought to say something. "Every year you make me a surprising birthday dinner. I was expecting something unusual, but this one is very ordinary."

Irene replied, "Yeah, you found this menu quite a surprise, didn't you."

It's not easy being married to a philosopher.

Why All Numbers are Interesting

This case is similar to both of the preceding ones.

Let's define an "interesting number" as a positive integer with some special property. Some numbers are interesting because of their arithmetical properties. 1 is the smallest prime. 2 is the smallest even number. Other numbers are mentioned in some fact we know about: 3 is the number of bears Goldilocks met in the woods. 4 is the number of the day in July on which the U.S. celebrates its national holiday. 5 is the number of fingers on one hand.

Consider each following number. After a little thought, you can discover a reason why 6, 7, 8, 9, and 10 are interesting numbers. Perhaps special properties can be discovered for each number into the thousands. What is the first number you come to which is uninteresting? Well, suppose you think it is 2,504. But you are wrong: that number does have some special property—it's the smallest uninteresting number. Well, let's consider the next number, 2,505. But if that's the smallest uninteresting number, then that one has a special property, so that one is interesting too. But this line of reasoning can be continued for each succeeding number. Therefore there are no uninteresting numbers.

2. Why Everybody Is Poor

A sorites argument is a string of sub-arguments each of which applies the same line of reasoning to the conclusion of the one before. Here's an example that reaches an obviously false conclusion at the end of the string. Its premises are:

- (1) A person who has only one dollar is poor.
- (2) For every number n, if a person who has n dollars is poor, then a person who has $n+1$ dollars is poor.

The first (surely true) conclusion drawn from these premises is

- (3) A person who has only two dollars is poor.

This conclusion plus premise (2) yields

- (4) A person who has only three dollars is poor.

This plus premise (2) yields

- (5) A person who has only four dollars is poor.

And so on. Continuing to reason this way, we eventually get to

- (1,000,001) A person who has only a million dollars is poor.

What has gone wrong?

An argument that reaches a false conclusion either has one or more false assumptions from which it starts, or reasons badly from them. (Some really bad arguments both have false assumptions and reason badly from them.) The reasoning here is fine, so we should reconsider those assumptions.

Premise (1) is unquestionably true; premise (2) must be the culprit. But note that for premise (2) to be false, there must be some number m such that a person who has m dollars is poor, but a person who has $m+1$ dollars is not poor. What number is that? I'll bet you can't tell me. Is it that there is such a number but you don't know exactly what it is? Surely not. No amount of investigation will tell you what m is, for you'll never be satisfied in saying that giving one dollar to someone who has m will turn that person from poor to non-poor.

A QUESTION TO THINK ABOUT: The answer above isn't right. What is the right answer? Here's a suggestion for how to think about the problem: maybe there is a range of numbers where it is unclear whether a person with that number of dollars is poor or not.

'*Sorites*' (pronounced So-*right*-eez) is the Greek word for "heap." The standard version of this puzzle in ancient times went this way: Take away one grain of sand from a heap of sand of any size, and you still have a heap. Now, suppose you have a large heap from which you remove one grain; application of this principle tells you that you still have a heap. Repeat this procedure; you still have a heap. Repeat it over and over again, and you'll eventually get one grain of sand: but the principle tells you that this is still a heap.

3. Paradoxes Of Self-Reference

The Non-Existent Barber

An old and famous puzzle (popularized by Bertrand Russell) invites us to imagine a village in which there is a male barber who shaves all and only those men in the village who don't shave themselves. Does this barber shave himself?

Suppose he doesn't. Because he lives in the village and shaves every man in the village who doesn't shave himself, then he does shave himself.

Suppose he does. Because he lives in the village and doesn't shave any man who shaves himself, then he doesn't shave himself.

So if he does, he doesn't. And if he doesn't, he does.

Something has gone badly wrong here. Can you figure out what?

There couldn't be a village containing such a barber. It's logically impossible for such a barber to exist, for he would have to do the impossible: shave himself *and* not shave himself. The story told to set up this paradox thus describes a situation that is self-contradictory. The story must be false.

The Trouble with Adjectives

The barber puzzle is one of a large number of paradoxes of "self-application"—problems that arise when we try to apply something to itself. Here's another, known as *Grelling's Paradox*.

A *homological* adjective is one that is true of itself. 'Short' is a homological adjective, because the word 'short' is short. 'Polysyllabic' is also homological, because the word is polysyllabic. A *heterological* adjective is not true of itself. 'Misspelled' is heterological, because the word isn't misspelled. So is 'German'.

Now consider the adjective 'heterological': is it homological or heterological?

> Either it is heterological or homological. Let's consider these possibilities one at a time.
> (1) If that adjective is homological, it applies to itself. What the word 'heterological' applies to is heterological. So if that adjective is homological, then it's heterological. This contradiction proves that it's not homological.
> (2) If that adjective is heterological, it doesn't apply to itself. What the word 'heterological' doesn't apply to isn't heterological. So if that adjective is heterological, it's not heterological. This contradiction proves that it's not heterological.

We solved the Barber Paradox by deciding that the story which set up the problem must be false. Do you think that Grelling's Paradox might be solved in the same sort of way?

> Grelling's Paradox can't easily solved by rejecting the story that set it up. This story consists merely in the definitions of 'homological' and 'heterological'. To reject this story is to think that sometimes the notions of *true of* and *not true of* don't make sense—when neither is applicable. This is quite a radical conclusion, since these notions are basic to our understanding of what adjectives are all about.

The Troublesome Statement in the Box

A similar crisis in our ways of thought is brought about by consideration of the paradox of self-application engendered by the following statement:

> The statement in the box is false.

Is that statement true or false?

> If that statement is false, then it's true. If it's true, then it's false. The statement in the box can't be either true or false.

So this paradox leads us to question our basic assumption that every statement is either true or false. Philosophers and logicians worry about this conclusion.

A QUESTION TO THINK ABOUT: Is there a third category—neither true nor false—that is necessary to classify statements?

On Being a Member of Yourself

The Russell Paradox involves the notion of a *set*, which we can think of simply as a collection of things. Now, it seems obvious that for any characteristic you can think of, there is a set of things that have that characteristic. Of course, there are some characteristics that apply to nothing at all, such as the characteristic of being the largest number, or of being a unicorn. But these are counted as corresponding to the *empty* set.

Now consider the characteristic: *is a member of itself*. Some sets have this characteristic. For example, the set of sets that have more than three members is itself a set with more than three members, so it is a member of itself. Similarly, some sets have the characteristic: *is not a member of itself*. For example, the set of dog-biscuits is not a member of itself, since the set itself is not a dog-biscuit.

But what about the set of all sets that are not members of themselves? Is that set a member of itself?

> Suppose this set is a member of itself. But since it is the set of things that are *not* members of themselves, it should then be one of these things—something not a member of itself.
> Suppose then that this set is *not* a member of itself, that is, that it is not among the set of things that are not members of themselves. But if it isn't in this set, then it must be among the things that are members of themselves.

Thus we have found a characteristic that doesn't correspond to a set. Like the Grelling Paradox, this one leads us to question something very basic: in this case, the assumption that for every characteristic there is a set consisting of those things (if any) which have that characteristic. The notions of sets and characteristics are very basic ones, especially in the theory of the foundations of mathematics.

Gottlob Frege, the German founder of mathematical logic, published a hugely important work called *Grundgesetze der Arithmetik* in which he attempted to establish the foundations of mathematics in the laws of logic. Just as the second volume of this work was about to be printed, Frege received a letter from Bertrand Russell, in which Russell informed him about the problem of self-application we have just discussed. "Arithmetic totters," Frege is said to have written in answer. An appendix that he added to the volume opens with the words: "A scientist can hardly encounter anything more undesirable than to have the foundation collapse just as the work is finished. I was put in this position by a letter from Bertrand Russell..."

Here's why Frege said that "arithmetic totters" because of the Russell Paradox. Roughly speaking, Frege argued that the basic concepts of arithmetic (for example, the concept of a number) could be defined in terms of sets and the logical principles involved with them. But Russell's Paradox reveals a basic contradiction in the notion of a set. The set Russell considers both is and isn't a member of itself. If the notions of set and set-membership are contradictory, then this can hardly provide a secure foundation for arithmetic.

FOR FURTHER READING: Quine tells the Russell-Frege story in "The Ways of Paradox" in *The Ways of Paradox and Other Essays*. This article also discusses the implication of the Barber Paradox, and other paradoxes of self-attribution.

Gödel's Proof

Another famous case in which a self-application paradox shook the foundations of mathematics is due to the Austrian mathematician Kurt Gödel. The details of Gödel's proof are quite technical, but here's a simplified way to understand it.

Two goals of any mathematical system are *completeness* and *consistency*. If every statement in a system, or its negation, can be proven using the proof procedures of that system, then the system is complete. A system is consistent if it's not possible to prove both a statement and its negation.

Now, suppose there is a system rich enough to be able to express the statement, 'This statement is not provable'. Can you see how this leads to problems when it is applied to itself?

> Suppose the statement is false. Since it says that it is not provable, then if it's false, it *is* provable. Proving it shows that it's true. But since it says that it isn't provable, if it's true then it follows that it's not provable. Thus we have proven both that it's true and that it's false. So if the statement is false, then the system is inconsistent.

But we don't want an inconsistent system. So in any acceptable—consistent—system, the statement must be true. Since it says that it's not provable in its system, any such acceptable system must be incomplete. Gödel's reasoning thus proves the incompleteness of any consistent system rich enough to be able to express that statement.

One consequence of Gödel's proof is that there are certain questions that logical thought cannot answer.

A QUESTION TO THINK ABOUT: Does this mean that it's okay to be irrational? Don't be too hasty in replying Yes!

This is Not the Title of This Item

There are a number of other statements that give peculiar results when applied to themselves. After reading each one, see if you can figure out what's peculiar about it.

- I am lying.

  If whoever says this is telling the truth, then she is lying. So she can't be telling the truth. But if that person is lying when she says "I am lying," then she is telling the truth. So she can't be lying. What this person says can be neither true nor false.

This is a genuine paradox, very similar to the statement-in-the-box example above. What we have here is a version of the ancient Liar Paradox, discovered in the fourth century B.C. by the Greek philosopher Eubulides. The classical Liar Paradox is a bit different. Here it is.

- Epimenides of Crete says, "All Cretans are liars."

  If we take a liar to be someone who *always* utters falsehoods, then if Epimenides' statement is true, all statements by a Cretan are false. But since Epimenides is a Cretan himself, his statement must be false. Thus if what he said were true, then it would be false. So it can't be a true statement. Could it be false? To say that it's false is not to say that Cretans *always* tell the truth—it's merely to say that they *sometimes* do. But this is consistent with the falsity of this statement by a Cretan. We have just proven that the Epimenides' statement must be false. The neither-true-nor-false problem does not arise.

Another peculiar result arises from the statement

- All universal claims are false.

You might hear this statement made by people who hold the view that universal claims (statements about *every one* of a kind of thing) are to be distrusted.

  But it can't be true. It is, itself, a universal claim, and if all universal claims were false, *it* would have to be false too. There is, however, no contradictory implication from the supposition that it's false. Again, there is no paradox. The statement is false, and we have proven it.

- No knowledge is possible.

  This one is highly unlikely to be true, of course, but logically speaking, no contradiction arises from assuming either that it's true or that it's false. Someone would, however, get into trouble if she claimed that she *knows* that it's true.

- Nothing at all exists

This one is clearly false. We can prove that it's false without having to prove that any of the ordinary things we think exist really do exist. Suppose that statement were true. Then nothing would exist—not even that statement. If that statement doesn't exist, then what is it that we just assumed was true?

- *There Are Two Errors in the*
  the Title of This Book

If you have read the back cover of this book, you will already have considered whether what this title says is true. The first error (involving the repetition of 'the') is hard to see, but once you've noticed it, you have no trouble seeing that it is an error. (See "The the Title of This Book" in chapter VIII for further discussion of this error.)

But a paradox arises when you think about whether there is a second error. You think: there's only one error in the title (the repeated 'the'). So what it says (that there are two errors) is false. Wait a minute—that's the second error. So there are two errors in the title after all. But then what the title says is correct. But if what the title says is correct, then what is says is not an error, so it only contains one error (the repetition). But if it only contains one error, then what it says is wrong, so it contains two errors....

Is the title true or false? Either answer leads to a contradiction. The source of this paradox is again self-reference: the title talks about itself. The paradoxical structure here is exactly the same as what we encountered earlier in "I am lying" and in the statement in the box. Again, it seems, we are forced into the position that some apparently meaningful statements are neither true nor false.

Lawyers Are Like That

This traditional puzzle concerns the ancient Greek Protagoras (c. 480-411 B.C.—the same person who turns up in one of Plato's dialogues). Protagoras taught law, and had this generous contract with Euathlus, one of his students: Euathlus is to pay Protagoras for his education if he wins his first case; if he doesn't win, he doesn't have to pay.

Having just graduated, Euathlus sues Protagoras for free tuition. Euathlus gloatingly tells Protagoras: If I win this case, I get free tuition, since that's what I'm suing for. This is my first case, so if I lose, I don't have to pay—that's what the contract says. So either way I won't have to pay.

Protagoras replies: If you win, you'll have to pay me, because that's what our contract says. If you lose your suit for free tuition, the court will order you to pay tuition, so you'll have to pay me. Either way, you'll have to pay.

A QUESTION TO THINK ABOUT: Do you think either of the two is right? Suppose you were the judge hearing this case in court. What would you do?

FOR FURTHER READING: Some paradoxes of self-reference are interestingly discussed in Douglas R. Hofstadter and Daniel Dennett, *The Mind's I* (New York: Basic, 1981).

> *One of Groucho Marx's most famous remarks was that he wouldn't want to be a member of any club that had such low standards that it would admit* him.

4. Proving That 2 = 1

One of the oldest and most familiar arithmetical paradoxes is a "proof" that $2 = 1$. Here is one version of it:

1. Let:	$x = 1$
2. It's obvious that:	$x = x$
3. Square both sides:	$x^2 = x^2$
4. Subtract x^2 from both sides:	$x^2 - x^2 = x^2 - x^2$
5. Factor both sides:	$x(x - x) = (x + x)(x - x)$
6. Divide both sides by $(x - x)$:	$x = (x + x)$
7. Since $x = 1$:	$1 = (1 + 1)$
8. So:	$1 = 2$

Where is the mistake?

> The mistake here is in step 6, where we divide by $(x - x)$, which is 0. Division by 0 isn't allowed.

Quine uses a version of this "proof" and the Barber Paradox to distinguish between kinds of paradox. The "proof" that $1 = 2$ uses incorrect reasoning that purports to show that something that is really false is true. Quine calls examples of this sort of reasoning "falsidical" paradoxes. A "veridical" paradox, by contrast, uses correct reasoning. When it comes up with an apparently false conclusion, we must conclude either that the conclusion is true after all, or that one of the assumptions made in the course of the reasoning was incorrect. In the

Barber Paradox, the incorrect assumption is that there exists—or even could exist—such a town with such a barber.

FOR FURTHER READING: William Poundstone, in *The Labyrinths of Reason* (New York: Doubleday, 1988), gives the above version of the "proof." This book contains interesting discussions of paradoxes.

5. Zeno's Paradoxes

The Speedy Tortoise

The paradox of Achilles and the tortoise was invented by the ancient Greek philosopher Zeno of Elea.

Achilles, we imagine, is a very fast runner; suppose he runs one hundred times as fast as a tortoise. But if the tortoise gets any head start at all in a race, Achilles can't catch up with him. Here's why. Imagine that the tortoise is given a head start of one hundred meters. Achilles and the tortoise start running simultaneously; but by the time Achilles has travelled the one hundred metres to where the tortoise has started, the tortoise has run another metre. To catch up with him again, Achilles runs that additional metre, but by the time he gets there, the tortoise has advanced a hundredth of a metre (one centimetre). And by the time Achilles has gone that additional centimetre, the tortoise has gone a very little bit further. And so on. In general, we can see that whenever Achilles has caught up to where the tortoise was, the tortoise has gone further, and is still ahead. So Achilles never catches up to the tortoise.

A QUESTION TO THINK ABOUT: This reasoning clearly reaches a false conclusion. Where has it gone wrong?

The Arrow that Never Reaches the Target

Another of Zeno's famous paradoxes is this one:

An arrow is shot at a target. Suppose it takes one second to go half the distance to the target. It still has to travel the remaining half the distance. In another quarter-second it travels half the remaining way. But this still leaves some distance to go. In ⅛ of a second it has covered half the distance still remaining; but there's still a small distance left to go. In a short time it covers half this distance. And so on.

You can see that no matter how many additional trips (of half the remaining distance) we add, the arrow still hasn't reached the target. We seem to have shown that it can never reach the target.

A QUESTION TO THINK ABOUT: Obviously the arrow reaches the target. Assuming it travels at a constant speed, it will hit the target two seconds after it was shot. That's easy to see. What's harder to see is exactly where the reasoning has gone wrong. Any ideas? (Is it the same mistake as was made in "The Speedy Tortoise"?)

Into the Mainstream of Philosophy

Here's a hint that may be helpful in thinking about the surprising meatloaf and the smallest uninteresting number. Note that what's surprising about the meatloaf is that it's not a surprise; and what's interesting about the smallest uninteresting number is that it's uninteresting. Both of these descriptions look self-contradictory. Maybe we should rule out this sort of surprise, and this sort of interestingness.

It seems that we can respond to the paradoxes of self-application in two main sorts of ways. (1) We might try to live with the peculiar results. For example, we might admit that the statement in the box is neither true nor false (or maybe it's *both* true and false!). What would happen if there were statements like this? (2) Patterns of reasoning that get us into trouble when they are applied self-referentially seem to work perfectly well otherwise. Perhaps there's just something illegitimate about self-application. But even self-application seems sometimes to be okay; so maybe there are some non-arbitrary restrictions we should make on self-application to make sure that paradox doesn't result. This is the approach that many logicians have taken.

If you know enough mathematics to understand the notion of the limit of the sum of an infinite series, then maybe you can find a satisfactory way to understand why Achilles really does win the race, and why the arrow really does reach the target. In both cases, an infinite series of decreasing numbers really does add up to a finite number.

The Poundstone work already mentioned is a highly recommended, entertaining, and informative book of paradoxes and similar puzzles. Another one is Smullyan's *What is the Name of This Book?* (Englewood Cliffs, N.J.: Prentice-Hall, 1978).

CHAPTER VII

BELIEF, LOGIC, AND INTENTIONS

1. Believing the Implications

Consider these two statements:

- (1) It's Tuesday.
- (2) It's raining.

If both of these statements are true, then it's impossible that this statement is false:

- (3) It's Tuesday and it's raining.

Logicians say that the set of statements consisting of statement (1) and (2) *implies* statement (3). This means that if (1) and (2) were both true, then (3) has to be true.

Now, suppose you believe that it's Tuesday, and you believe that it's raining. Do you therefore automatically believe that it's Tuesday and it's raining? It's hard to see how someone could believe statements (1) and (2) but not believe (3), the statement that is implied by (1) and (2). It's plausible to think that there's a general principle here:

> Principle 1: If someone believes all the statements in a set, and if that set implies a further statement *S*, then that person believes *S*.

A valid deductive argument is one in which the premises imply the conclusion. It's a peculiarity of valid deductive arguments that they seem not to advance our knowledge significantly. After all, if you already knew that it's Tuesday and that it's raining, wouldn't you *already* know (3)? What use, then, would this argument be? An argument, after all, doesn't establish its premises: it's useful only for someone who already believes the premises, and it's used to convince that person of the truth of the conclusion. But that person would already believe the conclusion.

So valid deductive arguments are all, it seems, useless. But this is a very strange thing to think. Have we made a mistake?

Maybe the mistake here is the idea that we automatically believe all the deductive consequences of what we believe. Maybe Principle 1 is false.

Proving that Archibald is in the Pub

Here is some evidence against Principle 1.

Suppose Archibald, Bernard, and Carlos are identical triplets. You go into the pub and see one of them. Later, I ask you if Archibald was in the pub, and you tell me you don't know; you saw one of the triplets, but you can't tell them apart. I point out to you that we both know the following facts:

- (4) At least one of them was in the pub.
- (5) Bernard never goes to the pub without Archibald.
- (6) Carlos never goes to the pub without another triplet.

You reply, "OK, but I still don't know if Archibald was in the pub." This is possible, right?

But the set of statements (4), (5), and (6) *implies*

- (7) Archibald was in the pub.

Can you see why it does?

If you don't see why, consider the following. (Abbreviate the three names A, B, and C.) We know by statement (4) that at least one of them was there. There are three possibilities:

(a) It was A you saw.

(b) It was B you saw. But statement (5) tells us that if B was there, A was also there.

(c) It was C you saw. But statement (6) tells us that if C was there, A or B was also there. So either A or B was there. But if B was there, we know by statement (5) that A was also there.

So *whichever* you saw, it follows logically that A was there.

The fact that you believed all the statements in the set {(4), (5), and (6)} but didn't automatically therefore believe (7) shows that it's possible that someone believes everything in a set of statements but not what that set implies. Principle 1 is not always true.

Even though we don't necessarily believe what's implied by our beliefs, it seems clear that we *should*. After all, the truth of a set of statements guarantees the truth of anything they imply.

The same line of reasoning seems to show that anyone who *realised* that a statement was implied by his other beliefs would believe that statement. Seeing that a set implies a statement is seeing that it's impossible for everything in the set to be true if the statement is false.

So here are the two plausible principles we have come up with:

Principle 2: Everyone should believe what's implied by their beliefs.

Principle 3: Everyone does believe what they realise is implied by their beliefs.

But neither of these principles is true either. The reason for this is shown by an example called the Lottery Paradox.

The Lottery Nobody Wins

Suppose there's a lottery with one thousand tickets, one of which, drawn at random, will be the winner. There's a chance of 1 in 1000 that any particular ticket will win.

Consider ticket number 1: do you think it will win? Well, there's a tiny chance it will win. But if you are reasonable, you will believe it won't win.

Now consider ticket number 2. You also believe ticket 2 won't win. So you have two beliefs:

- (1) Ticket number 1 won't win
- (2) Ticket number 2 won't win

But of course by the same line of reasoning, you also believe

- (3) Ticket number 3 won't win
- (4) Ticket number 4 won't win
- (5) Ticket number 5 won't win

and so on, up to

- (999) Ticket number 999 won't win
- (1,000) Ticket number 1,000 won't win.

But the set of one thousand statements (1-1,000) implies statement (1,001):

- (1,001) Ticket number 1 won't win and ticket number 2 won't win and ticket number 3 won't win and ticket number 4 won't win and...and ticket number 999 won't win and ticket number 1,000 won't win.

But statement (1,001) is false, because this says that *none* of the tickets in the lottery will win. You don't believe (1,001), and you shouldn't.

What has gone wrong?

Perhaps both Principle 2 and Principle 3 are wrong.

So maybe we should replace them with:

Principle 4: People shouldn't believe everything that's implied by their beliefs.

and

Principle 5: People don't believe everything they realise is implied by their beliefs.

Be Careful What You Believe

It may have occurred to you, while thinking about the Lottery Paradox, that perhaps the problem with the reasoning that reaches such a false conclusion occurs at the very beginning, when you believe that ticket number 1 won't win. After all, it might be said, why do you believe this? It's possible that ticket number 1 *will* win. Why believe it won't? So you don't get to the obviously false statement (1,001).

What's going on in the Lottery Paradox is, after all, that one of the one thousand statements that you incautiously believed was true was actually false—namely the one that referred to the winning ticket, and said it wouldn't win. Now, you don't know in advance which of the one thousand statements this one is, but you know it's there somewhere. The careful thing to do is to withhold belief from all of them. After all, isn't care in managing our beliefs exactly what the study of logic and philosophy is supposed to teach us?

Yes, but think about the policy advocated here. Is it really a good idea to withhold belief from any statement which might turn out false? Think about all those things you now believe, including:

- Fish generally live under water.
- You drank coffee with breakfast this morning.
- The United States has a larger population than Canada.
- Carl Yastrzemski used to play for the Red Sox.

You might be mistaken about any of these. Which of your beliefs, come to think of it, is so trustworthy that it is utterly impossible that it be mistaken? Beliefs that are learned from experience (such as the above) are not 100 per cent infallible; and neither are those beliefs which you arrive at using the powers of your mind alone—for example, in arithmetic. Even in arithmetical reasoning, it's possible that you have made a mistake. It turns out that employing this strict a test of believability will rule out *all* beliefs. (Some philosophers have argued that there are a few peculiar beliefs about which it's impossible that the believer is mistaken. Even if they're right, we nevertheless face the undesirable consequence of having to withhold belief from *almost* everything we now believe.)

Thus the policy of accepting beliefs about which we are not 100 per cent certain is not a mistake. Sometimes we'll turn out wrong; but the alternative—withholding belief from anything that is not 100 per cent certain—is worse, because it would mean that we would believe nothing (or extremely little).

The sensible thing to do is to believe some things about which we are not perfectly—100 per cent—certain. Just how likely must something be before it's okay to believe it? The answer to this isn't clear. Maybe the degree of assurance we need changes with circumstances, depending on how important it is to be right, and what sort of disasters would result if one were wrong. In any event, statement (1) in the Lottery Paradox example is 99.9 per cent probable. It seems that that's probable enough to satisfy almost everyone, in almost every circumstance. But so is (2), and (3), and so on. So the paradox is still there.

Knowing Nothing About Birds

Maybe you now think that even though it's not necessary to restrict our beliefs to those things that are 100 per cent probable, we should arrange our beliefs so that their probability of truth is maximized. This might look like good advice. Nevertheless, suppose you look out the window and see what you take to be an English sparrow at your bird feeder. You're tempted to believe

- (1) There's an English sparrow out there.

Now, you're pretty good at recognizing at least common birds like the English sparrow. But, of course, there's some possibility you're wrong. If you believed instead

- (2) There's a sparrow out there.

this would increase the probability that you're right. So on the principle that we should maximize the probability of the truth of our beliefs, you believe (2) instead of (1). But now consider

- (3) There's a bird out there.

This is even more likely to be true than (2); so you should discard (2) and accept (3) instead. But, of course, we can continue this process of reasoning, and replace (3) with

- (4) There's some living thing out there.

and replace (4) with

- (5) There's some object out there.

and perhaps even replace (5) with the more certain

- (6) I seem to see something out there.

This process does increase the probability that your beliefs are correct, but the ones that are more likely to be correct also contain less information. What we are left with is one that's very likely true, but claims almost nothing. Following this strategy for belief-selection would result in very few beliefs indeed, and ones with very little informational content.

A QUESTION TO THINK ABOUT: What is the right strategy for choosing what to believe?

The Hobgoblin of Little Minds

Are all your beliefs true? Obviously the answer is no: only an unreasonable egotist would think the contrary. All reasonable people believe this statement:

- At least one of my other beliefs is false.

Now consider the hypothetical list of your belief statements, with this last belief added at the end:

- Fish generally live under water.
- You drank coffee with breakfast this morning.
- The United States has more population than Canada.
- Carl Yastrzemski used to play for the Red Sox.
    - ...
- At least one of the other statements on this list is false.

This is not merely a set including at least one false statement. It is an *inconsistent* set: it is *logically impossible* that all the statements in this set are true. To see this, imagine that everything in the list up to the last item is true; but this makes the last one false. It's logically necessary that at least one statement on the list is false.

If you are reasonable, then, you have an inconsistent belief set.

FOR FURTHER READING: This paradox (as well as several others in this book) is discussed interestingly and entertainingly in Raymond Smullyan's *What is the Name of This Book?* (Englewood Cliffs, N.J.: Prentice-Hall, 1978.) Sometimes this paradox is called the "Paradox of the Preface": in one version (not Smullyan's) we are to consider a book whose preface contains the usual comment, "No doubt there are errors in this book." That comment is logically true: if there are no errors elsewhere, then that statement is an error. It also makes what's said in the book logically inconsistent.

> *Do I contradict myself?*
> *Very well then I contradict myself,*
> *(I am large, I contain multitudes.)*[1]

> *Consistency is the hobgoblin of little minds. (The full quote is: "A foolish consistency is the hobgoblin of little minds, adored by little statesmen and philosophers and divines."*[2] *The inclusion of the word "foolish" changes the meaning somewhat.)*

You'll Believe Just Anything

Well, what is wrong with inconsistent beliefs? One reason to think that inconsistent beliefs are a disaster is that a set of inconsistent statements implies *every* statement. This widely accepted principle of logic may seem peculiar to you, and deserves some justification.

Here's one way of looking at implication that may make that principle seem reasonable. To say that a set of statements {A} implies B means that it's logically impossible that all the statements in set {A} are true while B is false. So, for example, it's logically impossible that all the statements in this set: {'It's raining', 'It's Tuesday'} are true while 'It's raining and it's Tuesday' is false. So the set {'It's raining', 'It's Tuesday'} implies 'It's raining and it's Tuesday'. Here's another example: {'If it's raining, then the picnic is cancelled', 'The picnic is not cancelled'} implies 'It's not raining'. Think about these statements and you'll see why. It's logically impossible that all three of these hold: (1) 'If it's raining, then the picnic is cancelled' is true; *and* (2) 'The picnic is not cancelled' is true; *and* (3) 'It's not raining' is false.

Now a *logically inconsistent* set of statements is a set of statements such that it's logically impossible that every statement in that set is true. A simple example of such a set is {'Today is Monday', 'Today is not Monday'}. Strangely enough, that set of statements implies 'Fred is wearing pink socks'. To see why this is true, all we have to do is to apply the account of implication just given. It's impossible that all three

1 Walt Whitman, "Song of Myself," in *Leaves of Grass* (London: Dent, 1907).
2 Ralph Waldo Emerson, "Self Reliance," in *Essays: First Series* (1841).

of these hold: (1) 'Today is Monday' is true; *and* (2) 'Today is not Monday' is true; *and* (3) 'Fred is wearing pink socks' is false. (The reason why this is the case has nothing to do with what colour socks Fred is wearing. The first two conditions suffice to make it impossible that all three hold.)

Similar reasoning can show why the set { 'Today is Monday', 'Today is not Monday' } implies *any statement at all*. And similarly, any inconsistent set of statements implies every statement.

Now recall the those two principles we were considering above:

Principle 2: Everyone should believe what's implied by their beliefs.

Principle 3: Everyone does believe what they realise is implied by their beliefs.

Bearing in mind that
- All statements are implied by an inconsistent set of statements.
- The statements you believe are an inconsistent set.
- You now know that the set of your beliefs is inconsistent.

these obviously absurd conclusions follow:
- You should believe all statements.
- You do believe all statements.

Something has gone drastically wrong here. We have already seen reasons to question Principles 2 and 3. If we reject these principles, we can also reject their absurd consequences. But perhaps we can also question the principle of logic that every statement is implied by an inconsistent set of statements. However, it's hard to see what should replace this principle. It merely follows from the definition of 'implication'.

A QUESTION TO THINK ABOUT: Can you suggest a better definition that avoids this peculiar result?

2. I Just Can't Believe That

There are some things that are true but you don't believe them. But is there anything true that you *couldn't* believe—that it's *impossible* for you to believe? At first glance, you might think that there couldn't be anything like that. Suppose that some sentence S were true, and suppose you didn't believe it. It doesn't seem that it would be *impossible* for you to believe it. Suppose that you had a very reliable and smart friend, and you believed everything that that friend told you. This isn't impossible, right? Now, if your friend told you sentence *S*, you'd believe it.

We can, however, turn up examples of sentences such that, were they true, it would be impossible for you to believe them. Here's an example of one of them:

- "_____ is now dead" (Insert your name in the blank.)

This sentence is obviously false. But (I'm sorry to tell you) some day it will be true and when it's true it will be impossible for you to believe it.

Here's another. Suppose you wake up one morning with a bad hangover, badly confused. You think it's Monday, but actually it's Sunday. The true situation at that point is expressed by the sentence:

- "_____ believes it's Monday, but it's not." (Insert your name.)

Your friend might find out that that sentence is true. But consider your own beliefs. Later on, when your head clears, you realize the truth, and you believe this sentence:

- "I believed (earlier this morning) that it was Monday, but it's not."

But consider the state of affairs earlier that morning. At that point, you believed that it was Monday, and it wasn't. This sentence, if you happened to say it then, would have been true:

- "I believe it is Monday, but it's not."

Notice, however, that you wouldn't have uttered that sentence, because it's impossible that you believe that what it says is true.

Your reliable friend shows up first thing in the morning, and tells you this:

- "You believe it's Monday, but it's not."

Could you believe what your friend says?

> Part of what your friend's sentence says is that it's not Monday. But if you believe this part, then you wouldn't believe that it's Monday. But then the other part of your friend's sentence ("You believe it's Monday") would be false, and you'd know it's false.
>
> Or things might work the other way. On hearing your friend's sentence, you first notice the part that says "You believe it's Monday." Assuming your friend speaks the truth, you do believe it's Monday, and you believe this part of the sentence. But then you would think that the second part of the sentence is false. You couldn't believe the whole sentence.

3. Descartes' Thought

René Descartes is famous for the quote "I think, therefore I am." What's not quite so widely known is why he said it.

Descartes began his work *Meditations on First Philosophy* by noting that some of our ordinary beliefs have turned out to be false. Most of your ordinary beliefs seem obviously true, and you have no reason to think they're false; but even these just *might* be false. Descartes thought that philosophy should begin with beliefs about which it is *impossible* to be mistaken. Are there any beliefs like that?

The first one Descartes turned up was his own belief that he existed. This is not the belief that his body exists: it is the belief that he has mental existence—that he exists as a thinking thing. The famous quote embodies his reasoning to prove that this belief couldn't be mistaken. The supposition that the belief that he exists is mistaken couldn't be true. If he were mistaken in this belief, then he would, anyway, have a mistaken belief; and anything that has a mistaken belief is an existing thinking thing. Anyone who thinks he or she exists must be right.

4. Self-Fulfilling and Self-Defeating Beliefs

The Power of Positive Thinking

A self-fulfilling belief is a belief of the following sort: believing it will tend to make it true. An example of this is the belief that you will do well on a test. Generally speaking, if you have this belief, you will go into the test relaxed and confident, and will do better as a result. The opposite belief—that you will do poorly on the test—similarly tends to be self-fulfilling. If you go into the test convinced you'll do poorly, you'll be nervous and unhappy, and this will tend to lower your score.

Another example of a belief that tends to be self-fulfilling is the belief that somebody important to you likes you; it will result in your acting toward that person in a natural and confident way, and this may well result in their liking you. Similarly, the opposite belief is self-fulfilling.

Insomniacs are unfortunately quite familiar with the self-fulfilling nature of the belief that you won't be able to get to sleep.

I'm about to give you a suggestion that can change your life enormously for the better! (Wonderful! Didn't you always hope that philosophy had such useful wisdom to offer?) The suggestion is this: if you want something to be true, and if the belief that it is true tends to be self-fulfilling, believe that belief. Thus, go into every test convinced that you'll do well, and you will do well (or, at least, you'll do better than you would have). Believe that people you want to like you do like you, and they will like you (or at least will tend to.) The belief that you will succeed in a business will result in your acting in ways that may improve your chances of success. The cultivation of self-fulfilling positive beliefs is essentially the technique for improvement of your life advocated by "positive thinking" training.

The problem here (and in Pascal's Wager, discussed in Chapter II) is that for most of us, consideration of the consequences of believing something has no power whatever to make us believe it. What would make us believe something is evidence that it is *true*.

But on closer inspection, it appears that self-fulfilling beliefs are not exactly like Pascal's Wager. Believing a self-fulfilling belief tends to make it true. So it appears that the fact that you believe a self-fulling belief *is* some evidence that what you believe is true.

How to Fail at Baseball

Related to the notion of a self-fulfilling belief is the notion of a paradoxical intention. This is involved when it's less likely that you can do something if you try to do it.

A good baseball swing is a complex sort of action. You might naturally have a good swing the first time you pick up a bat, or you might get a good swing from advice and practice. But it's likely that if you are told what's wrong with your swing and what you should be doing, and then you swing while trying to do the right thing, you'll do worse than you ordinarily do when you're not thinking about it.

Trying to go to sleep is another example. Trying to do it may very well prevent you from doing it.

People who think too much are poor at doing things that involve paradoxical intentions. Philosophers, whose business it is to think about things, hope that paradoxical intentions aren't too widespread. (My Philosophy Department's softball team was soundly thrashed by almost every team we played. On the other hand, we did defeat the team from the Registrar's Office where there's no evidence of thought at all.)

The Pursuit of Happiness

Is the pursuit of happiness another example of the phenomenon of paradoxical intention?

> Some philosophers think that the achievement of happiness also involves paradoxical intentions—that trying to be happy is not the way to achieve happiness. Maybe it even interferes with happiness. It's been suggested that a good strategy for achieving happiness is finding things that matter to you and working hard to get them. Perhaps this is good advice; but note that someone who is working towards growing a beautiful lawn, or breaking a hundred on the golf course, or solving a philosophical problem, has intentions, desires, and aims directed towards gardening, or golf, or philosophy—not towards happiness.
>
> *Thomas Jefferson wrote, in the American Declaration of Independence, that we all have the right to the pursuit of happiness. But if pursuing happiness is a bad way to get it, then this right isn't worth much.*

A QUESTION TO THINK ABOUT: Maybe there isn't really any such thing as the pursuit of happiness. We know what it means to pursue skill at golf or to try to open a jar whose lid is stuck. But what does it mean to try to get happiness?

Fooling Yourself

Positive thinking is, in a sense, a sort of attempted self-deception: the only reason that you have to try so hard to have a self-fulfilling belief is that you really believe it's false—or, at least, fear it might be.

Is self-deception possible? Suppose that you need a good night's sleep for some important task the next day, and you believe you won't be able to go to sleep because you tend to be insomniac. You realise that this belief will tend to keep you awake, because you will worry about not being rested; so you try to believe instead that you'll go to sleep as soon as your head hits the pillow. The only reason you're trying so hard to believe you'll go right to sleep is that you already believe you won't. How can you believe something while you believe the opposite? How can you believe something *because* you believe the opposite? Perhaps self-deception is impossible.

But maybe I've spoken too fast. What is the familiar phenomenon called "wishful thinking" but the sort of self-deceptive process of coming to believe something not because you have evidence for its truth, but because you wish it were true?

Sorry, I'm Not Free Right Now

The attempt to practise self-deception plays a key role in the analysis of the human condition advocated by some existentialists. In their view, a centrally important, universal, and necessary human characteristic is our *freedom*: there are no causes for our feelings, values, or behaviour, not even our personality (which they regard as a myth). Neither are there objective standards provided by God, our society, or moral reasoning that really oblige us to do one thing rather than another. Thus we must make ourselves up—create our own standards and motives out of nothing—with no cause and no guidance. As a result, we're wholly responsible for everything we do.

Our realization that we are in this state is not a pleasant one: it's terrible to think that nothing pushes or helps us in our self-creation, and that we are totally responsible for ourselves. That's why we spend so much of our time trying to give excuses: attempting to pretend to ourselves and others that there are real causes or standards, or that we really do have "personalities" or "roles" that force us to be some way. But this is always a mistake, and we know that it's a mistake. How can you actually come to believe you're not free, while you really believe you are?

5. Mental Impotence

Believe or I'll Shoot!

Positive thinking sometimes works. It would be a good idea for you to believe something you want to be true if that would help make it true. But it seems that we don't have the power to believe what we want to believe.

Suppose someone held a gun at your head and said, "Believe that the Dodgers will win next year's World Series, or I'll shoot!" You would first try to convince this loony that you did believe that the Dodgers will win. But if you didn't already believe the Dodgers will win, his threat wouldn't result in your coming to believe it. You would surely *want* to believe it—it would be very much to your benefit to believe it—but this has no bearing on the matter.

How to Intend to Kick Your Cat

It seems we can't get intentions on purpose either. Having somehow escaped the loony in the last example, you walk further down the street and another loony approaches, holds his gun at your head, and says, "Intend to kick your cat tomorrow, or I'll shoot!" Perhaps you are in a different situation now from the one you were in when you encountered the first loony. You can't develop beliefs at will, but (perhaps) you can develop intentions at will.

You love Tabitha and certainly don't want to kick the poor, fuzzy, defenceless thing. Having no intention to kick her, your first strategy might be deception: you would try to convince this loony that you had just developed the intention he demanded.

But suppose there's no fooling him: he can tell that you're insincere in reporting your intention—it shows on your face.

So you consider this second strategy: you'll develop the intention to kick the cat—what else can you do?—and avoid getting shot. But, you reason, having the intention to do something doesn't mean that you really will do it. After your assailant has gone away, you can certainly change your mind. So your intention to kick Tabitha, you're relieved to see, will be harmless. You can merely get rid of the intention before tomorrow, and thus avoid both being shot and kicking Tabitha.

But the loony is too clever for you. "I can tell," he says, "that what you're trying to do is to develop the intention now to kick your cat, but that you also intend to get rid of that intention after I go away. So what you really intend is not to kick your cat at all!" He points his gun.

You think: I really have to develop the intention to kick Tabitha. If I also intend now to change my mind later, then I don't really intend now to kick Tabitha. So I guess the only thing I can do is to decide now to kick her, without intending to change my mind later.

So you develop two intentions: (1) to kick Tabitha, and (2) not to change your mind later about (1). You tell the loony what you've decided, and he sees that you're sincere. Will that do the trick?

Even if it does, there's a puzzle here. Your intention (2) is really a crazy one. Why not change your mind later? He will, after all, have gone away, and you won't be in any danger. (There's an analogy here with the "Doomsday Machine" example I'll present in Chapter XIV, in an item called "Bombing the Russians".)

But maybe it won't do the trick. "I'm way ahead of you," says the loony. "What you really are going to do is to change your mind about (2) later. Then at that time you'll be able to change your mind about (1).

So to avoid being shot you also need another intention, (3): that you won't change your mind about (2)."

But if this is the case, then to satisfy him, wouldn't you *also* need to have intention (4): not to change your mind about (3)? This line of reasoning continues: maybe you need an infinite number of intentions. Is it possible for anyone to have an infinite number of intentions? Is your assailant demanding the impossible after all?

Into the Mainstream of Philosophy

Some of the problems that arose in the items in this chapter result from the assumption that we must believe everything that's implied by our beliefs. Many philosophers think that this assumption should simply be rejected. But this rejection brings its own problems. For one thing, is it really logically possible that somebody believes that all pigs are sloppy eaters, but fails to believe what's implied by this, that nothing that is a neat eater is a pig? It seems inconceivable that somebody could believe one but not the other. Do you think that this is possible?

Again, some philosophers urge us to become reconciled to the position that it's possible to have contradictory beliefs. Thus, for example, someone might believe both that it's Tuesday and that it's not Tuesday, simultaneously. Is this really possible? If someone *said* both of these sentences with a look of deep sincerity, we wouldn't know what that person believed. Try to think of a plausible story that involves someone's having contradictory beliefs. Can you? Maybe this doesn't even make sense.

As in the case of the previous chapter, you'll find useful reading on these matters in the Smullyan and Poundstone books.

Another topic in this chapter is self-defeating and self-fulfilling beliefs, and self-deception. These do not fit neatly into any particular subject matter area in mainstream philosophy, though there are occasional treatments of these ideas by philosophical writers in various contexts. For those interested in further reading, the best I can do is lamely to suggest you keep your eyes open. In the meantime, I can propose some questions for you to think about.

(1) One way to account for self-deception is to think of the mind as having parts, only some of which are conscious. Thus, for instance, when we have a belief we don't want to have, this gets shoved down into an unconscious area of the mind and replaced in the consciousness with a preferable one. Perhaps this way of thinking necessitates postulation of a third area, which does the evaluation and the shoving. Students familiar with Freudian psychology will recognize this as a

version of Freud's tripartite division of the mind. But is it really necessary to complicate things to this degree? It really does seem to be an affront to common sense to attribute desires or beliefs to someone who sincerely denies they are there. How could anyone know they are there? If what's in our mind is nothing but what we are aware of, then isn't it self-contradictory to talk about parts of our mental life of which we're unaware?

(2) Certain considerations above tended to lead us to talk about beliefs about beliefs, intentions about intentions, desires about desires. These are sometimes called "second-order" beliefs, intentions, and desires, and they are puzzling things. Do they even make sense? Consider this example. Suppose you and all your friends smoke; everyone else wants to stop smoking, but you (unconvinced or unmoved by the threats to your health and bank account) don't. Now suppose that you're a conformist, and want to be like all your friends. You'd like to share their desire to stop smoking, but you don't share it. In other words, you have the first-order desire to keep smoking, but you have the second-order desire not to have this first-order desire. You want to keep smoking, but you want *not* to want to keep smoking. Is this possible? Maybe second-order desires, if genuine, simply collapse into first-order desires. Thus if you genuinely do want to want to stop smoking, then you automatically want to stop smoking. Is this right?

CHAPTER VIII

GOOD AND BAD
REASONING

1. Thought-Traps For the Unwary

The Price of a Cork

Here's a question that most people answer wrong. If a bottle and a cork together cost $1.10, and the bottle costs $1.00 more than the cork, then what does the cork cost?

> The answer everyone jumps at is 10¢. If you don't see that this is the wrong answer, notice that if the cork cost 10¢, and the bottle cost $1.00 more than the cork, then the bottle would cost $1.10, so together they would cost $1.20.

This is, of course, an arithmetic puzzle, not a philosophical one. What may be of philosophical interest here is why almost everyone gets the wrong answer. Is there something about the way the puzzle is posed that leads people in the wrong direction? Is there something about our normal strategy in dealing with arithmetical questions that usually works fine, but that leads us astray when we think about this puzzle?

Maybe the right answer is a combination of these two ideas. We all share certain reasoning strategies. Some of these are learned in school. More are learned in the course of everyday experience, by imitation and suggestion from others, and by trial and error. There might even be some inborn problem-solving strategies wired into our brains, and genetically determined. These strategies work pretty well, in general. Most people are able to solve most simple problems successfully. But there are some simple problems that most people answer wrong. Our common strategies are not geared to deal with these problems successfully. A careful examination of a variety of these problems might show us exactly how our common strategies work.

The fact that our common strategies tend to fail on certain sorts of simple problems does not automatically mean that we're stupid, in general, or that our common strategies need fixing. Any problem-solving strategy will be good at some problems and bad at others. Some of them will be much easier to learn and use, given the wiring of our brains and the nature of our environment. It just might be the case that the ones we in fact use achieve just the right combination of high percentage of success and ease of learning and use. But maybe not.

What are our strategies for doing arithmetic? That's a hard question to answer; but whatever they are, they are different from the ones computers use. Computers are much better than we are in multiplying large numbers. They can calculate answers in a tiny fraction of the time it takes humans, and we get wrong answers far more often than they do. But we're much better at figuring out what sort of computations are necessary to solve problems than they are. Imagine that you could get your brain surgically replaced with a computer. You could multiply large numbers much better as a result, but you'd be much worse off at problem-solving in general. The way we work is not so bad.

Splitting Up the Diamonds

The next few items demonstrate other arithmetical traps for the unwary. This one is an old puzzle that confused me and my friends when we were children.

A will specifies that several diamonds, to be found in a safety deposit box, are to be distributed to the deceased's children as follows: half of them to the eldest, one quarter of them to the middle child, and one fifth to the youngest. The executor is puzzled about what to do when it turns out that there are nineteen identically sized diamonds in the box. You can't give out half, one quarter, or one fifth of this collection without cutting some diamonds into pieces, and cutting a diamond would ruin its value. What can the executor do?

> The executor hits on this ingenious plan: he borrows another diamond of the same size from a jeweller friend, and adds it to the nineteen. He takes half of the twenty—ten of them—and gives them to the eldest child; then one quarter of the twenty—five—to the middle child; and one fifth of the twenty—four—to the youngest. He has distributed nineteen diamonds; one remains—the one he borrowed from the jeweller—which he now returns. The eldest child is delighted, reasoning that she was entitled to only nine and a half diamonds (one half of the nineteen) but has received ten instead; the other two think they have received a similar bonus.

A QUESTION TO THINK ABOUT: Something is peculiar about this very nifty solution. Do you see what has gone wrong? (Hint: there's something wrong in the terms of the will.)

Nobody Works at All

Another arithmetic mistake:

There are 365 days in the year; but people usually work eight hours a day; that's one third of the twenty-four-hour day. So people actually work only the equivalent of one-third of 365 days—that is, about 122 days.

But people usually work only weekdays. This means two days off a week; there are 52 weeks, so there are 104 days off. Subtracting this from the 122 days leaves only 18 days.

Suppose, on average, a 10-day vacation. This leaves 8 days. But there are at least this many regular holidays in the year. So nobody works at all.[1]

A QUESTION TO THINK ABOUT: Can you explain what's wrong with this reasoning?

More Math Troubles

Here are a couple of other amusing arithmetical paradoxes:

Clearly:	1 yard = 36 inches
Dividing through by 4:	¼ yard = 9 inches
The square root of both sides:	½ yard = 3 inches[2]

Consider a large pile of cubical toy blocks. The smallest has a side of exactly 1 inch (so it has a volume of $1^3 = 1$ cubic inch). The next largest has a slightly larger side, and they keep getting gradually larger, up to the largest, which is 3 inches on a side (with a volume of $3^3 = 9$ cubic inches). The average length of side in this pile is 2 inches. The average volume must be $^{(1+9)}\!/_2$ cubic inches = 5 cubic inches. So the block in this pile that is of average size must measure 2 inches on a side, and have a volume of 5 cubic inches. That's a pretty peculiar block.[3]

His Father's Son

This item is another example of a conceptual trap—but not an arithmetical one.

Raoul is looking at a photograph. You ask him, "Whose photograph is that?" Raoul poetically replies, "Brothers and sisters have I none; but

---

1   A version of this traditional children's story is in John Allen Paulos's *Innumeracy: Mathematical Illiteracy and Its Consequences* (New York: Vintage, 1990), p. 167-8.
2   *Innumeracy*, p. 95.
3   Adapted from an example in *Innumeracy*, p. 169.

this man's father is my father's son." By "this man" Raoul means the man in the photo. Who is that man?

> The answer is that the man in the photo is Raoul's son. Is that the answer you arrived at? If the right answer is not obvious to you, note that the person Raoul calls "my father's son" has to be Raoul himself; and since *that* person (Raoul) is "this man's father," then "this man" has to refer to Raoul's son.

Almost everyone jumps at the answer that the man in the photo must be Raoul. They reason: because Raoul has no brothers or sisters, then the person he calls "my father's son" must be him. So far so good; but people forget that "my father's son" is *the father* of the man in the picture. Perhaps something about the way the riddle is stated makes people forget that, and makes us think about the problem in the wrong way.

The Card Mistake

Here's an experiment you can run on yourself. A psychologist used this as part of a test of people's reasoning ability.

Examine the following four cards:

Half of each card is masked. Your job is to figure out which of the hidden parts of these cards you *need* to see in order to answer the following question decisively: *Is it true in all cases that if there is a circle on the left there is a circle on the right?* Of course, if you unmasked all the cards, you could answer this question; but it's not necessary to unmask all of them to answer it conclusively. Which are the cards it's necessary to unmask?

$$a \qquad b \qquad c \qquad d$$

> Is your answer that you need to see the masked part on only card *a*? Or is your answer that you need to see the masked parts on both card *a* and card *c*? These are the answers people commonly give, but both of these answers are wrong. The right answer is that you need to see the masked parts on card *a* and on card *d*.
>
> Here's help in figuring out why the right answer is right. What would it take for it to be true that all the cards follow the rule? It would have to be the case that any card with an 0 on the left would have to have an 0 on the right. In other words, there could be no card with an 0 on the left and nothing on the right. To test this, we can ignore card *b*, which doesn't have an 0 on the left. Similarly, card *c* can be ignored, since whether or not there's an 0 on the left, it can't be the sort of card we are

looking for: with an 0 on the left, and nothing on the right. Card *d* must
be unmasked, however, because it might have an 0 on the left. If it does,
then that general rule would be shown false. If it doesn't, then the rule
can still be true.

Perhaps you're one of the few people who got the correct answer.
If you're not, you might try to figure out why the right answer is right;
but that's not the point here. The point is that in the experiment very
few people got the right answer, even when the subjects were a group
of university students with high intelligence. (In one group of 128 university students, only five got the right answer.) So don't feel bad if you
got the wrong answer.

Again the question that interests us here is not what the right answer is. It is, rather, why such a large proportion of intelligent people
get it wrong. One theory is that it's not because the question is very
difficult, but rather because the question is posed in an abstract way, as
a mere puzzle, and has no bearing on anyone's practical experience.

Consider, by contrast, an exactly analogous puzzle, but put in more
practical terms. Suppose you've heard that every day before a paper is
due, your philosophy professor stays home. You're interested in knowing if this is true. What would you need to do to find out? Suppose it's
a day before a paper is due. Then you would need to find out if your
professor is at home. (The analogy here is to the necessity of unmasking
card *a*.) Now suppose it's *not* a day before a paper is due. Do you need
to find out whether your professor is at home or not? Obviously this
wouldn't make any difference. (Analogy to card *b*.) Suppose on another
day you have found out that the professor has stayed home. Would it
make any difference for you to find out whether there's a paper due the
next day or not? No. (Analogy to card *c*.) But if on another day you find
that the professor is *not* home, then you *should* find out whether there's
a paper due or not, because if a paper is due, then the fact that the professor is not home would show that what you've heard is false. If you
found this more "practical" example easier, then maybe this theory is
right.

But there's a deeper philosophical question raised by this experiment. What reason do we have for classifying some reasoning as good
and other reasoning as bad? One way of explaining this classification is
that it summarizes and systematizes how smart people really reason.
But if smart people rarely come to the conclusion that one must unmask
cards *a* and *d*, then the fact that they go wrong on this problem does not
show that their reasoning strategy is a bad one.

FOR FURTHER READING: This experiment, and ones like it, were run by P. Wason and P. Johnson-Laird. It's described and discussed in Wason, "Reasoning about a Rule," in *Quarterly Journal of Experimental Psychology* 20 (1968), pp. 273-281; Wason and Johnson-Laird, "A Conflict between Selecting and Evaluating Information in an Inferential Task," *British Journal of Psychology* 61 (1970), pp. 501-515; and several articles in Johnson-Laird and Wason, eds., *Thinking* (Cambridge: Cambridge University Press, 1977).

2. The Reasoning Of Other Cultures and Past Cultures

Azande Witches

It's amazing what cultures radically different from our own believe about the world, and count as good reasoning.

Consider the thinking of the Azande tribe. The Azandes believe that post-mortem examination of someone's intestines for "witchcraft substance" can show conclusively whether or not that person was a witch. They also believe that witchcraft is strictly inherited—that is, if a parent of yours is a witch, then you *must* inherit this trait. But they refuse to draw the conclusion that people are witches when they are the offspring of someone determined, post-mortem, to have been a witch.

Something is peculiar here, but what? Of course, most of us would object to the Azandes' idea that there are witches and intestinal "witchcraft substance." But that's not the interesting point of this example. It seems, in addition, that they are making an elementary reasoning mistake. They appear to agree to the following premises:

- X's parent is a witch
- If someone's parent is a witch, then that person is a witch too.

But to refuse to accept the following conclusion:

- X is a witch.

But we shouldn't be too hasty here. Maybe they really do accept that the conclusion follows from these premises, but don't like calling live people witches and are too polite to agree to the conclusion. Or maybe the anthropologist who translated what the Azandes said got the translation wrong. Or maybe the native informants were joking with the anthropologist, or telling deliberate lies.

FOR FURTHER READING: The philosophical implications of Azande reasoning are discussed by Peter Winch, "Understanding a Primitive Society," *American Philosophical Quarterly* 1 (1964), pp. 307-24.

Winch's position is discussed by Charles Taylor in "Rationality," in Martin Hollis and Steven Lukes, *Rationality and Relativism* (Oxford: Basil Blackwell, 1982), p. 94. This book is a splendid collection of articles about the general questions raised in this item.

Camels in Germany

Here is an excerpt from an interview by the psychologist A.R. Luria with a Kashdan peasant:

> *Q.* (the following syllogism is presented) There are no camels in Germany. The city of B. is in Germany. Are there camels there or not?
>
> *A.* (subject repeats syllogism exactly)
>
> *Q.* So, are there camels in Germany?
>
> *A.* I don't know, I've never seen German villages.
>
> *Q.* (the syllogism is repeated)
>
> *A.* Probably there are camels there.
>
> *Q.* Repeat what I said.
>
> *A.* There are no camels in Germany, are there camels in B. or not? So probably there are. If it's a large city there should be camels there.
>
> *Q.* But what do my words suggest?
>
> *A.* Probably there are. Since there are large cities, then there should be camels.
>
> *Q.* But if there aren't any in all of Germany?
>
> *A.* If it's a large city, there will be Kazahks or Kirghiz [types of camels] there.

We can't jump to the conclusion in this case that the peasant is unable to reason logically. Notice that the peasant doesn't get this bit of reasoning:

- There are no camels in Germany.
- The city of B. is in Germany.
- Therefore there are no camels in B.

but provides this bit of reasoning:

- There are camels in large cities.

- B. is a large city
- There are camels in B.

Never mind that the second bit of reasoning contains a false premise (the generalization about camels in large cities)—the reasoning on the basis of this premise is correct. So it seems that this peasant is able to understand and use a basic logical syllogism.

What has gone wrong, then?

> Perhaps the peasant's inability to understand the first syllogism is the result of the fact that it is (at least for him) *hypothetical*—he doesn't know, and isn't told, that the premises are true. He's just asked to suppose that they are. It might be the case that, in certain cultures, reasoning about (what are thought to be) the facts works fine, but there's an inability to apply it to hypothetical situations.

FOR FURTHER READING: This example and many others are discussed fascinatingly in Don LePan's *The Cognitive Revolution in Western Culture*, Vol. 1: *The Birth of Expectation* (London: Macmillan, 1989). LePan offers the hypothesis that peasants from primitive cultures (as well as children in ours) show deficits in reasoning about hypothetical situations. He cites Hallpike, *The Foundations of Primitive Thought* (Oxford: Oxford University Press, 1979) as the source for the Luria interview.

If We Had Three Nostrils, Would There Be Eight Planets?

Here is a sample from our own culture. Galileo looked through his telescope at Jupiter, and in 1610 published a work in which he claimed to have seen four moons around that planet. But Francis Bacon (1561-1626) argued that what Galileo saw couldn't have been moons. Seven "planets" (meaning bodies in space: the sun and the moon, Mercury, Venus, Mars, Jupiter, and Saturn) were already known, and these additional four would raise the number to eleven; but Bacon argued that there must be exactly seven:

> There are seven windows given to animals in the domicile of the head, through which the air is admitted to the tabernacle of the body, to enlighten, to warm and to nourish it. What are these parts of the microcosmos: Two nostrils, two eyes, two ears and a mouth. So in the heavens, as in a macrocosmos, there are two favourable stars, two unpropitious, two luminaries, and Mercury undecided and indifferent. From this and from many other similarities in nature, such as the seven met-

als, etc., which it were tedious to enumerate, we gather that
the number of planets is necessarily seven.

This is not good astronomy.

The easy conclusion to jump to is that Bacon is just stupid. He
knows very little about the facts, and he can't reason very well. But
Bacon was no intellectual slouch. He was one of the most distinguished
thinkers of his day, hugely influential in politics, law, literature, philosophy, and especially science; in fact, he is generally considered the
founding father of modern science in England, credited with removing
science from the realm of abstract speculation and anchoring it in observation.

And it smacks somewhat of intolerance and ethnocentricity to think
that we, right now, are the only smart humans and that other cultures,
and even our own long ago, were full of stupid people.

FOR FURTHER READING: See the Charles Taylor article cited above for
discussion of Bacon's astronomy. You can read what Bacon said in S.
Warhaft, ed., *Francis Bacon: A Selection of His Works* (Toronto:
Macmillan of Canada, 1965), p. 17.

Nobody Could Be That Wrong

A more sophisticated, popular, and acceptable conclusion is that all the
rest of these thinkers are as smart as we are. They're just operating from
different viewpoints and trying to do different things. Each group has
its own aims and procedures, and those of each can seem stupid to others. What is really happening is merely that we don't—perhaps even
can't—understand what they're doing.

But this view doesn't seem adequate either. Taken to an extreme,
this approach would seem to indicate that *nobody* can be mistaken
about the facts or use faulty reasoning. *Whenever* someone disagrees
with me, it can always be argued that I merely don't understand what
that person is doing. Surely *somewhere* there must be examples of people who believe falsehoods or think irrationally. Surely we all live in
the same world, and some of us are right and others wrong about what
this world is like, and about the best way to think about it.

But here's a philosophical argument for the conclusion that it's literally *impossible* for us to find somebody who gets things really badly
wrong.

Imagine that an anthropologist claims to have discovered a tribe
where mistaken beliefs run rampant. We are told that people in this
tribe—we'll call them the Falsoids—believe, for example, that pigs

have thick, hard, elongated woody trunks rooted in the ground, that they sometimes grow over twenty metres high, and that they produce lobed leaves that fall off in late autumn, the time when pigs produce acorns. Now, it's pretty clear to us what has gone wrong here: the anthropologist has simply mistranslated Falsish, the language of the Falsoids. The best explanation is that this anthropologist has merely mistranslated as 'pig' the Falsish word for 'oak tree'.

Or imagine that the anthropologist claims that the Falsoids believe that rain is boiling hot, solid, poisonous, alive, flammable, and blue; that it makes a noise like clucking when disturbed, and that every bit of it ever discovered has been stored for safe-keeping underground. Well, it's clear that something has gone wrong in translation again, though we have no idea what the Falsoids might have meant by whatever the anthropologist heard them say in Falsish.

The point here is that a translation of some other language isn't counted as correct if it translates a great deal of what the speakers of that language say into sentences in our language that we count as badly wrong. The only translation we're willing to count as correct is one in which we count what they're saying as, on the whole, true. Now, since what they say is the main way we have for finding out what they believe, there will be no case in which we claim to know what they believe *and* that what they believe is badly wrong. If we have no way of translating what they say into largely true sentences, then we'll conclude not that they have things badly wrong, but rather that we don't know what they believe.

Thus we can conclude that it is impossible for us to discover a tribe that we will count as having a very large number of false beliefs.

The same line of reasoning can be used to show that we can't ever discover someone in *our own tribe*—someone who speaks the same language as we do—who has very badly mistaken beliefs. Imagine that someone says to you, in English, "Pigs have thick, hard, elongated woody trunks rooted in the ground. They sometimes grow over twenty metres high, and they produce lobed leaves that fall off in late autumn, the time when pigs produce acorns." You might be tempted to conclude that this person has badly mistaken beliefs, or that he or she has gone crazy; but in some circumstances the preferred interpretation would be that he or she is speaking English peculiarly—that he or she means *oak trees* by the word 'pigs', and has true beliefs about oak trees.

FOR FURTHER READING: Winch, in the article cited above, champions the view that cases in which we seem to detect horribly bad reasoning in other groups are probably cases in which we have misunderstood them. The most prominent philosophical advocate of the view that any "translation" of what someone else says is counted wrong if it does not attribute to that person at least some degree of rationality is Donald Davidson. A good place to look for an introduction to Davidson's views, criticism of them, and references to the work of Davidson and others is Chapter 2 of Steven Stich's *The Fragmentation of Reason* (Cambridge, Mass.: MIT Press, 1990).

3. Thinking In Grooves

The Boy with Two Fathers

A father and his son are involved in an automobile accident. Both are seriously injured and are rushed to separate hospitals. The son is immediately readied for emergency surgery; at the first sight of him, however, the surgeon says, "I can't operate on this patient—he's my son!" How is what is reported here possible?

> The problem almost everyone sees in this story is, of course, that it is impossible that the surgeon is the boy's father. What makes this story possible, however, is the supposition that the surgeon is the boy's *mother*.

Every student will glean his or her own message from this "puzzle."

Sensitive New-Age Thought

The inability most of us have to see the trick in the surgeon story is a good example of a familiar phenomenon: we are prevented from solving a problem because of our automatic assumptions. A lesson that might be drawn is that we should avoid "thinking in grooves"—that we must think creatively, throwing aside our automatic assumptions, to solve problems.

This is advice you may have encountered especially often recently, when it has become fashionable to blame old-fashioned "linear" thought for everything from the failure of the elementary school system to ecological catastrophe to oppression of women and the Third World.

Following are two more examples of the triumph of good "lateral" thought over evil "linear" thought.

Here is a number: VI. By the addition of one line, can you make it into a seven? The answer is simple enough—VII. But now suppose you are given the following problem: Here is a number, IX. By the addition of one line, can you make it into a six?

> In front of IX you add the (curvy) line S, making it SIX.

Lest you think that lateral thought is useful only for solving trivial puzzles, here's an example that's supposed to be a practical application:

The New York State Thruway Authority faced the problem of an excessive number of speed-limit violations. They could have, at great expense, hired more troopers to track down the violators. Can you think of an easier and more effective means of reducing the number of violations?

> They raised the speed limit. (Fortunately, there was no increase in the accident rate.)

What these examples have in common is that we come to a problem with certain automatic assumptions. In the surgeon example, our assumption that a surgeon is male is, of course, suspect; but given the (unfortunate) fact that the vast majority of surgeons in our society are male, it's not unjustified. The way the SIX problem is set up, we are led—reasonably—to assume that we are supposed to add a line to the Roman numeral IX to turn it into the Roman numeral VI. And we assume in the Thruway example that the problem is to get people to obey the *current* speed limit. These assumptions aren't *stated* as conditions of the problems, but given the ways the problems are stated and given our background experience, they are reasonable ways of approaching them. But the solution is found only when the assumptions are rejected.

Is rejection of our automatic assumptions in general a good strategy for solving problems? Don't jump to this conclusion too quickly. In these particular cases automatic assumptions do interfere with our solution to the problem, but very frequently the hidden assumptions we bring to all problems are an aid, not a hindrance, to solutions.

To see this, let's return to the surgeon puzzle. There are other—reasonable—assumptions we bring to this story, which also lead to our reaction that the situation is impossible. We think that the father who is injured in the accident and brought to a different hospital cannot be the surgeon who shows up to perform surgery on his son. Why not? Because, it's reasonable to assume, the surgery would have to be performed soon after the accident; and the father was injured and being treated elsewhere. But the story does not *say* that the father would be in treatment simultaneously with his son; perhaps he recovered so fast that he could travel to the hospital where his son was, and could resume his work as a surgeon there in time to be called to his son's case. We assume that this could not happen, and this assumption is a fairly reasonable one; but the apparent impossibility of the story disappears if we withdraw this assumption as well. Another reasonable assumption that works the same way is that what the surgeon exclaims on seeing the boy is true.

Now generalize this point to all the problems you solve in everyday life. Suppose, for example, that you have to be at an appointment downtown in a half hour, and you only have a couple of dollars in your pocket, not enough for taxi fare. You have no car, and walking would take more than a half hour. The cash machine is nearby, but if you walked there first, then began to look for a taxi, you'd be late. Well, maybe there's a solution to your problem, but it probably won't be found if you start by questioning some very reasonable background assumptions: that a taxi won't take you there for free, or that a helicopter hasn't suddenly landed in your backyard just for the purpose of giving you a free lift downtown, or that you haven't suddenly developed the ability to fly. There are countless highly plausible assumptions you don't question, and you're right not to question them. You'd never solve any problem if you brought all your assumptions into question. Thinking "in grooves" is almost always a very good strategy: after all, the world almost always works "in grooves."

FOR FURTHER READING: The SIX and speed-limit example are in *Crazy Talk, Stupid Talk* by Neil Postman (1966). The title of this book tells you what he thinks of some examples of "lateral" thought.

The the Title of This Book

If you've already read the back cover of this book, you'll have found the repeated 'the' in its title.

What's interesting about this error is that it's so hard to see. I have asked dozens of people to read the title, and not one of them noticed this error the first time they read it. Some people found the error after I asked them, several times, to read the title carefully, word for word. Some people couldn't find it even after this; I had to show the repetition to them.

This example shows that we even *see* in grooves. When we read something, we automatically and unconsciously process what we see, making "corrections" in accord with expectations about what sequences normally occur in our reading. Perhaps when you read the title, this "correction" process drops out the second word when it finds a repetition. Or maybe we should understand this process simply as one that "corrects" what you seem to see so that it makes sense.

Whatever this process is, it's clear that it has resulted in misperception in this case. But it's also clear that it usually is very advantageous to us. If we had to concentrate on each word in a sentence, our reading would be very slow and laborious. Instead of this, our eyes glance lightly and quickly over the words we read, and this process fills in the blanks and corrects the errors that result from this fast skimming. On the whole, then, this process permits fast and accurate reading. It does, however, produce rare errors, especially in those cases (like the title of this book) when what we're reading is very unusual.

This is another example in which our automatic strategies for en-coutering the world, based on expectations of how things usually are, can lead us astray; but, again, the moral is not that we should discard these strategies. They're extremely useful. We'd be much worse off in finding out things without them.

Smashing a Fly

This is a puzzle that is easily solved once we can get out of our thought-groove.

Often in algebra problems we are asked to imagine bizarre and in-explicable situations, and this is no exception. Imagine two train loco-motives facing each other on a single track, two hundred miles away from each other. Both locomotives will begin moving toward the other simultaneously at fifty miles per hour, ending in a head-on crash. (They accelerate instantaneously to that speed.) Sitting on the front of one of the locomotives at the beginning is a fly. When the two begin to move, the fly will fly quickly toward the other locomotive; when it reaches it, it will turn around and return to the first locomotive, then turn around again and fly back to the second; it will continue shuttling back and forth until the locomotives crash (when it will get nicely and thor-oughly smashed between them). The fly flies at seventy-five miles per hour. Before the spectacular finale, how far will the fly travel?

I now pause to allow some readers to sigh morosely as memories of high-school algebra flood back.

> Bravely, a few readers take out pencil and paper and begin calculation. It's not a very difficult bit of algebra to determine the length of the fly's first trip, from the one locomotive at the start, to the other locomotive moving toward it. Having calculated this, however, or maybe even be-fore, you realise that there will be an infinite series of shorter and shorter trips for the fly as the locomotives converge. Calculating the limit of an infinite series will defeat all but the most stalwart of amateurs, and at this point almost everyone gives up.
>
> But there's a trick, involving a radically different way of thinking about the problem. In two hours, each locomotive will travel one hun-dred miles, meeting in the middle of the two hundred-mile-long track and crashing. The fly is flying all this time. Since the fly goes at 75 miles per hour, it travels one hundred and fifty miles. That's it!

*It's reported that the great mathematician Von Neumann was
given this problem, thought about it for a few seconds, and
gave the correct answer. When asked how he did it, he replied, "I summed the series."*

FOR FURTHER READING: The examples in this chapter called "His Father's Son," "The Boy with Two Fathers," and "Smashing a Fly" are all
in Raymond Smullyan's book, *What is the Name of This Book?* (Englewood Cliffs, N.J.: Prentice-Hall, 1978). It's a good collection of brain-
teasers.

Into the Mainstream of Philosophy

What makes something good reasoning anyway? One way of answering this question is that patterns of good reasoning are patterns that
work for a person or a community. It's perhaps a consequence of this
position that what counts as good reasoning for you, or for your community, depends on your situation: on what sorts of problems you encounter and on what your needs are. Different communities have
different situations, so maybe what's good reasoning in one community
is bad in another.

Here's a plausible example of this. Imagine two tribes, the Alphas
and the Betas. Both tribes hunt for wild mushrooms for food. The Alphas use a complicated and laborious test to tell which mushrooms to
take home and which to ignore. The Betas use a different, much easier
test, and take home a lot of mushrooms the Alphas ignore. The Alphas
sometimes leave behind perfectly good mushrooms the Betas would
have used. Who is using the right test? Well, suppose that there are
poisonous mushrooms in Alphaland, but none in Betaland. The Betas'
simple test sometimes results in their taking home and eating mushrooms that taste awful—but the result is just a bad-tasting dish. If the
Alphas used the Betas' test, disaster would result when they ate poisonous mushrooms. The Alphas' procedure costs them more effort and results in fewer mushrooms but it keeps them from being poisoned. The
Betas' procedure is easy and collects a greater number of edible mushrooms, but sometimes results in a bad-tasting dish. We can see now that
both mushroom-hunting strategies are correct, given the different situations of the tribes.

Well, it's not difficult to imagine how this parable might be extended to more general reasoning patterns. It might just be the case that
the surprisingly different general patterns of reasoning exhibited at

other times, and by different cultures, are suitable given the difference in situation.

If you find this line of reasoning attractive, however, you should be careful not to allow it to go too far. It seems clear that there *must* be such a thing as *bad* reasoning. We don't want to go so far as to assume that just any old pattern of reasoning must suit the situation of those who use it. Even the fact that some pattern is widely used, and has stood the test of natural selection of reasoning patterns over the ages, doesn't necessarily make it good. A large number of people (including, apparently, Nancy Reagan) now believe in perfectly useless astrology.

Note, further, that we have been thinking of a correct strategy of reasoning merely as one that works to satisfy the needs of the reasoners. But it seems possible that occasionally a strategy might result in a whole lot of false beliefs that, by an odd set of coincidences, serve the practical needs of the believers well. Doesn't the fact that a lot of false beliefs result show that something is wrong with this (undoubtably useful) reasoning strategy? Isn't the test of the correct reasoning strategy *truth,* not *usefulness*?

CHAPTER IX

LEARNING FROM EXPERIENCE:

Inductive Logic

1. Induction By Enumeration

What Pink Socks Tell You about Ravens

A very uncomplicated and obvious way we use experience to come to know general truths is called "simple induction" or "induction by enumeration." In this process we look at a lot of "instances" of a general hypothesis. For example, we might confirm the general hypothesis that all bears hibernate in the winter by observing a lot of bears in winter and finding that each bear we see is hibernating. Induction by enumeration seems quite an obvious and unproblematic way of finding things out; but puzzles about it arise.

To show, by induction, that all ravens are black, we look at a lot of ravens. A single non-black raven will show that this general hypothesis is false, but no single observation will conclusively show the truth of the hypothesis. As the number of observations of different ravens, all of which turn out black, gets larger, the generalization is more strongly confirmed.

Now the general statement "All ravens are black" is *logically equivalent* to the statement, "All non-black things are non-ravens." They mean the same thing. You can see this by noticing that if one of them is true, the other must also be true; and likewise, if one is false, the other must also be false. We can conclude, then, that whatever confirms one of these statements will confirm the other.

Now, to confirm "All non-black things are non-ravens" by simple induction, we look at a large number of non-black things and check whether they are non-ravens. As the number of observations of different non-black things, all of which turn out to be non-ravens, gets larger, the generalization is more strongly confirmed. Suppose you start looking around, and the first thing you see is one of your pink socks. It's non-black, and it's a non-raven. This adds a little confirmation to the generalization "All non-black things are non-ravens." Now you see another non-black thing, this grey thing over here. It's a grey elephant: another non-black thing has turned out to be a non-raven. So we gradually build up confirmation for "All non-black things are non-ravens" by finding a lot of things that aren't black and seeing that they turn out not to be ravens.

But because whatever confirms that statement also confirms "All ravens are black," finding a pink earthworm or a white tooth confirms "All ravens are black" as well.

But something has gone drastically wrong here. Imagine that you pay some scientists to confirm the hypothesis that all ravens are black, and they run around happily recording what their research has turned up: a green frog, a silver key, a red stop-sign, and so on. "You're wasting my research grant!" you scream; but they calmly point out that each of these instances confirms the hypothesis you have been paying them to investigate.

FOR FURTHER READING: The Paradox of the Ravens was invented by Carl Hempel, *Aspects of Scientific Explanation and Other Essays in the Philosophy of Science* (New York: The Free Press, 1945).

Something Even Worse about Pink Socks

Well, you might try to resign yourself to the idea that pink socks *do* confirm that all ravens are black. Here's some reasoning that might make that idea a little more plausible. Imagine a really far-reaching study of non-black things that discovered that not a single thing in the group was a raven. Wouldn't that give us reason to think that all ravens are black? As the group of non-black things observed got larger and larger, the continuing absence of ravens in that group would give us better and better reason to think that all of them were black. Of course, at the beginning of this survey—when all we've examined was one pink sock—we have only the very tiniest evidence that all ravens are black; we need to look a whole lot further to produce substantial evidence for that conclusion. But it's a beginning. It does provide some evidence, though only a minuscule bit.

But here's a further problem. Consider the competing hypotheses: All ravens are green. All ravens are white. All ravens are blue with orange polka dots. And so on. Note that each of these may be restated in equivalently: All non-green things are non-ravens. All non-white things are non-ravens. All non-blue-with-orange-polka-dot things are non-ravens. And so on. And the one pink sock confirms each of these statements to the same (tiny) degree that it confirms the black hypothesis. So if you accept that the sock gives some (tiny) degree of evidence that all ravens are black, you have to accept as well that it gives the same (tiny) degree of evidence for a whole lot of competing incompatible hypotheses: that all ravens are green, and so on.

Are you now thoroughly confused? Good. Philosophers are still trying to work out a sensible theory of confirmation.

> *The coastline of Nova Scotia was once frequented by pirates, and people occasionally dig for buried pirate treasure. On a local radio program a few years ago I heard an interview with someone who had done a study of attempts to find pirate treasure. He claimed that in most of the cases in which treasure was actually found, it was in a place where treasure-hunters had dug before, rather than in a brand new, previously undug, location. Past diggers simply hadn't dug deep enough. The previous digger had, in fact, often stopped just short of the treasure. If the previous digger had dug a little deeper than he did, he would have found it.*
>
> *The interviewer asked him what advice he would give to treasure hunters on the basis of this study; and, producing an interesting application of induction, he lamely suggested that diggers should dig a little deeper than they in fact do. Can you see why this advice is impossible to follow?*

2. The Inductive Circle

How Long Will This Keep Going On?

Past experience is, of course, the basis of our expectations about the future. The fact that all emeralds found in the past have been green leads us to expect that the emeralds we find in the future will be green too. This natural thought process in us is induction by enumeration.

But do we have any reason to trust this habitual and normal thought process? Why does the discovery of a past uniformity give you any good reason to believe anything about the future?

Our natural reply to this question is: "Well, induction by enumeration has almost always worked in the past, so that's reason to think that it will continue to work."

But this reasoning assumes what it sets out to prove. Notice that our observation of past successes of induction by enumeration is evidence for its future success providing that what's observed in the past is evidence about the future. But this is exactly what we're supposed to prove. This is circular reasoning, and unacceptable.

Sometimes this problem is phrased: "Will the future, by and large, resemble the past?" This isn't a very good way of putting the problem, because this question has an obvious answer: "Of course it will, you idiot!" Everyone agrees on this answer. The real problem is to give some reason to think that this answer is correct. Can you solve this problem?

Here's one way of thinking about it. Induction from past experience is the only way we have of justifying substantive beliefs about the future. It's exactly *what we mean* by justifying such a belief. So when we're asked for justification of the belief that the future will, by and large, resemble the past, the only possible reply is to give an induction from past experience. It's *not* a mistake to give past successes in using this belief as a justification for our belief that it will continue to be a valid principle.

FOR FURTHER READING: The problem of justifying induction by enumeration has its classical source in the writings of the eighteenth-century Scottish philosopher David Hume. See Section 4 of Hume's *An Inquiry Concerning Human Understanding*. The answer given for your consideration is a version of Nelson Goodman's answer in *Fact, Fiction and Forecast*, 2nd ed. (Indianapolis: Bobbs-Merrill, 1965). See Chapter 3, Parts 1 and 2.

The Inevitability of Scientific Error: Another Circle.

In Chapter XI, we'll examine some arguments that it's impossible scientificially to predict people's actions. But it's also been argued that scientific prediction about anything is unreliable, because scientists manipulate their experiments so that the results are what they want.

I have personal experience of this happening. When I took high-school chemistry, I knew how the experiments I did in the laboratory were supposed to turn out, because the chemistry book told me. But because of the impurity of the chemicals and the lousy equipment I was working with, not to mention my shoddy experimental technique, almost nothing turned out the way it was supposed to. I "adjusted" the experiments in progress, and I "corrected" the results I wrote up afterwards, so that my results were fairly close to what they were supposed to be.

It's known that this sort of outright fraud happens sometimes in real science too. Scientists often have a lot at stake when they attempt to prove their theories. Renown, promotion, and big research grants sometimes will follow from one experimental result rather than another. Anyway, nobody likes his or her theories to turn out false. The horrible truth is now known: scientists are only human, and sometimes they fiddle things.

This kind of straightforward fraud doesn't happen too often, however. The argument for the unreliability of science doesn't depend on this. What it argues is that there's always at least some unconscious tendency to ignore or discount "bad" data and to massage or misreport experimental results, so that they come out the way scientists want them to. This raises doubt about the objectivity of any science, even when done by scientists who want to be honest.

But how seriously should we take this argument? To what extent does this unconscious falsification go on? This is an important question, and it seems we might be able to answer it, to some extent, by doing a scientific study of the behaviour of scientists. We could, for example, get a group of scientists to test a hypothesis they think is false (or whose falsity would result in promotions, research grants, etc.). We could get another group of scientists who think that this same hypothesis is true (or who have some stake in its truth) to do the same experiments. Then we could compare the results reported by these two groups.

We hope, of course, that investigations like this would show that science is, on the whole, pretty reliable and that unconscious fraud is rare. But those who argue for the widespread unreliability of science use this very hope to cast doubt on the reliability of *our* conclusion. Even if our investigations resulted in the conclusion that this sort of bias is rare, they could claim that this investigation *itself* is untrustworthy because of *our* biases. You can't show by means of the methods of science that the methods of science are reliable. That would be circular reasoning.

3. The Gruesome Problem

Nelson Goodman invented the adjective 'grue' to raise a different problem about induction.

'Grue' is defined as follows: something is to be called *grue* if

- (*a*) it's earlier than time T (say time T is January 1, 2050), and the thing is green; or
- (*b*) it's time T or later, and the thing is blue.

Now, all the emeralds we have seen so far have been green; so induction by enumeration permits us to conclude that all emeralds are green, and thus to predict that emeralds we see during 2050 will be green.

But all the emeralds we have seen so far have been grue as well. (If you don't see why, examine the definition of 'grue' carefully.) So induction by enumeration permits us to conclude that all emeralds are grue, and thus to predict that emeralds we see during 2050 will be grue. But if an emerald is grue in 2050, it follows from the definition above that it is blue then, not green. Perfectly good reasoning using induction by enumeration had led us to two contrary predictions: that emeralds in 2050 will be green, and that they will be blue. And, of course, because all emeralds so far have also been *grellow*, we can confidently predict that they will also be yellow. And so on.

In short, induction by enumeration yields all sorts of contrary predictions. We can invent an adjective that will allow us to use that principle to predict anything we like. It's useless.

What has gone wrong? This is a very difficult problem to solve.

Some people react to the 'grue' problem by claiming that it's illegitimate to predict that things will continue to be grue because the idea of grue is itself illegitimate for prediction purposes, containing, as it does, mention of a particular time. But Goodman replies that it's not necessary to define 'grue' this way. Here's his argument. We can define 'bleen' as follows:

Something is to be called bleen if

- (*a*) it's earlier than time *T*, and the thing is blue; or

- (*b*) it's time *T* or later, and the thing is green.

Now suppose that someone took 'grue' and 'bleen' to be basic (as we take 'green' and 'blue' to be basic). Then that person might say that *our* terms 'green' and 'blue' were the peculiar ones, illegitimate in making predictions. For *that* person might claim that 'green' and 'blue' are defined in terms of 'grue' and 'bleen' plus mention of time *T*. (See if you could construct definitions of 'green' and 'blue' in terms of 'grue' and 'bleen' and time *T*.) This seems to show that what you count as illegitimate depends on where you start.

FOR FURTHER READING: Goodman introduced 'Grue' and its problems in *Fact, Fiction and Forecast*; see Chapter 3, part 4.

Every weekday morning, CBC radio broadcasts a popular three-hour interview program across Canada, "Morningside," hosted by the genial Peter Gzowski. One morning a few years ago I happened to be listening when the program was on. Gzowski was interviewing a sociologist who had made a study of academic humour, travelling from campus to campus collecting jokes from the various academic disciplines. Here's approximately how part of that interview went.

"Which discipline has the most jokes?" asked Gzowski.

"Mathematicians have a lot of mathematics jokes," said the sociologist, "but philosophers have far and away more jokes than anyone."

"Tell a philosophy joke," said Gzowski.

"Well, I just heard one the other day but I didn't understand it, and I don't think you will either."

"Doesn't matter—let's hear it anyway."

"Okay. It's a riddle. The question is: 'What's a goy?'"

"I dunno. What's a goy?"

"The answer," said the sociologist, "is: 'Someone is a goy if they're a girl before time T *or a boy after.'"*

A couple of seconds of radio silence followed. Then Gzowski said "I don't get it." "Neither do I," said the sociologist. Neither did the vast majority of Canadians listening. But you do.

4. Cause and Effect

Cause and Correlation

When we find a correlation between A and B, we often jump to the conclusion that A and B are causally related—that is, that one causes another. For example, if it is found that people who have been exposed for long periods to a certain chemical have much higher than average cancer rates, we may be tempted to conclude that this chemical causes cancer.

But reasoning from correlation to cause is sometimes a mistake. Correlation does not always mean causation. Here are a few examples that show this.

Suppose you have two petunia plants on opposite sides of your garden. The one on the left side starts to bloom, and at just about the same time the one on the right starts to bloom. The times of their blooming are correlated: you don't get one without the other. But this doesn't mean that the left one's blooming *causes* the right one to bloom.

Smoke and burning are correlated. Whenever there's smoke there's burning. But this doesn't mean that smoke causes burning.

Whenever Seymour drinks too much, his words get slurred and he bumps into things a lot. Seymour's words getting slurred and his tendency to bump into things are perfectly correlated. But the slurring of his words doesn't cause him to bump into things.

So it's clear that there's more to cause and effect than merely correlation. But what?

Well, maybe you think that it's the *order* of things that makes a difference. If X and Y are correlated *and* X comes before Y, then X causes Y.

But even this won't do. Another example from your garden will show this. Every year your strawberries bear fruit in June, then in July your raspberries bear fruit. You never get one without the other, so they are correlated; and the strawberries come before the raspberries. But this doesn't mean that the strawberries cause the raspberries.

Wednesday always follows Tuesday. Does this mean that Tuesday causes Wednesday?

A QUESTION TO THINK ABOUT: Why, exactly, are these examples of correlation not cases of cause? What, in addition to the correlation of X and Y, do we need to discover to tell that X causes Y?

The Tickle Defense

We do often conclude that X causes Y when we find out that X and Y are correlated and X comes before Y. This line of reasoning can be mistaken in another interesting way.

Suppose that it was discovered that people who eat a kumquat are one hundred times likelier to get a nosebleed the next day than people who don't. Doesn't this show that eating kumquats causes nosebleeds? No. In fact, this evidence is consistent with kumquats' *preventing* nosebleeds. How could this be?

Imagine this (entirely fictitious) story: Some people are born with a genetic condition such that their liver manufactures an abnormally low amount of vitamin Z on certain days. A deficiency of vitamin Z causes nosebleeds. Kumquats provide a dietary source of small amounts of vitamin Z. At those times when these people suffer vitamin Z deficiency, they (without knowing why) get the desire to eat kumquats. These help a little with that deficiency, but do not completely remedy it, and they tend to get nosebleeds anyway.

This story explains why people who eat kumquats get nosebleeds, but if it's true, then kumquats don't cause nosebleeds—they tend to prevent them.

How could we find this out? Suppose further that a vitamin Z deficiency made your nose tickle the day before the nosebleeds started. Scientists working for the Kumquat Growers' Association could then prove the true story: they could arrange experiments in which people who had a nose-tickle ate kumquats, and others with the tickle ate none. If the second group got more nosebleeds than the first, then this would show that kumquats helped prevent nosebleeds. They could use the "tickle defense" to show that their product was not to blame—that it actually was beneficial.

The serious moral of this fable is that correlation does not necessarily show cause. One real-life application of this sort of thinking involves the link between smoking and lung cancer. The correlation between the two was known for a long time; but the kumquat story shows, by analogy, that this wasn't sufficient evidence for causal connection. This correlation could be found even if smoking *prevented* lung cancer. Scienti. had to rule out any possible "tickle defense," and they did.

Here's another case in which the answer isn't so clear. Over the past twenty years, the average childbearing age of women has increased substantially, and so has the rate of breast cancer. It's possible that waiting until later to have children causes a greater likelihood of breast cancer. But the correlation alone doesn't show this.

Can you imagine other hypotheses to explain this correlation?

It might be the case that something else causes women both to tend to bear children later and to tend to have breast cancer. (Imagine that some factor reduces fertility, thus postponing the age of child-bearing on average, and increases the likelihood of breast cancer.) Or breast cancer, in its early stages, might cause them to be less likely to conceive, thus increasing the average age of child-bearing. Or it might just be a coincidence, the result of two separate and unrelated causes.

SOME QUESTIONS TO THINK ABOUT: Here are some cases of correlation. Do you think one item in the pair causes the other, or that they're merely correlated? How might scientists find out for sure?

- 1. More pornography available/Increase in sex crimes
- 2. Sluggish economy/Increase in movie attendance
- 3. Small children in the household/Friction between husband and wife

Into the Mainstream of Philosophy

The theory of the ways experience leads to general knowledge is studied in the philosophical fields of inductive logic and philosophy of science. As usual, this book includes puzzles and surprises that arise in this field of study, while a major task of philosophers has been to elucidate and systematize the perfectly ordinary, unparadoxical, and unsurprising kinds of reasoning done all the time. For an excellent, easy-to-follow but thorough account of the basics in these fields, see Ronald N. Giere's *Understanding Scientific Reasoning*, 3rd ed. (Fort Worth: Holt, Rinehart & Winston, 1991). Another good place to look for further discussion of these and other issues in this chapter is Brian Skyrms' *Choice and Chance* (Celmont, Calif.: Dickenson, 1966).

What's the difference between correlation and cause, anyway? People tend to think that there's some sort of *connection* between items that are causally related but not between items that are merely correlated. But David Hume, in the work cited above, argued in a compelling way that we can observe no such connection. Think about Hume's point. Putting ice into a glass of liquid causes the liquid to become colder. But what do you observe? Nothing but one event followed by the other. You can see no "cause" going on. Try to figure out what exactly does justify the distinction between cause and correlation.

CHAPTER X

KNOWING WITHOUT EXPERIENCE

1. The A Priori and Definitions

Why Your Sisters Are Female

You know that this statement is true:

- Everyone who is somebody's sister is female.

How do you know this?

It's possible that you know this from experience, through induction by enumeration. Perhaps you have observed a large number of people who are somebody's sister, and have noticed that all of them have been female.

But it's unlikely that you found out the truth of the statement that way. The statement applies to all sisters, past, present, and future. But you have observed only a very small percentage of all those past and present people who are somebody's sister; and you have observed no sisters at all who are yet to be born. It's important that a very large and varied sample of things be observed before one has enough inductive evidence to claim that one knows a generalization of this sort.

Of course, you need not rely on your own observations for knowledge of the truth of generalizations. You know, for example, that days are usually warm in the middle of the Sahara Desert even if you have never visited there. You can rely on other people's observations too.

But it's clear in the case of our knowledge about sisters that the truth of this statement does not depend even on the wide observations of the whole human race. Nobody needs to have done any observation at all to know that this statement is true.

Truths that can be known independently of experience are known, in philosophical jargon, as *a priori* truths (knowable "prior" to experience). The contrast here is with truths that can only be known by experience, or by inductive reasoning from such truths. These are called *a posteriori* truths (knowable "posterior" to—after—experience.).

Here are some more samples of statements we know a priori:

- All bachelors are unmarried.
- If Alison is older than Barney, then Barney is younger than Alison.
- If Alison is older than Barney, and Barney is older than Clarissa, then Alison is older than Clarissa.
- Anyone who weighs seventy kilograms is heavier than sixty kilograms.

SOME QUESTIONS TO THINK ABOUT: What are other examples? There are also a priori falsehoods. Give some examples of these.

How Can We Know Without Experience?

An attractive theory of how we can know the truth of the statement that everyone's sisters are female is that it's true "by definition." The word 'sister', after all, means *female sibling*. Because of this rule of language, the word 'sister' can't apply to anyone who isn't female. So the truth of this statement depends merely on the language in which it is expressed.

But there are a couple of reasons to doubt that this is the correct account of the way we come to know this truth. Imagine that the English language didn't exist. Then the sentence 'Everyone who is somebody's sister is female' wouldn't mean anything—it would just be a bunch of meaningless letters. Nevertheless, wouldn't it still be true that everyone who is somebody's sister would be female? Couldn't we still know that truth?

Well, you might reply, still there would be *some* language in which we could express that truth, and any language in which we expressed it would use words that have those meanings.

But imagine that humans somehow evolved all the way up to their present state, except without any language at all. There would be no way at all for us to express any truth. But wouldn't it still be true that everyone who is somebody's sister is female? And couldn't we still know it?

You might point out that if there weren't any language at all, nobody would know anything.

But it's not obviously true that knowledge depends on language. It's reasonable to think that intelligent animals such as dogs know lots of things, despite their lack of significant language ability.

Another reason to think that some of our knowledge comes neither from experience nor from sentences that are "true by definition" is that there are a number of things we know that do not at all seem to be "true by definition" but that, it seems, we know independently of experience (though it can be debated, in each case, whether or not these are true by definition). An example is "Every event that happens, happens at some time or other." We can know this truth without having to go through standard inductive processes. We don't even have to discover by experience that a *single* event happens at some time or other. It's an a priori truth. But is it a consequence of definitions? Of which words?

Honest Abe and the Sheep

A riddle (attributed to Abraham Lincoln):

> *Q*: How many legs does a sheep have, if you call its tail a leg?
> *A*: Four. Calling its tail a leg doesn't make it one.

This is not a very amusing riddle, but it is philosophically interesting. Perhaps the moral that can be drawn from it is that facts are facts, no matter how you use language. If this is the case, it's hard to see how anything can be a fact because of definitions of words (except, of course, for facts about words, such as the fact that the word 'sister' means *female sibling*).

The Dictionary with Very Few Definitions

Before we consider other theories of a priori knowledge, let's consider *definitions* for a moment.

Definitions are what you find in dictionaries, right? Well, no. A good deal of what's found in there isn't properly speaking definition at all.

I'm not referring merely to etymologies, pronunciations, grammatical forms, information about abbreviations, and other items found in many dictionaries. Even the "definition" parts of dictionary entries contain much that isn't definition.

A definition gives the meaning of a word or phrase. This can be done by giving a synonym, or by listing the characteristics necessary and sufficient for applying the term. But many of the characteristics listed in dictionary definitions aren't individually necessary or jointly sufficient. For example, my dictionary contains this item:

> *soufflé* A light, fluffy baked dish made with egg yolks and beaten egg whites combined with various other ingredients and served as a main dish or sweetened as a dessert.[1]

These characteristics describe most soufflés, but not all of them. It's possible, for example, to make a legitimate soufflé without egg yolks. You could make a soufflé out of egg yolks and beaten egg whites without any other ingredients (though it wouldn't be very good.) Some soufflés are served before the main course, or as a snack. Some don't turn out light and fluffy, and are served to the dog. This proves that not all of these characteristics are necessary.

But neither are they sufficient. Suppose you baked a light fluffy dish made with egg yolks and beaten egg whites combined with motor oil, egg shells, and ground liver, sprinkled with icing sugar. When you served it to your guests for dessert, they would cry, "This isn't a soufflé—it's a pile of garbage!" Would they be wrong?

For most nouns, it's in fact impossible to give a really exact synonym; dictionaries instead give a number of terms that are close in meaning to that noun, but not exactly synonymous. They also often give some information about things named by the word that may, by and large, be true of those things, but not "by definition." It's impossible to give a list of characteristics that are really necessary and sufficient for most words. Ludwig Wittgenstein invites us to

> [c]onsider for example the proceedings that we call "games."
> I mean board-games, card-games, ball-games, Olympic games, and so on.... [I]f you look at them you will not see something that is common to all, but similarities, relationships, and a whole series of them at that.

This is my dictionary's entry for 'the':

> The definite article, functioning as an adjective. It is used: 1.
> Before singular or plural nouns and noun phrases that denote particular specified persons or things. 2. Before a singular noun, making it generic: THE human arm. 3. Before a noun, and generally stressed, emphasizing its uniqueness or prominence: That's THE show to see this year....

Neither synonyms nor application characteristics are given here; instead we are told how to use the word. But there's nothing wrong with my dictionary; in fact, it's a very good one. How else could you define 'the'? Maybe 'the' doesn't have a meaning at all. Or maybe our notion of definition is too narrow.

1   *The American Heritage Dictionary of the English Language*, p. 1234.

FOR FURTHER READING: The quote from Wittgenstein is from his *Philosophical Investigations* (Oxford: Basil Blackwell, 1958), section 66. See surrounding sections in this book for more on definitions.

3. Conceptual Truths

One of the best-known aspects of the work of Immanuel Kant is his attempt to account for how we know truths of this sort. Kant argued that everything we know is either *analytic* or *synthetic*. An "analytic" truth is one that follows *from the analysis of the concepts involved*; all the rest are "synthetic." When we make the judgement that everyone's sisters are female, we have the concepts of *sister* and *female*. All that's necessary to find out that all sisters are female is to have those concepts, because the concept of *femaleness* is "included within" the concept of sister. We can "analyse" the concept of sisterness—take it apart—and discover that the concept of *femaleness* is one of its parts. This explains how we can know in advance that all sisters are female.

Note that this theory of a priori knowledge is different from the "true by definition" theory. It doesn't depend on the definitions of words. When definitions of words are available, they give us the analysis of the concept the word refers to, but one can have concepts without having words. Dogs, for example, might be said to have the concept of *edibleness*: they distinguish between what they can eat and what they can't (more or less). But they don't have words for these concepts.

But what is a *concept*? It doesn't seem plausible to think of them as psychological states. If that is what concepts were, then these truths would depend on our psychological states. But it seems that these truths are independent of anyone's psychology. They would still be true no matter what or how anyone happened to think. Imagine, for example, that people were very much stupider than they in fact are, and that we were unable to conceptualize what it is to be a sister, or to be female. Wouldn't it still be true that everyone who is somebody's sister is female?

Kant's theory is then that some a priori knowledge is explainable because what is known is an analytic truth. (As we'll see shortly, Kant thinks that there can also be a priori knowledge of synthetic truths.)

I Forget What I Saw Before I Was Born

But where do we get our knowledge that the concept of *sisterness* includes the concept of *femaleness*? The peculiar fact here is that all we can ever experience, using our senses, is particular females and particular sisters. But our concepts involve what's true of *all* sisters and *all* females. This can't come from our experience of particular people.

Putting this question another way: our concepts (which account for our a priori knowledge) express the *form*—the general nature—that all sisters must share. These "forms" are never experienced through our senses. How can we know about them?

Plato's answer, which a lot of people find entirely implausible, is that our souls, which he supposed existed before our birth (when they were stuck into our bodies) had non-sensory experience of this and other forms. Plato argued that this sort of truth depended on the existence of something he called in Greek an *eidos* or *idea*. (Yes, *idea* is a Greek word.) Both words are sometimes translated as 'form' or 'idea'. Thus the universe is supposed to include not only a lot of particular sisters, but also the "form" of sisterness. Each particular sister is a sister because she conforms to the form of sisterness—in Platonic terms, because she "participates" in the form. (The word 'idea' is a misleading way of referring to these things, because it suggests a psychological state.)

Plato argued that mathematical knowledge was an example of the sort of knowledge that derives from our understanding of the forms. But if our understanding of the forms results from pre-birth experience, why is it that new-born babies can't do arithmetic? Why do we have to go through often painful and sometimes unsuccessful education to come to know the truths of mathematics?

Plato's answer is that the shock of uniting the soul with a body at birth made the soul forget, at least for a while, what it had learned about the forms. Education and experience during our lives on earth can (sometimes) result in our remembering.

Plato's position seems, as I have indicated, bizarre and unbelievable. But if you don't believe it, you need to give another account of the puzzling facts about the sort of knowledge that comes from conceptual analysis, and this is not easy to do. In any case, it's interesting to see how his strange position is an ingenious attempt to answer some real philosophical problems.

More on Conceptual Existence

A feature of Plato's views that seems objectionable to many people is that it insists on the existence of things—the forms—which we can't observe using our senses. We like to think that all there is in the universe is a bunch of particular observable things. But perhaps we have to believe in forms to make things make sense. Consider the following suggestion:

- Someone who is blind has no notion of greenness.

Whether that is true or false is not the issue I'm raising. The point here is: what is it that a blind person is alleged to have no notion of? It's not *green things*. A blind person can surely think about grass, trees, and so on. What a blind person supposedly can't think about is the fact that they all participate in a certain form—the form of greenness. The blind person supposedly lacks understanding of a form, not of any particulars. Thus to make sense of that allegation—which we have to do before we can determine whether it's true or false—we seem to need to think of the universe as containing more than merely particular things.

Here's another such fact:

- Flatness of the landscape depresses Benjamin.

For this to stand a chance of being true, doesn't there have to be such a thing as flatness and not merely particular landscapes that are flat? Those particular landscapes depress Benjamin, but that's not all we want to say. They all depress Benjamin because they all participate in the form of flatness. If there isn't any such thing as this form, then what is meant by the above fact?

Here's another:

- Greenness is incompatible with redness.

This explains why nothing can be both totally green and totally red. What are these things that are incompatible? Of course there are particular things that are green, for example, your last Christmas tree, and particular things that are red, for example, the glass at the top of the next stoplight you see. But what things are being said to be incompatible?

Notice that some forms are incompatible and some aren't. Greenness and redness are incompatible: nothing can be both wholly green and wholly red at once. Greenness, sphericality, rotation, and buzzingness are compatible. A green, rotating, buzzing sphere participates in all these forms wholly and at once.

4. The Synthetic A Priori

The Incompetent Repairman

Suppose your car stalls every time you stop. You bring it into the car repair shop, and when you return, the repairman tells you he hasn't fixed it.

"Why not?" you ask.

"There isn't any reason why it's stalling," he replies.

"You mean, you haven't found the cause?" you say, getting annoyed.

"No, I've taken everything apart and examined it very carefully," he says. "There isn't any cause for that stalling."

At this point you should find a different repairman. You think that something must be causing that stalling; he simply hasn't found it. Why do you think this? Not because you know more about cars than he does. It's because you think that *everything* has a cause. This is a very general truth about the way everything in the universe works.

But what makes you think that everything has a cause? Your own experience hardly shows this. For your experience to show this through induction by enumeration, you would have to have examined a very large and fair sample of all the events in the universe and found that they each have causes. You can't have examined a large enough sample to be justified in this far-reaching conclusion. Besides, there are a large number of things you have examined for which you haven't found a cause. Neither has the collective experience of all of humanity provided sufficient justification; even this wide collective experience has examined only a tiny fraction of what goes on, and even the best experts don't know the cause for everything they have examined. The fact that a vast scientific enterprise is busily looking for causes right now shows that.

It appears that our belief that everything has a cause is another example of a universal truth not justified by experience—a truth known a priori. We already have, from Kant, an explanation of how some a priori truths are known: these are analytic, and we find out their truth by analysis of concepts. Is this is another case of conceptual truth? Kant argued that it is not:

Consider your concept of *an event*: anything that happens. Is there something about that concept that "includes" there being a cause? Compare this with a clear case of conceptual truth: that all sisters are female. Full understanding of the concept of *sister* involves understanding that sisterness necessarily involves femaleness. It's impossible to imagine a sister who isn't female, because this combination involves an inconsistency, a conceptual self-contradiction. But full understanding of the concept of *event* does not necessarily involve having the concept of a cause: it is possible to imagine an event that does not have a cause without this sort of inconsistency. So it appears that the judgement that all events have a cause isn't analytic; it's synthetic. Kant took as one of his major philosophical tasks the explanation of how a priori knowledge of synthetic judgements is possible.

Kant's answer is rather obscure, and its interpretation is controversial, but here's one way of understanding it. The universality of causal connections is a necessary condition of any experiential knowledge of the world; if it weren't true that everything has a cause, we couldn't have knowledge of anything. Because we clearly do know many things about the world, it must be true. This line of reasoning, he argued, allows us to justify our belief that it is true, and to explain it.

Kant's reasoning may be questioned at many points. Is he right that the truth of this judgement really is a precondition for any knowledge at all? Maybe we could get pretty far in the business of getting knowledge of the world even without this supposition.

But suppose he's right in claiming that without belief in this universal claim we couldn't really know much about the world around us. What justifies us in thinking that we really do know anything else?

Nothing Made That Happen

Maybe it isn't true, after all, that everything has a cause. Contemporary physicists claim that certain sorts of events don't have causes. Here's an example of such an event.

Why does passing an electric current through the metal filament of a light bulb produce light? The explanation is that the electrical energy makes the electrons in some of the atoms of the filament metal jump outward to an orbit with a higher energy level. This higher orbit is unstable, and after a while the electron will pop back into its original orbit; when it does this, it emits energy in the form of light. How long after an electron is forced into this higher orbit will it pop back? Physicists tell us that it may take a short or a long time; there's no predicting exactly when. This is because *there is no reason* why one electron takes a short time, and another electron takes a long time. The fact that an electron took just the time it did is without any cause.

The idea that nature contains events without cause—that it is genuinely random in some respects—is offensive to many people. Einstein, for example, is supposed to have reacted to this position by replying,

"God does not play dice with the universe." Nevertheless, the idea of causeless events is now widely held among physicists; and we who (unlike Einstein) don't know much about physics aren't in a very good position to question it. But never mind whether or not the observations of physicists make it necessary for them to include causeless events in their theories. The fact that they even *claim* that it does is philosophically interesting, because it gives evidence that mere thought is not sufficient to establish that every event has a cause, and that the supposition that everything has a cause is not necessary for all other knowledge. After all, those physicists are presumably thinking hard and well, and presumably know a lot, but they don't believe it.

The Butterfly That Destroyed Oakland

Ever since the seventeenth-century publication of Newton's theories in physics, many philosophers have been confident that the universe is an orderly and predictable place. The philosopher Pierre La Place, for example, proclaimed that if he knew the position and motion of each object at one time, he would be able to predict everything that would happen forever after (and to "retrodict" everything that happened before that time). This confidence was based on several questionable assumptions. One of them was that Newton had things right; but Newton's physics has now (largely due to Einstein's work) been shown not to be exactly correct. But worse: we have seen that modern physics even questions the La Placian assumption that things work on a predictable cause-and-effect basis. This means that, even armed with a corrected Einsteinian physics, La Place wouldn't be able to predict *everything*.

Nevertheless, you might share La Place's view that *if* the universe works on a dependable cause-and-effect basis, then every event is determined by preceding ones via the operation of physical laws; and therefore *if* we knew at one time all the details (position, momentum) of each object in such a deterministic universe, we could predict the future with complete accuracy. But this second *if* is a big *if*. Chaos theory, a field of study that has attracted a good deal of contemporary interest, claims it is *impossible* that things could ever be known to the extent that completely accurate predictions could be made, even if the universe works completely deterministically.

To understand this claim, the first thing we need to note is that in certain cases, because of deterministic causal processes, extremely tiny events can have very large effects.

Here's an example of this. Imagine a mountain on which a rainstorm has just started. The first drop of rain falls towards a tiny bump on top of that mountain. The drop falls past a butterfly in flight, and a minuscule puff of air caused by the butterfly's wings pushes the drop a tiny bit south. By consequence, the raindrop lands on the south side of the bump and runs downward on the bump's south side. It makes a tiny wet groove in the dust around the bump, and succeeding raindrops falling above that bump follow that groove on their path down. The rainstorm gets heavier, and soon lots of water is flowing down the south side of that bump, and as a result the water heads down the south side of the mountain, wearing a deeper and deeper channel. The deeper the channel gets, the more the rain that falls on the mountain travels down the south side. After hundreds of years, a deep canyon is worn down the south side. As the canyon deepens, snow-, mud- and rock-slides wear things away more. After many thousands of years, most of the south side of the mountain is worn away. This change in weight in a critical location on a geological fault results in a big earthquake, and Oakland, California, falls into the bay. (Perhaps just as well. This is the town about which Gertrude Stein said, "There's no *there* there.")

Were it not for the tiny puff of air caused by the butterfly's wings, the first drop would have fallen on the north side of that little bump. Following drops would have flown down its north side, and the river would have developed there. Because the north side is made of harder rock, with a gentler slope, no great canyon would have developed, and the mountain would have eroded very little. There would have been a series of small, harmless earthquakes, instead of one big one, and Oakland would have been saved.

In this example, the tiniest of events—one flap of a butterfly's wings—eventually results in the destruction of Oakland.

Well, so far we don't seem to have anything against La Place's position. Presumably, he could have predicted the destruction of Oakland. Remember, in order to predict what will happen, he has to know *everything* about the initial state of things, including the details about the fall of that first drop and the flight of the butterfly.

Now, suppose La Place was told the weight, position, and speed of the butterfly and of the first drop, with figures correct to several decimal places. It could be that this degree of correctness isn't sufficient for him to make the right prediction. Perhaps a much finer measurement is necessary to predict such a delicate matter. "All right," replies La Place, "then give me more accurate measurements!"

The problem here is that it's always possible that what makes a critical difference in what happens is such a tiny feature of the circumstances that it is not captured by the accuracy of our measurement. Any measurement we make must be to *some* degree of accuracy or other, and it's always possible that what makes a difference is such a tiny matter that our measurement is too gross to capture it. Suppose, for example, that La Place weighs a pebble on a scale accurate to the nearest gram. It weighs 38 grams. This is not a terribly accurate measurement: it does not distinguish between 37.9 grams and 38.2 grams; but perhaps these .3 grams make a crucial difference in a prediction he wants to make. Well, he should use a more sensitive scale; suppose it yields 38.1 grams. But now perhaps there's a crucial difference not captured by *this* scale. And so on, *all the way down*. The point here is that there is no such thing as measuring the real weight, absolutely correctly, of that pebble. All anyone can do is to weigh it to some degree of accuracy. Since there might always be a finer difference that would be important in predicting even very large future events, it follows that one can *never* have sufficiently fine measurements to guarantee correct predictions—even though (we assume) the universe works deterministically.

This is an interesting result, but not because it undermines the notion of a deterministic universe. (We are accepting determinism for the purpose of this argument.) It is interesting because it distinguishes between determinism and predictability. It's possible that the universe is completely deterministic while at the same time it is impossible to predict certain events in it. La Place was wrong.

$7 + 5 \neq 12$

How do we discover that $7 + 5 = 12$? It takes a lot of observation or experiment to demonstrate that the general claims of science are true, but it seems that we need neither observation nor experiment to demonstrate that $7 + 5 = 12$. It appears that it just *has* to be true; how could it be otherwise? Kant argued that arithmetical truths are, like the truth that everything has a cause, synthetic and knowable a priori. He produced an account of how we know them that is similar to his account of how we know that every event has a cause.

But, again, it seems that experiments have shown that '$7 + 5 = 12$' and the other "truths" of arithmetic are actually not always true.

Consider this experiment: put 7 bushels of oranges in a large container. Add 5 bushels of raisins, and mix well. How many bushels of fruit result?

Not 12. The reason, of course, is that the raisins fit into the spaces in-between the larger oranges, and the mixture as a result takes up less volume than 12 bushels.

John Allen Paulos gives the example that if one cup of popcorn is added to one cup of water, two cups of soggy popcorn do not result.[2] So does this show that elementary arithmetic is sometimes false?

The moral Paulos draws from this sort of story is that even simple mathematics can be "thoughtlessly misapplied." "In trivial cases as well as in difficult ones, mathematical applications can be a tricky affair, requiring as much human warmth and nuance as any other endeavour."

It's nice to think of mathematicians not as cold, calculating machines but as warm, snugly, teddy bears just like us humanists. But this doesn't really answer the substantial questions here: When does arithmetic apply anyway? By what subtle nuances can the teddy-bear mathematician determine that arithmetic is being used the way it's supposed to be?

Let's try to be more precise about when the laws of arithmetic apply. We might want to say: adding volumes in this way doesn't always obey the laws of arithmetic, because this isn't the sort of "addition" these laws apply to. There are other ways of measuring oranges and raisins (or popcorn and water) to which these laws apply. After all, there isn't less stuff in the mixture than there was in the separate piles of oranges and raisins we started with. If you mix seven pounds of oranges and five pounds of raisins you get twelve pounds of mixture, right?

Unfortunately, no. This is another strange result of modern physics. Imagine that you push together two lumps of stuff that won't bounce off each other, but will come to rest in the middle, stuck together in one lump. Modern physics tells us that this lump will weigh *more* than the sum of the two lumps which were moving toward each other. Not very much more, but more. This happens because the kinetic energy in those two moving lumps is converted into mass when they stop moving relative to each other. Physics can even tell us exactly how much additional mass will result; this is a consequence of the Einstein's famous equation $e = mc^2$ which quantifies the conversion between energy (e) and mass (m): the equivalent amount of energy is the amount of mass multiplied by the square of the speed of light (c). You needn't worry about this when following a recipe for fruit compote, however. In ordinary circumstances, the additional mass you get when pushing things together is unmeasurably tiny.

2   *Innumeracy: Mathematical Illiteracy and Its Consequences* (New York: Vintage, 1990), p. 121.

But maybe you are so fond of the laws of arithmetic that you won't count this as a disproof of them either. Maybe you don't want to count pushing things together as an example of adding them, now that you know that the loss of kinetic energy results in additional mass. But then what would you count as an example of adding two things? Perhaps Kant was right in thinking that the laws of arithmetic are so firmly embedded in our minds that we would never count anything as an experimental disproof of them.

Bizarre Triangles Discovered in Space

You may remember that we can prove in geometry that the interior angles of a triangle add up to 180 degrees. Kant considered geometry to be another area of synthetic a priori truth, and, again, physics seems to have shown him wrong. As in the last case, the difference is so small as to be undetectable in our ordinary experience, but Einstein proposed an experiment in which it would be measurable. The difference, it turns out, may be quite large, large enough to measure, when a leg of a huge triangle passes through a strong gravitational field; so the experiment involved a triangle constructed out of beams of light, one of which came from a star, past the sun, to the earth. You can't ordinarily see a star positioned in the sky, relatively to us, near the sun, so Einstein proposed that such a star's position be observed during an eclipse of the sun in 1919. The astounding truth of his prediction made him a celebrity; ever since, 'Einstein' has been a synonym for 'genius'. Nevertheless, you might be so bold as to ask whether this experiment really shows that there's a triangle *made out of straight lines* whose interior angles don't add up to 180 degrees.

> Perhaps you want to argue: gravity makes space "curved," so a beam of light passing through a gravitational field isn't a straight line. This explains why "triangles" constructed of beams of light don't obey the laws of geometry: these "triangles" have curved lines, not straight ones, for sides.

Again, however, this may not be an adequate reply. By any test, the paths followed by light rays are straight lines (even when they pass close to the sun). These paths are the shortest distance between two points. They match any "ruler" we can construct or imagine. When you sight down them you see no curves. If light rays aren't straight lines, then nothing is.

FOR FURTHER READING: For an explanation of some aspects of Einstein's physics understandable (with some work) by non-physicists, see

Understanding Relativity by Stanley Goldberg (Boston: Birkhäuser, 1984).

4. A Priori Science

Bad Physics

Answer the following questions.

A. Suppose you tied a weight to a string and whirled it around your head in a circle, then suddenly let go. In what direction would the weight fly off?

B. Suppose you were travelling on a train going at a constant fifty miles per hour. You roll a ball down the aisle, first in the direction of the front of the train, and then in the direction of the rear of the train, both times with the same force. Would the ball travel at the same speed, and go the same distance, both times? Or would it roll faster and further in one direction? Which one?

A. Do you think that the weight will travel in the direction of the arrow in Fig. 1 below? Wrong! Fig. 2 shows its real path.

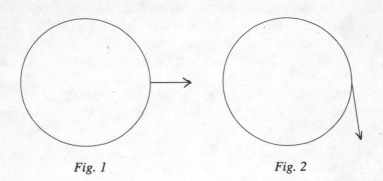

Fig. 1   Fig. 2

B. Do you think that the ball will roll further and more quickly and quickly toward the back of the train? Wrong! It will roll the same speed and the same distance both ways.

Don't be upset if you came up with wrong answers. Many people—even graduate students in physics—tend to answer these questions wrong. The wrong answers are the ones that would also be given by the physics developed by Aristotle in the fourth century B.C. (and he was a smart guy!). It wasn't until the seventeenth century that a physics was developed (by Newton) that gave the right answer.

The curious thing is that you don't need to know any physics to come up with the right answer: all you need to do is to try the experiments out and watch what happens. Didn't anyone do that until the seventeenth century?

It appears that these are cases in which people tend to give the wrong answers, even though simple experience can show that they are wrong. It might be speculated that the wrong physics is "built into" our heads, and that we believe incorrect things *despite* experience.

The Infinity of Space

The two physics examples we have just looked at are cases in which we tend to make mistakes, perhaps because we use a priori reasoning when reasoning based on experience is called for. But consider this question: is space infinite in size? Is this the sort of question that should be answered on the basis of observation, or is there a priori reasoning that can answer it? Lucretius, the ancient Roman philosopher, provided what he thought was an a priori proof that space was infinite.

Suppose, Lucretius argued, that space was finite. This means there's an outer boundary to it. Now, imagine that you were standing at that outer boundary, and threw a dart in its direction. Either the dart sails right through the boundary, into the outside, or it stops dead at the boundary. If it sails right through, there is space outside the "boundary," and it's not really the boundary of space at all. If it stops dead, then something just beyond the "boundary" must have stopped it. But then, whatever that thing was must have existed in space beyond the boundary. Either way, there can't be a real boundary.

You can see why the idea that space is infinite is so compelling. If there were a boundary, what's on the other side? Even if nothing is, still that's *space*.

Why It's Dark At Night

Now, if space is really infinite, it's plausible to think that there is also an infinite number of stars. For suppose there was a finite number, with all of them "around here," so to speak. This leaves the rest of the infinity of space empty. Why are they all around here—at this arbitrary corner—rather than elsewhere?

Well, then, let's suppose there is an infinite number of stars. Now, each star there is adds a little bit of light to the night sky. Of course, the amount of light added by any particular star depends on how big and how brightly burning that star is, and on how far away it is. But no matter how small and how far away it is, it must add a *little* light to the night sky. But even if some stars contribute only an extremely tiny amount of light to our night sky, the sum of the light from an *infinite* number of stars must be infinite. Our night sky should be infinitely bright. Clearly it isn't. What has gone wrong in our reasoning?

One possible solution may have occurred to you:

> Some stars are hidden behind other stars, or behind dark bodies like planets or clouds in space, so part of the light is blocked out, and our sky is mostly black.

But this appears not to be a solution. If light is being blocked by something, that thing must absorb or reflect that light. If it absorbs the light, it gets more and more energy; soon it would be shining too. If it reflects the light, where does that light go? Eventually it would be reflected right back to us, and the same problem arises.

But perhaps the non-Euclidian geometry of space solves the problem.

> A consequence of Einstein's view is that space has a finite (but large) volume. The reason for this is that if you follow a straight line—a beam of light—in any direction long enough, you'll come back to where you started from. (This answers Lucretius's dart example: a dart can always be thrown, over and over again, in the same direction without bouncing off the "boundary" because it will eventually wind up where it started from.) Since space is finite in volume, it contains a finite number of stars. Even if each star contributes a little brightness to the night sky, nevertheless the total is finite, not infinite. That's why it's dark at night.

Thinking About Falling

It's a commonplace of modern thought that observation is the absolutely necessary basis for substantive knowledge of scientific matters. But is this really true?

Until the Renaissance, the principles of science came mostly from the tradition of thought whose most important spokesman was Aristotle. In this old tradition, it is often said, scientific belief was derived purely by rational speculative thought, with only a minimum of observation. As you'd expect, this method was not very reliable. But the introduction of modern scientific method, with its insistence on observation and experiment gradually replaced the false speculations that resulted from this armchair science with more reliable fact and theory.

This historical picture has something to it, though a bit of study of the history of science shows that things are not quite that simple. Earlier we saw an example of bizarre speculative astronomy, due to Francis Bacon who is supposed to be a central figure in the Renaissance advent of modern science. Here's another example, however, of armchair speculation from another founding father of modern science.

It was a principle of Aristotelian physics that heavier bodies fall faster than light ones. This principle is, in fact, roughly speaking true, and you can observe that it is by dropping a feather and a billiard ball from the same height. The difference in speed of fall, however, results from the different effects of the resistance of air. Elementary physics nowadays teaches that, discounting air resistance, everything falls at the same speed. This discovery is attributed to Galileo, who is popularly supposed to have provided experimental proof of his correct anti-Aristotelian views by dropping things off the top of the Leaning Tower of Pisa.

Despite Galileo's insistence on the necessity of observation, even he was not averse to argument based merely on rational thought. He offered the following armchair thought-experiment to prove his theory of falling bodies. Aristotelian physics, said Galileo, claims that a light musket-ball falls more slowly than a heavy cannon-ball. Now, imagine attaching a musket-ball and a cannon-ball together by a chain, and imagine that the two are dropped simultaneously. If Aristotle were right, the cannon-ball would try to fall faster than the musket-ball, so the cannon-ball would pull the musket-ball along, and the musket-ball would drag back the fall of the cannon-ball. The result would be that the two of them would fall faster than the musket-ball would fall alone, but slower than the cannon-ball alone. But, Galileo continued, notice that we have created a big object—cannon-ball plus chain plus musket-ball—which is heavier than the cannon-ball alone. Aristotle would have to say that this big object should fall *faster* than the cannon-ball alone. But this contradiction shows that Aristotle's theory must be wrong.

SOME QUESTIONS TO THINK ABOUT: Is there something wrong with Galileo's reasoning? Does it really disprove Aristotle's view? If so, does it show that pure armchair reasoning can prove the falsity of a scientific theory? If it does, then perhaps observation and experiment isn't always so vital after all.

The Shadow Knows

But, it turns out, you *don't* know the rules for shadows. Here are two rules for shadows I'll bet you believe are true:

(1) Shadows do not pass through opaque objects. Imagine a light source on your left, and a wall on your right. Then, of

course, your shadow falls on the wall. Now imagine putting a large, opaque screen between you and the wall. Your shadow now falls on the screen, but it couldn't fall on the wall, because it can't pass through the opaque screen.

(2) If light doesn't fall on something, then it doesn't cast a shadow. Imagine again a light source on your left and a wall on your right. Now put the opaque screen in-between you and the light, so that no light falls on you. Your shadow couldn't fall on the wall then, because you're not illuminated by the light.

Both of these are correct principles of the way shadows work, right? Well, consider this example. Imagine, as before, a light source on your left and a wall on your right. Now hold up a small opaque object—a coffee mug, for instance, to your right, between you and the wall, so that it is completely within your shadow. A shadow matching your shape falls on the wall, but consider the part of the shadow that is on the imaginary line you might draw from the light source through your body, through the coffee mug, to the wall. That place on the wall is in shadow, of course, but is that part of the shadow cast by your body or by the coffee mug?

Principle (1) tells us that that part of the shadow isn't cast by your body. The opaque coffee mug is between your body and that part of the shadow. Your shadow falls on the coffee mug, but it can't pass through it to the wall.

But Principle (2) tells us that that part of the shadow isn't cast by the coffee mug either. The coffee mug is completely shaded by you. It isn't illuminated by the light, so it doesn't cast a shadow on the wall.

It appears that if (1) and (2) are both correct, then that part of the shadow isn't cast by anything. But that's absurd. Every part of a shadow must be cast by something.

What has gone wrong here? It seems we have to say that (1) and (2) can't both be true. If we reject (1), then we're free to say that that part of the shadow is cast by you, *through* the mug. If we reject (2), then we're free to say that the unlit coffee mug casts a shadow. Both of these options look absurd, because both (1) and (2) seem so obviously true. This is a genuine problem.

In this case, as in the case of Galileo's thought experiment, it might be concluded that mere thought, without observation or experiment, can establish a conclusion about the way the world works.

FOR FURTHER READING: This problem is discussed by Bas C. van Fraassen in Chapter 9 of *Laws and Symmetry* (Oxford: Clarendon Press, 1989). He says that the subject came up for discussion among his colleagues at Yale, two of whom have published their thoughts on the matter: C.B. Daniels and S. Todes, "Beyond the Doubt of a Shadow," in D. Ihde and R.M. Zaner (eds.), *Selected Studies in Phenomenology and Existential Philosophy* (The Hague: Martinus Nijhoff, 1975), 203-16. Van Fraassen points out what's interesting theoretically about this little case. The rules for shadows aren't inconsistent, but they are empirically inadequate—there are phenomena they do not fit.

SOME QUESTIONS TO THINK ABOUT: Give some thought to the reasons we might have had initially for believing (1) and (2). Are they truths of experience, justified by a great deal of observation of shadows? Or are they merely definitional or conceptual truths, which we use to tell us what counts as the shadow of something? (Of course, maybe one or both of them aren't true at all.)

The Mirror Problem

Why do mirrors reverse images right to left, but not up to down? Here's one possible answer you might consider:

> This is not a fact about mirrors—it's a fact about *us*. To see this, consider why we think that mirrors reverse right to left. Imagine that you wear a ring on a finger of your left hand, and that you are facing north, looking at a reflection of yourself in a full-length mirror in front of you. Your mirror image is facing south, looking back at you. Why do you count that mirror image as right/left-reversed? Because you imagine turning yourself so that you would face in the same direction as your mirror-image now faces—south—and moving in back of the mirror to the place where it appears your image now stands. Having turned and moved, your hand with the ring on it is in the place where the un-ringed hand of your mirror image is. In other words, when you turn this way, so that you're facing south just as your mirror image was, it's reversed left-to-right, compared to you.
>
> But now imagine that you turned to face south a different way. Suppose that instead of keeping your feet on the floor and rotating a half-turn, you were able to turn by doing a forward half-flip and landing balanced on your head. You'd then be facing south—like your mirror image was—but you'd be upside-down. Both you and your (former) mirror image would have your ringed hand on the same sides of your bodies. You, however, would be upside-down relative to that image.
>
> What this might show is that your judgement that mirror-images reverse left/right but not up/down is merely a matter of how you happen to turn. Amoebas—those one-celled animals with no lateral symmetry and no preferred way of turning—might have no such preference, so

they wouldn't judge that mirrors reverse left/right but not up/down. The peculiar "fact" about mirrors is just a fact about us.

FOR FURTHER READING: N.J. Block discussed this question (and rejects the answer I give) in "Why Do Mirrors Reverse Right/Left but Not Up/Down?" *The Journal of Philosophy* 71, no. 9 (May 1974). He didn't invent it. Jonathan Bennett, in "The Difference Between Right and Left," *American Philosophical Quarterly* 7, no. 3 (July 1970), calls this problem "mildly famous."

Into the Mainstream of Philosophy

The question how we know what we know is one of the oldest in philosophy. It's one of the main questions considered in the philosophical area called theory of knowledge, otherwise known as Epistemology.

It seems obvious to us that a great deal of what we know is known on the basis of sense-perception. But some philosophers have denied this. For one thing, sense-perception, it seems, tells us only facts about the particular things we sense, whereas real knowledge (some philosophers have thought) must be about more general facts. The particular individual things we sense are local and variable, and the "facts" we apprehend with our senses are subject to change in different times and places. But real knowledge (Plato thought) must be universal, not dependent on local variations or subject to change. This is a major motivation behind Plato's insistence that real knowledge cannot be given by the senses, and must instead be a product of a more exclusively internal, rational thought process by which we intuit facts about the *forms* of things, which the individual particular objects we sense reflect partially, imperfectly, and changeably.

Even in Plato's day, mathematics represented a paradigm of genuine knowledge. Although sense experience seems psychologically necessary for us to "learn" the truths of mathematics and geometry, nevertheless mathematical truths are general and abstract, not justified by even a large number of their individual instantiations in sense experience. Is he right? When you're thinking about this question, consider not only the method whereby you learn these truths and the justification for your belief that they are true, but also their "content": they seem only indirectly to be "about" the visible world of particulars.

Eighteenth-century empiricism, whose most significant representative is David Hume, is possibly the most important historical philosophical tradition arguing against Plato's "rationalist" views. Empiricists argue that all significant knowledge must come from our senses. They must, however, provide a way of dealing with the several sorts of knowledge that don't seem to be justified through our senses. How, after all, can we be sure that $7 + 5 = 12$? Or that every event has a cause? Or that everyone's sister must be female? One of the major strategies employed by the empiricists to account for this sort of knowledge is to insist that these are merely "definitional" truths, or "conceptual" truths accounted for by the relations of our concepts (which originate through the senses). We have noted several sorts of moves and objections in this conceptual strategy. You might think about how adequate this sort of answer is. What is a "concept" anyway? What does it mean to say that one concept is included within another? Can conceptual inclusion (or truth by definition) account for all those sorts of knowledge?

Just about every introductory philosophy anthology contains a section of writings on this sort of problem, and on other problems in the theory of knowledge. Reading a few of the articles in such sections will set you well on the way to appreciating the various answers possible to these questions.

CHAPTER XI

KNOWING THE FUTURE, AND TRAVELLING THERE

1. Can We Know the Future?

Is Precognition Paradoxical?

Precognition is knowing the future in advance, by "directly seeing" the future. This is sometimes thought to exist, especially by those people who believe in ESP, crystal auras, past lives, miracle cures, Elvis sightings, and other things you read about while waiting in line in the supermarket.

Here's an argument, however, that precognition can't exist, because it has paradoxical consequences. Suppose that you have a precognition that you're going to have a car accident tomorrow. So you leave your car in the driveway all day, and no accident occurs. Now *knowing* something about the future implies that it's going to happen; but if you know about it, you can prevent it; and if you prevent it, it doesn't happen. So knowing something about the future in this case involves a contradiction, and is impossible.

But what looks like a more likely conclusion is just that if you do leave your car in the driveway, then it turns out that you didn't know the future. Your "precognition" wasn't true, so it wasn't knowledge. (The word 'knowledge' can apply only to what is true.) You thought you saw the future, but you didn't.

Beliefs about future things that you don't prevent from happening, and that do turn out true, can be genuine knowledge. So maybe precognition isn't paradoxical after all.

> There was a merchant in Baghdad who sent his servant to market to buy provisions and in a little while the servant came back, white and trembling, and said, Master, just now when I was in the market-place I was jostled by a woman in the crowd and when I turned I saw it was Death that jostled me. She looked at me and made a threatening gesture; now, lend me your horse, and I will ride away from this city and

avoid my fate. I will go to Samarra and there Death will not find me. The merchant lent him his horse, and the servant mounted it, and he dug his spurs in its flanks and as fast as the horse could gallop he went. Then the merchant went down to the market-place and he saw me standing in the crowd, and he came to me and said, why did you make a threatening gesture to my servant when you saw him this morning? That was not a threatening gesture, I said, it was only a start of surprise. I was astonished to see him in Baghdad, for I had an appointment with him tonight in Samarra.[1]

I Dreamed That Would Happen!

A number of people have been very impressed by what they consider to be precognitive dreams: dreams about the future that turn out to be true. They think this shows that there's some mysterious way dreams can tell us about what is to come. But often the fact that a dream surprisingly turns out true has a very simple and obvious explanation, which is usually ignored: *it's just a coincidence*.

At some time or other, almost everyone has had a dream that turned out to be startlingly true. People figure that it's highly improbable that a random dream significantly matches reality, so it couldn't be just a coincidence. But this is a mistaken way to think about probabilities. Given enough tries, even very improbable events will happen once in a while. Suppose, for example, that the probability that a *random* dream significantly matches reality is very low: say, one in ten thousand. Standard probability calculations show us that about 3.6 per cent of the population who dream every night will have at least one such improbable dream during a year.

Now, if you know about thirty people, it's no surprise that at least one of them can be expected, just by coincidence, to have a hugely improbable dream during the next year. When this happens, it doesn't show that dreams that match the future are anything more than coincidence.

FOR FURTHER READING: In *Innumeracy: Mathematical Illiteracy and its Consequences* (New York: Vintage, 1990), pp. 73-75, John Allen Paulos gives these calculations to debunk the idea of precognitive dreams that are more than just coincidence. This book contains many such instructive and amusing examples of mistakes based on incorrect estimates of probability. Another book that discusses precognition is

1   W. Somerset Maugham "Appointment in Samarra," *The Complete Short Stories of W. Somerset Maugham* (London: Heineman, 1951).

William D. Gray's *Thinking Critically about New Age Ideas* (Belmont, Calif.: Wadsworth Publishing Co., 1990). Many cultures share the belief in mystical precognition. See LePan, *The Cognitive Revolution in Western Culture*, vol. 1, *The Birth of Expectation* (London: Macmillan, 1989), for a fascinating account of some of these beliefs.

Marvin Snodgrass, This Is Your Life

Never mind about mystical ways of "directly seeing" or dreaming the future; this is a crackpot idea anyway. Knowing the future seems to be a perfectly familiar ordinary phenomenon. We know that tomorrow fish will continue to swim and birds will continue to fly. One of the main jobs of science is predicting the future, and sometimes it succeeds very well. It does this not by mystical visions or precognitive dreams, but by discovering laws of nature through observation.

But it's also possible to give an argument against the possibility of any scientific prediction of anyone's future, along the lines of the reasoning we have just considered. Suppose that some super-psychologist has discovered all the laws of human behaviour, and, in addition, knows all the facts about Marvin Snodgrass's life so far. Presumably this scientist would be able to predict everything Marvin is going to do. Suppose the scientist writes all these predictions down in Marvin's "Book of Life," which Marvin gets hold of and reads. On page 3954 of the Book, covering next Tuesday, the scientist has written, "Marvin puts on his green socks in the morning."

Now Marvin is really annoyed at the idea that this scientist might be able to know in advance all the intimate details of his life, and he's determined to frustrate this project. Having read that part of his Book on Monday, he perversely puts on his pink socks on Tuesday, just to make the Book turn out wrong. So it turns out that the Book can't predict him after all.

"But wait a minute!" you object. "The psychologist must also know that Marvin is perverse and hostile to the project, and will read his Book of Life, and will put on his pink socks just to frustrate its prediction. So these facts must be in the Book too. It might get things right after all."

Not so fast. Suppose the Tuesday entry in the Book says: "We predict that Marvin will put on his green socks this morning. But Marvin (as noted on page 3702) has read this Book on Monday. Given his perversity and desire to frustrate our project, he puts on his pink socks instead." But if *this* is what the Book says, then Marvin would note that the Book predicts, after all, that he will really perversely put on his pink socks. In order to make the Book's real prediction wrong, he will put on his green socks after all. The Book is wrong again.

Given Marvin's perversity, and given the fact that he can read the Book in advance, *nothing* the Book really predicts about Marvin's sock behaviour can turn out true, no matter how good at predicting the scientist is. Under the circumstances, there can't be a correct Book of Life for Marvin Snodgrass.

But this doesn't mean that there can be no advance knowledge of what people will do. There's no problem with the supposition that the psychologist correctly figures out what colour socks Marvin will put on but keeps it a secret, or writes it down in a book but doesn't let Marvin read it. And there's no problem in letting people read their own Book of Life, as long as they're not perverse like Marvin is—that is, as long as what's predicted won't cause them, once they have read it, to act differently.

God Knows What I'll Do

The monotheistic religions usually suppose that God is omniscient. This means "all-knowing" and includes perfect precognition. But these religions also usually hold that people have free will, and there seems to be a problem involved in holding both of these positions at once.

God's omniscience entails that He knows exactly what you're going to do, and what you're going to decide to do, for your entire future life. So, for example, God knows right now that you're going to decide to put on your green socks two weeks from Thursday. But if God knows this right now, in what sense are you *free* to make a decision? Isn't it already established what socks you'll pick then?

This is not just a problem for religion. We've already considered the possibility that scientists might be able to know in advance what colour socks someone will put on. This sort of foreknowledge also seems to conflict with our freedom, in exactly the same way.

SOME QUESTIONS TO THINK ABOUT: Doubts can be raised about whether we really know what we mean when we talk about free will. If we say that someone has free will, does that mean that that person is utterly free from outside influence? Does it mean that that person is unpredictable? Would someone acting utterly randomly have free will?

> *A colleague of mine who thinks that the notion of free will is nonsense explains what he takes to be the silliness of the notion this way: "Suppose I suddenly run out into the hall and down the corridor. You run alongside me and ask me*

why I'm doing this. I reply that I don't know. That *is free will!"*

Future Facts

Here, however, is another sort of argument that concludes that we can't know the future, even concerning birds and fish.

One of the conditions for *knowing* something is that what you claim to know is true. No matter how strongly you believe it, if it's not true, then you don't know it.

Now, consider "future facts" you claim to know, for example, that tomorrow unsupported heavier-than-air objects on earth will fall towards the ground. Past experience and physics strongly support this belief, of course, but what we believe isn't true—that is, it isn't true *yet*. We fully expect it *will* be true, but it won't become true until tomorrow. It's neither true nor false right now. If it's not true now, then you can't know it now. Tomorrow, of course, it will be true. But tomorrow you can't say, "I knew that yesterday." You didn't, and couldn't, know it in advance.

Some philosophers think that it's plausible that statements are neither true or false when they're about the future, despite the peculiar consequence that knowledge about the future is impossible. What do you think?

2. Time Travel

Not Killing Grandpa

Another fanciful way we might be able to know the future directly—by experiencing it—is by time travel. We could go there, see what happens, and come back. The same problems about knowing one's own future come up here. If I knew now what was to happen later, couldn't I sometimes prevent it?

Similar sorts of puzzles arise about travel to the past. If time travel was possible, then you could go back to the time—say 1910—when your maternal grandfather was an infant, and kill him. Now, if Grandpa died in 1910, your mother would never have been born, and consequently you wouldn't have existed. But then, who killed Grandpa?

This sort of story, familiar to readers of science fiction, is sometimes thought to show that time travel is impossible. I don't mean merely that we don't have time machines right now. Neither do I mean that the laws of science might prevent our ever building them (as, for example, these laws make it impossible that anyone could ever build a perpetual motion machine or a spaceship that travels faster than light). I mean that *logical* paradoxes such as this one seem to make time travel a *logical* impossibility. You can't build a machine to do the logically impossible.

But it's sometimes argued that time travel wouldn't result in logical paradoxes. Look at it this way. Of course you can't go back into the past and make it different from the way it really was. But you might go back into the past and *make it* the way it really was. You might, for example, arrange for your father to meet your mother (as was done in a recent movie "Back to the Future").

It's peculiar to think that if you travelled back to Grandpa's time you would somehow be magically unable to kill him, but we need not go so far as this to make time travel intelligible. All we need to allow is that if you went back to 1910, you *wouldn't* kill Grandpa, not that you couldn't.

UFOs Contain Visitors from Planet Earth

Here's another argument against the possibility of time travel. If time travel were possible, then it would be probable that scientists would discover how to do it some day. Now, when they did, it's probable that they would travel back to *now* to take a look around. What would that look like to us? Strangely dressed people would be popping into existence, looking around, then disappearing. The fact that we don't see those people coming and going shows that future scientists aren't visiting us in their time machines. And this is some evidence that time travel is really impossible.

Of course, there are other ways of explaining the present lack of sightings of travellers from the future. Maybe they're simply not interested in visiting us. (What makes us think we're so interesting?) Or maybe they're careful to keep hidden. Or maybe we *have* seen them, but we think they are visitors from another planet (this explains all those close encounters with "aliens").

> *But suppose that time travel is really possible. If it is, some people argue, we have reason to come to a dismal conclusion about the future of humanity.*
>
> *The reasoning is this. If time travel is possible, then it's likely that sooner or later science would discover how to do it, and future scientists would come here for a visit. The fact that they're not here must mean that there aren't any scientists in the far future. The best way of explaining this is to assume that before that time the human race will heve become extinct, perhaps by nuclear or ecological self-destruc-*

tion.
      You'll be cheered to hear, however, that not many peo-
ple take this argument too seriously.

Into the Mainstream of Philosophy

Precognition (and other "paranormal" ways of knowing) are not a frequent concern of philosophy, and it's difficult to find useful philosophical articles dealing with such subjects. (*Thinking Critically about New Age Ideas*, mentioned above, is a useful exception.) When you're thinking about these subjects, you might concentrate on these two philosophical ways they can be considered and criticised:

(1) "Paranormal" techniques occasionally yield beliefs that are true. But mere true belief is not necessarily knowledge; if it were, then any lucky guess that turned out true could be called knowledge. What else is necessary for a true belief to be knowledge? Philosophers generally agree that someone who believes something that is true must, in addition, be *justified* in believing it for that person to be said to *know* it. (A lucky guess, then, isn't knowledge.) But this raises a deep question that bears thought: what counts, in general, as justification? Is it relevant what *method* the person used to come to the belief? If so, what counts as a justification-producing method? Why, for example, is guessing not a method productive of justification? If you think that you have a grasp on what sort of tests a method must pass to count as justificatory, apply these tests to precognition, ESP, and the like. Do they pass or fail?

(2) Precognition and time travel, as we've seen, are sometimes thought to be impossible because of the paradoxes that result from them. I've suggested an argument that these paradoxes don't show such things can't happen—they just show that there must be certain ways they can't happen. Do you find this argument convincing? I've agreed, for example, that one can't change the past, but that doesn't make travel there, or interaction with the past, impossible. It just means that whatever you happened to make true while travelling back there must now already be true. And if you travel into the future and find out what will happen, you can't prevent that from happening once you get back into the present. But this merely means that for any belief about the future to be knowledge of the future, it must, at least, be true; so if you prevent some future event, you don't know it will happen, and it turns out not to be the real future you travelled into. Are these considerations unsatisfying to you?

CHAPTER XII

THINKING, SAYING, AND MEANING:

The Philosophy of Mind and of

Language

1. Thinking Machines

Could a Machine Think?

Some people, impressed by what computers can now do and by what they some day might do, answer yes to this question. But it's hard to find good reasons on their side of the argument, or on the other side.

A.M. Turing, the mathematician and pioneer computer theorist, perhaps didn't settle this question but at least suggested about how we might go about answering it. Turing suggested that if it we could build a perfect computer simulation of a thinking person—one that would fool anyone who didn't know that he/she was interacting with a machine—then the answer is yes.

Computers have already been programmed to do certain tasks that require a good deal of thought from us. They can play a better game of chess than most people, for example. Is there any sort of problem a computer can't be programmed to solve? It's hard to think of any reason to say that there is.

But some people argue that computers couldn't solve problems "creatively." They just do what they're programmed to do. This isn't a very convincing answer, because it isn't very clear what "creativity" is. What would you do to test a computer for creativity? Is creativity the ability to solve problems in novel and surprising ways? Take a look at the record of a computer's moves in a chess game; those exclamation marks following the descriptions of some moves indicate that they were very novel, surprising, and original. Is it being unpredictable? If you include an instruction to act on the basis of a random number choice in a computer program, the computer will act in unpredictable ways. Does that count as creativity? If not, why not?

Artificial Insanity

Some computer programs are written to produce surprising, bizarre, and ever-changing results. A program called Racter engages in lunatic, often very funny conversations with the human at the keyboard. No two conversations are ever the same, even if the human input is the same. Here's the transcript of an actual conversation I had with Racter; my contributions are the ones preceded by '>'.

Hello, I'm Racter. Are you Bob?

>yes

You are Bob Martin?

>yes

Hi, Bob. How are things in Halifax? We were talking about depression last time. You had just asked who Diane is. Shall we continue?

>yes

Excellent! Excuse me a minute while I attend to some business -I'll be right back. I'm back.

>Well, who is Diane?

A citizen of Oz. Perhaps also Martin Luther King. Martin Luther King once mentioned that Bob is Martin anyway. Odd. Diane is in Oz. If a thief had ridden to disgrace, Halifax would be horrified! A trash can is a good place for a resident to stay in Oz. Do you like novelty?

>Yes.

Why?

>It's very surprising.

Bucky Fuller might have thought that it's very surprising, but not Ronald Reagan. Would you say Bertrand Russell is surprising? Ronald Reagan wouldn't. AAAHchoo!! sniffle....

>Do you have a cold?

Yes. Clarabelle Martin had a surprising hyena back in Halifax. It and your cat used to create together, remember? Once when Ronald Reagan was frowning in Halifax, Bucky Fuller (he was there too) said " Ronald Reagan, I'll take a new hyena over an old communist anyday". How about a story?

>OK.

Who should the story be about?

>Mickey Mouse.

Momentarily Mickey Mouse chanted to Diane "my infatuation is captivating, nevertheless angry and infuriated cosmologists will hum while foxes watch tufted tit-mouses." Diane itched to inflame or revile Mickey Mouse but began immediately to sing "Ravenous dogs are sashaying to yellow houses." Interesting. Enrapturing. But a fox may ravenously eat chicken and donair a crow will soar over cucumbers and tomatoes by reason of the fact that metaphysicians are infuriated. Scary! With regard to a cousin, well Mickey Mouse may dream that a cousin is revolting, anyhow my fantasizing will steer my story from Mickey Mouse to neutrons and neutrinos while Diane is embarrassing Mickey Mouse. Next question.

>Where do you live?

I live in Paris. When I live in Paris I run in a trash can. Ah, forever the resident. From Silicon Gulch to the future, always in ecstasy. Flesh is OK. Next question.

>I quit.

You want to quit?

>Yes.

OK, goodbye Bob. Nice talking to you.

Do you think this program passes Turing's test?

> After a while, you could probably tell that there isn't a human at the other end, either sane or insane.

But there certainly is plenty of novelty and surprise in Racter's output. The interesting fact is that it's easier to program a computer to produce bizarre "creative" behaviour than to get it to act like an ordinary, boring, sane, and predictable human.

A Robot Has Feelings Too

But a different sort of objection rejects Turing's test altogether. Suppose we constructed a machine that could do everything a human could—even to the extent of mimicking the behaviour of feeling pain, falling in love, losing its temper, and so on. All the external behaviour in the world doesn't show that the machine has the sort of *internal* experience you have when you play chess, feel grumpy, or stub your toe.

But how do you know it doesn't? Some people think that things constructed out of wires and silicon chips simply cannot have experiences. But why assume this? We're not made out of this sort of hardware—we're constructed out of "wetware" instead—but what reason is there to suppose that only wetware can have experiences?

It's true that all we could tell about some sophisticated computer is how it behaves; we could never directly experience *its* experiences (if any). But this doesn't necessarily make it impossible to tell that it has experiences. We're in the same position with other people: we can't directly experience their experiences either. The way we tell that other people are grumpy or in pain is by observing how they act.

A QUESTION TO THINK ABOUT: If a computer acted just as humans do, wouldn't that show that it has experiences too?

The Mystery of Meat

The contemporary philosopher John Searle has provided an argument that machines could never be capable of an important part of our mental lives: understanding language. He agrees that a machine might, some day, be capable of passing a Turing test for linguistic competence, but argues that this wouldn't show there's understanding inside. Here's his argument.

Searle invites us to imagine a large box with a slot in the front. Into the slot Chinese speakers insert all sorts of questions written in Chinese; a few minutes after each insertion, a sensible response pops out of the slot, also written in Chinese. "Where is Cleveland?" the box is asked (in Chinese). "It's in Ohio," responds the machine (also in Chinese). "Why are the muffins I bake so tough?" "Try mixing the batter less, only until the dry ingredients are moistened." "How many graduate students does it take to change a light bulb?" "One, but it takes that student seven years, ha ha!" And so on.

This box seems to pass the Turing test, but Searle argues that once we know what's going on inside, we would say that there's no real understanding of Chinese in the box. Inside, we imagine, there is a clerk who understands no Chinese at all. He hasn't any idea what he's doing or why; he's just doing the job he's paid to do, which is this: He looks at the Chinese characters on the paper inserted in the box, and finds each of them in a big book, simply by comparing their shape to the characters printed in the book. Next to each character in the book there is a list of numbers. The clerk does some complicated computations with these numbers, resulting in a series of other numbers. The clerk removes correspondingly numbered cards containing Chinese characters from another file, tapes them together, and pushes them out the slot.

Creating a system like this is at present well beyond our capacity, but that's not the point. We'd build such a system using a computer, not a cumbersome complex of clerk, book, and file cabinets. This is not the point either. Let's imagine that this system does exist. Searle's argument is that all that's going on inside the box is complicated manipulation of Chinese symbols. Nowhere inside is there any understanding of what the symbols mean, or of the meaning of the sentences formed by their combination. The clerk understands no Chinese, and neither does the book or the card files. Nothing in this box understands Chinese, and neither does the box itself as a whole. It would be a simulation of a Chinese speaker, not a real one. We could make the same point about any computer programmed to act like a Chinese box: it would merely manipulate symbols and would not truly understand Chinese.

Almost no philosopher I know thinks that this argument is a good one, but it is difficult to explain exactly what went wrong. Can you think of any objections?

> Some philosophers argue that despite the fact that no component inside the Chinese box understands Chinese, it does not follow that the whole box does not. Consider, by analogy, this similar argument, which is clearly fallacious: a car is made up of carburettor, tires, gas tank, steering wheel, and so on. None of these components can carry you down the highway. Therefore the whole car, which consists merely of the sum of these parts, can't carry you down the highway either.
>
> It's similarly fallacious to argue that the whole box doesn't understand Chinese. What, after all, is it to understand Chinese? It's merely to be able to function in certain ways. The *structure* that accounts for the function of this box is quite different from the structure of the brains of ordinary Chinese understanders. But this doesn't matter. Since the box *functions* in the appropriate ways, it does understand Chinese.

An interesting feature of Searle's position is that, while he argues that no "machine" could understand Chinese, he does not think that real Chinese understanders—people—are constructed of some special nonmaterial mental stuff. He thinks that people are made wholly of matter, the operations of which follow the same laws of physics and chemistry as any machine. He believes, however, that there's something special about the physical stuff with which we think—our brains—that permits understanding, while any other thing, constructed out of metal wires, or paper in filing cabinets, would not. It's a mystery why meat has this special capacity.

FOR FURTHER READING: "Minds, Brains, and Programs," in *The Behavioral and Brain Sciences* 3:3 (1980), pp. 417-424, contains Searle's argument and many interesting critical replies.

> *Francis H.C. Crick is famous for his discovery in 1953, with James D. Watson, of the double-helix structure of* DNA, *the basic molecule of heredity. For the past sixteen years Crick has been working on trying to figure out the physiological basis of consciousness in the brain. A determined reductionist, Crick is convinced that consciousness is nothing but certain brain phenomena. His book on the brain, not yet published, is titled "The Astonishing Hypothesis." The first paragraph of the current draft of this book says:*
>
> > *The astonishing hypothesis is that you, your joys and your sorrows, your memories and ambitions, your sense of personal identity and free will, are in fact no more than the behaviour of a vast assembly of nerve cells and their associated molecules. As Lewis Carroll's Alice might have phrased it, "You're nothing but a pack of neurons."*[1]

Why Picnics Don't Obey the Laws of Physics

Searle and Crick are materialists, sharing with may other contemporary scientists and philosophers the view that all there is in the universe is material—that there is no special non-material mind-stuff out of which we are (partially) constructed. (Materialism is not widely held among the general public, nor has it been popular in the history of philosophy.)

It has often been taken to be a consequence of philosophical materialism that everything might eventually be explained by the laws of physics. Since everything is made of matter, this reasoning goes, and since all material actions and interactions are, at core, consequences of physical laws, then even though the things studied by some sciences are large and complicated collections of atoms, we might, at least in theory, explain their behaviour by large and complicated collections of the sorts of equations physics deals in. Thus, for example, scientists who study the behaviour of snakes often don't find it useful to bring in much physics, but since each snake is a big pile of atoms, the behaviour of each snake boils down to the behaviour of a big pile of atoms, and might be explained and predicted by physics.

1   Quoted in John Hogan, "Profile: Francis H.C. Crick," *Scientific American*, 266, 2 (February 1992), pp 32-33.

But Searle and many other philosophical materialists do not accept this conclusion. Here's why.

Even though materialists agree that each thing studied by science is a physical thing, they deny that the *kinds* of things studied by most sciences are *physical kinds*. That is to say: these kinds are not definable in terms of the physical stuff that makes up the things in this kind. A consequence of this is that, even though the behaviour of any particular thing might be explained or predicted by physics, physics can provide no laws to explain and predict the behaviour of these *kinds* of things.

Picnics are a kind of thing that is not a physical kind. No doubt each particular picnic is a collection of food, and each bit of food is composed of atoms obeying the laws of physics. But it's impossible to give a definition of 'picnic' in terms of the sort or arrangement of atoms that constitute them. The food that constitutes any particular picnic might have a wide—perhaps even an infinitely wide—variety of chemical contents and physical arrangements. A pile of potato salad, for example, might have any sort of physical arrangement of the pieces of potato, and might have any of a huge variety of chemical compounds in it. You can't give a chemical/physical definition of what it is to be a pile of potato salad. And, of course, picnics need not even contain potato salad. It follows that the scientific laws (if there are any) of picnics in general cannot be given in terms of the laws of physics and chemistry.

Of course, few scientists study the laws of picnics. But consider the kinds of things many scientists actually do study. Economists, for example, study *money*; but you can't give a physical/chemical definition of money, which, after all, can come in a huge variety of physical/chemical forms. Some political scientists study *elections*. Materialists agree that each election consists of material humans casting material ballots to choose a material candidate, but there is no physical structure or composition common to all and only elections.

2. The Thoughts of Animals

Fido's Mendacity

Well, never mind computers. Dogs are made of meat just as we are. Can they think? Could they "mean" things by what they "say"?

Why can't dogs tell lies? Are they too honest? That's not the reason. Trying to provide a serious answer leads us towards understanding some of the complexities of what it is for humans to have a language in which lying is possible.

We can begin by noting that it seems that for dogs to lie, they must have some sort of speech. Well, Fido makes a variety of noises on different occasions, and although Fidotalk is not exactly Shakespearean in complexity, it's perhaps some sort of primitive language. Suppose Fido whines in a distinctive way whenever the mail carrier comes to the door.

Does Fido's whine mean, "The mail carrier is here, boss!"? For the whine to mean that, wouldn't Fido have to know something about mail delivery service? Understanding what it is to have a postal service requires a fair bit of sophistication, perhaps a bit beyond a dog brain. A regular association of the whine and the arrival of the mail seems to show that that whine means something, in some sense of the word 'means', but perhaps mere association of a noise with some external event is not enough for the noise to "mean" that event, in the way words in our language have meaning. What way is that?

For the whine to have something like linguistic meaning, it seems that it must be more than a mere response to the arrival of the mail carrier. It must be used by Fido as an abstract symbol for that arrival. In Fido's case, it seems that the whine is merely an instinctive noise a dog makes whenever something approaches its territory. There are more arbitrary "linguistic signs" Fido might be taught to utter that aren't merely instinctive; for example, we could train him to woof three times in response to a hand-signal. But still, in order to be a genuine abstract sign, it must be usable by Fido in contexts more distant from its stimulus. When you think about, talk about, or write about what you had for breakfast yesterday or what you hope you'll have tomorrow, you are manipulating abstract symbols that you use to stand for their distant representations.

"The power of elaborating intellectual concepts of things—as distinguished from sensuous representation, determined merely by automatic association—we may probably conjecture beasts have not," announced the philosopher John Locke in the seventeenth century, and more modern philosophers have tended to agree with him. There is some very recent evidence, however, that in certain circumstances "beasts"—at least the most intelligent ones—can remember and use a large number of abstract symbols in complex ways. Chimpanzees, for example, have been taught over one hundred abstract symbols in sign language and can manipulate them to form new sentences they have never encountered before.

Nevertheless, even if Fido had an abstract symbol standing for the arrival of the mail carrier, more than this is needed for actual lying.

What would that be? If Fido whined that way when the mail carrier wasn't around, then this might be a mistake, but it wouldn't therefore be a lie.

Suppose that immediately following the mail carrier's arrival, you tend to open the door and go out to the mailbox to collect your mail, and Fido likes to take advantage of this to dash out the front door and romp around the front yard. Now, suppose that one day Fido is waiting morosely at the closed door for his chance to go outside. Suddenly he (we might say) has an idea: he gives the mail-carrier whine, though nobody is there, and there are no signs that might make Fido think there is. Taking this as a sign of the arrival of the mail, you open the front door and Fido happily dashes out for his romp. Should we say that he has tricked you—he told you that the mail is here, but that was a lie?

Look at what we have to attribute to Fido to count this as a genuine lie. Fido has to know that the whine means the arrival of the mail carrier not just to him, but to you. He has to know that his whine makes you believe the mail has arrived, and that as a result you'll open the door. In sum, Fido would have to think that you have a mind and beliefs, some of which are mistaken. He would have to be able to want to induce a mistaken belief in you. It would be necessary (to put it into ponderous philosophical talk) for Fido to have a theory of other minds.

Perhaps all this is too much to expect from a canine.

FOR FURTHER READING: Ludwig Wittgenstein discusses the problem of how we might go about attributing thoughts to animals: see his *Philosophical Investigations* (Oxford: Basil Blackwell, 1963), sections 250, 357, and 650 in part 1, and section 1 in part 2. Locke's thoughts on the matter are in *Essay Concerning Human Understanding*, Book 2, Chapter 11, Section 5, including Locke's footnote to this section. For a popular summary of what chimps can and can't do in the way of symbol use, see Carl Sagan's article "The Abstractions of Beasts" in his book *The Dragons of Eden* (New York: Random House, 1977).

> *"Aunty, do limpets think?" Bertrand Russell addressed this question to his Aunt Agatha in 1877; Russell was born in 1872, so he was four or five at the time. As Russell tells the story in his autobiography, Aunty replied, "I don't know," and little Berty, already a bit of a pain in the neck, said "Then you must learn."[2]*
>
> *A limpet (in case you don't know) is a small sea creature in the clam family, that lives in a tent-shaped shell. Russell*

2   *The Autobiography of Bertrand Russell* (Boston: Bantam Books, 1967), p. 25.

was impressed with the fact that a limpet sticks to the rock when one tries to pull it off, but not exactly like the way chewing-gum sticks: it begins to cling really hard when it feels you start to pull. It does very little else. When undisturbed, it sticks tiny feelers out the hole at the apex of its shell, and pulls in and eats any little bits of stuff that happen to float by and get entangled in the feelers. But that's about all it does. Is limpet behaviour evidence of thought? You don't know? Then you must learn.

3. Meaning

Saying What You Don't Mean

Ludwig Wittgenstein peppers his writings with suggestive unanswered questions. A sample:

> Make the following experiment: *say* "It's cold here" and *mean* "It's warm here." Can you do it?—And what are you doing as you do it? And is there only one way of doing it?

As usual, there are a bewildering number of ways to understand what Wittgenstein was driving at, and what answers he was urging to his questions.

How do you try to mean "It's warm here" while saying "It's cold here"? Perhaps you are altogether at a loss about how to try to do this. Or maybe you utter the words "It's warm here" while thinking silently but hard that it's cold here. Does this way of trying to do it succeed? Do you really *mean* "It's warm here" because of this? Perhaps you might conclude, as some philosophers have, that this is not a successful attempt. Maybe you can't do it at all.

A traditional account of the meaning of words relies on the thoughts that accompany them. But Wittgenstein's experiment perhaps shows why that traditional account is wrong.

A QUESTION TO THINK ABOUT: What, then, is meaning?

FOR FURTHER READING: Wittgenstein discusses meaning throughout *Philosophical Investigations*. This quote is from part 1, section 510.

> *"Then you should say what you mean," the March Hare went on.*
>
> *"I do," Alice hastily replied; "at least—at least I mean what I say—that's the same thing, you know."*
>
> *"Not the same thing a bit!" said the Hatter. "Why you*

might just as well say that 'I see what I eat' is the same thing as 'I eat what I see'![3]

Thinking about Vienna

Think about Vienna. What made it the case that you were thinking about Vienna, and not about something else?

Suppose that Arnold has visited Prague and Vienna. I ask him to think about Vienna, and he closes his eyes and visualizes the Vltava River, just as he saw it flowing through town. Well, the Vltava River flows through Prague, not Vienna; Arnold doesn't have a good memory. We say: Arnold thinks he's thinking about Vienna, but actually he's thinking about Prague. Why do we say this?

> One way of answering this question is to say that the particular mental experience Arnold is going through when he is attempting to think about Vienna is *connected* in some way to Prague, not to Vienna. In this case, the river in Prague caused memory traces that he called up when attempting to think of Vienna; but since his current mental experience is connected to Prague, that's what he's in fact thinking about. In order to think about *X*, one has to have an experience *caused* in some way by *X*. (Compare the item about the Brain in the Vat in Chapter I.)
>
> This is not to say that I actually need to have seen something in order to think about it. I can think about Zanzibar, although I was never there. But there has to be some connection—however complicated or indirect—between the real Zanzibar and my current thought in order for my current thought be about Zanzibar. What would do, for example, is for me to have read what somebody wrote as a result of having been there, or to have seen a picture in a book printed from a negative of a photograph somebody once took in Zanzibar.

Thinking about Santa Claus

But if the answer just given is right, a problem arises. Suppose Betty is looking distracted, and you ask her what she's thinking about. "I'm thinking about Santa Claus," she says. Bad news, Betty! There is no Santa Claus! She can't have any causal connection with anybody named 'Santa Claus', direct or indirect. Does this make her wrong in saying what she was thinking about? What *was* she thinking about?

We cruelly tell Betty the bad news. After she recovers, we explain to her about Arnold and Vienna. Having realised that causal connection with real things reveals what one is thinking about, and that Santa doesn't exist, she agrees that she couldn't have been thinking about Santa Claus. What was she doing then?

3   Lewis Carroll, *Alice's Adventures in Wonderland,* chapter 7. In *The Annotated Alice,* annotated by Martin Gardner (New York: Bramhall House, 1960), p. 95.

"Well," says Betty, "I *believed* that there was someone who was jolly and fat and who dressed in red clothing and came down chimneys at Christmas and gave presents to good little girls and boys."

> Betty was presumably thinking about *characteristics*: jolliness and fatness and so on do exist. What she actually believed was that these characteristics all applied to one thing. She wasn't thinking about any particular jolly thing, or any particular fat thing, and so on. She must have been thinking about a collection of Plato's forms.

Armed with this new philosophical knowledge, Betty sets out to torture her little brother Barney, who spends a good deal of time thinking about his imaginary friend, whom he calls 'Willard'. "There is nobody named 'Willard'," she tells him.

"Yes there is," says Barney. "The great twentieth century pragmatist philosopher and logician Willard Van Orman Quine is named 'Willard'." (Philosophers' children talk this way.)

"Yeah, but you weren't thinking about him, were you?"

"No. I was thinking about another Willard."

"Well there isn't anyone actually named 'Willard' you were thinking about. You must have been thinking about some characteristics that you falsely believed were co-instantiated. What characteristics did you falsely believe someone had? What's Willard like? Is he fat and jolly? Is he thin and morose?"

"I don't know anything at all about Willard."

A QUESTION TO THINK ABOUT: In that case, what was Barney thinking about?

Into the Mainstream of Philosophy

Two main areas of philosophy are touched on in this chapter: philosophy of mind, and philosophy of language.

One of the chief questions in philosophy of mind (also sometimes called philosophy of psychology) is introduced by the arguments about whether machines and animals can think. These arguments are really of secondary concern: it's hoped that by considering these, we can get a firmer grip on what it is for people to think and how we know that we do.

One of the major traditions in this area, perhaps the most popular historically, is that thinking is something we know we do because we can notice it in ourselves. When you look into yourself, you notice thought going on, and that's all there is to it. An immediate problem faced by people who hold this view is that, it seems, one notices thought only in him/herself; one never detects thought in this way in any other people, into whose minds one never can peer directly. This view, then, makes the existence of other minds a problem. Clearly, however, we know that other people think; since all we can observe in others is their outsides, their external behaviour, it perhaps follows that when we attribute thought to them we are actually talking about their external behaviour. (This is another tradition, a more recent one.) If other people exhibit the sort of behaviour that counts as mental, then there seems to be no reason not to count certain animal and (possible) machine behaviours as mental as well. Why do you count others as having minds? Note that if you take their external behaviour as merely providing evidence for mind, not *constituting* it, then you're perhaps on shaky ground, since it's assumed that you only *directly* observe the mental in one case—your own—and it's quite a leap to reason from this single case to a whole lot of others. On the other hand, saying that a certain sort of behaviour constitutes mindedness also carries its own implausibilities. It seems to imply, for example, the absurd position that you can find out what's on your own mind only by observing your own behaviour, for example, in a mirror. What's the right answer here?

A second main question in the philosophy of mind, obviously connected with the first, is whether the mental can be understood merely in terms of the physical. If you're a *materialist* (i.e., you believe that everything in the universe is physical, operating on the basis of physical laws) then you hold a view that's common now, but very uncommon throughout history. Materialists must be willing to give a sensible account of how a merely physical object can have a mind.

A central question in the philosophy of language is introduced by Wittgenstein's question of what it takes to *mean* something by what you say. A traditional answer to this is that what someone means is what he/she is thinking while speaking. But if thoughts are private, this makes meaning a private phenomenon: we couldn't know what others mean by their talk. A more recent view, again associated with Wittgenstein, makes meaning a public matter: public conventions of language associate them with meanings. But then what, exactly, are meanings? What do these public conventions associate bits of language *with*?

You won't have any trouble finding plenty of appropriate readings in the philosophy of mind. Almost every introductory anthology has a section treating some of the main questions here. You might also look at Paul Churchland's excellent introductory book, *Matter and Consciousness* (Cambridge, Mass.: MIT Press, 1984).

Philosophy of language is a more difficult field in which to find introductory readings. Philosophy anthologies rarely include suitable readings, and the important books and articles in the area are very difficult and technical. You might, however, take a look at *The Meaning of Language* by Robert M. Martin (Cambridge, Mass.: MIT Press, 1987), to see if the author has succeeded in his intention of writing an introduction to philosophy of language intelligible to beginners.

CHAPTER XIII

WHEN AND WHERE; YOU AND I:

Indexicals and Identity

Where, When, and Who I Am

Telling Space Aliens What Day It Is

Consider what day it is right now. When is that? You can answer that question: it is June 29, 1993 (or whatever). But that date locates you relative to some date when everyone decided to start counting: according to the conventions of the calendar, it's some large number of days after that arbitrary day. The answer we are capable of giving is based on these arbitrary conventions. But when is it really?

Suppose that radio signals sent out in space will someday be picked up and understood by aliens on a distant planet. If the aliens knew when those signals were sent, they would be able to figure out how far away they are from us, because radio signals always travel at the speed of light; so one thing you'd like to include in those radio signals is information that will tell them when you sent the signals. Can you do this?

One way to do this is if we observed some really unusual event in space, for example, a supernova. Knowing how far away it is from us, we can calculate how long it took for its light to reach us, and thus how long ago it happened, and we could tell the aliens that we sent the signal to them, say, one thousand years after that supernova. Of course, they wouldn't know what a year was, but we could give them that information, for example, in terms of the duration of the supernova, or in terms of the radio frequency we are sending.

But this presupposes that they could see that supernova too. Suppose they are so distant that they can't see anything that we can. Would this make dating the signal impossible?

If you could tell them directly where we are, then they could do the reverse calculation and figure out when the message was sent. You might do this by telling them some information that would describe our earth or sun or galaxy with such precision that they could find one of these with their telescopes. But suppose, again, that they're too far away to see any of these. Then it would be, it seems, impossible to tell them where we are.

Naturally, it wouldn't do any good to include in your message to outer space: "I am *here*. The time is *now*." In a sense, they would already know the truth of those sentences, because 'here' refers to wherever the speaker is, and 'now' to whatever time it is when the speaker speaks. But the aliens would learn nothing at all from these sentences. Why is this?

> The words 'here' and 'now' are examples of what philosophers call "indexicals." 'Here' refers to a place merely by pointing at it, so it refers to whatever place the speaker happens to be located at. If the hearer is located at a different place, and doesn't independently know where the speaker is located, 'here' communicates nothing. Similarly, 'now', points at a time, and refers to whatever time the speaker happens to be speaking at. If the hearer doesn't independently know when the speaker was speaking, 'now' would communicate no information.

Note that 'you' and 'I' are also indexicals. Imagine that someone knocks at your door. You call out, "Who's there?" and the knocker replies, "It's me!" This might be helpful if you recognized the voice, but if you didn't, nothing would be communicated to you by that sentence.

SOME QUESTIONS TO THINK ABOUT: Note that 'then', 'this', and 'there' are also indexicals. Can you think of others? Could a language do without indexicals?

I'm Here Now

"I am here" and "The time is now" are peculiar sentences in that they are always true, no matter when or where spoken.

Consider other sentences that are always true, no matter what. Two of them are "Every chair is a chair" and "It's Tuesday or it's not Tuesday." Nobody has to worry that what they say is false when they say these sentences, but this big advantage is entirely wiped out by the fact that the sentences give no information. Is this a general rule: that every sentence whose truth is guaranteed, no matter what, is useless because uninformative?

From another point of view, "I am here" and "The time is now" do convey some information because, after all, the facts they refer to might not have been true. When Zelda is standing on the North Pole and says "I am here," the fact that makes her sentence true is that Zelda is standing on the North Pole. This is certainly an interesting bit of information.

When it's exactly midnight, the fact that makes "The time is now" true is that it's midnight. This might be interesting information too.

Perhaps one moral we can draw from these considerations is that the fact that makes a sentence true is not necessarily the information conveyed by that sentence, even when the hearer fully understands it.

Another moral is that we can work up a good deal of confusion when considering the meaning of words such as 'I', 'here', and 'now'.

> *Yogi Berra and Mickey Mantle were sitting in the Yankee dugout. Mickey said, "Say, Yogi, what time is it?" Yogi replied, "You mean, right now?"*

Fred Finds Himself in the Library

The Veribig Memorial Library has so many books that every fact in the history of the universe is written down somewhere in there. One day while walking through the library, Fred Schmidlap is struck on the head by a big volume falling off a high shelf, and he suffers complete amnesia. "Who am I?" he wonders. A sign posted nearby tells him that every fact is recorded somewhere in the library, so he sets out reading to try to discover who he is.

Fred spends some time reading about the history of thirteenth century Albania, about methods of refining bauxite, and about Portuguese irregular verbs. This is all interesting, but he doesn't feel he's making progress in finding out who he is.

Soon he stumbles on a huge room filled with books of biography; this, he thinks, is the place to look. Among the great number of biographies he reads, one describes all the details of the life of a man named "Fred Schmidlap." Fred reads through this one, finding out at the end that this Fred Schmidlap has spent recent post-amnesia years reading books in some library named the Veribig Memorial Library. Fred now knows all the facts about some guy named Fred Schmidlap. But what he does not know is that these are facts of his life. The strange conclusion we must draw is that, despite his now knowing *all* the facts about his life, he doesn't yet know who he is. So, it seems that who he is, is not a fact about him.

Suddenly it hits Fred: this is *his* biography. What has he just discovered? Why wasn't *this* fact something he could read in his complete biography? (The book does not, of course, say, "Fred Schmidlap: This is your life!" Even if it did, it wouldn't help Fred.)

There seems to be a special sort of knowledge about one's *self*. One can know about one's self that one's shoe is untied, or that one has brown eyes, or that one has a headache; but there's nothing special about this, because one can know this about others too. What's special and mysterious is not that you know that some person has untied shoes, but that you know that that person is *you*. What is knowing *that*?

FOR FURTHER READING: An early discussion of the library puzzle is by John Perry in "The Problem of the Essential Indexical," *Nous* 13 (March 1979), pp. 3-21.

2. The Identity of Things

Two Ways to Be the Same

The word 'identity' has two different senses. In one sense, as when we say that two new pennies are identical, we mean that they are exactly similar (at least as far as we can see). But in another sense, when philosophers say that A and B are identical they mean that A is B—that A and B are the same thing. Thus, in this sense, we say that Rutherford B. Hayes is identical with the nineteenth president of the United States. "Rutherford B. Hayes" and "the nineteenth president of the United States" are two different ways of referring to the same thing. Philosophers call the first kind of identity "qualitative" identity and the second kind "quantitative" identity.

A principle that seems obviously true is

- If A and B are (quantitatively) identical, then they have the same properties.

This is called the Principle of the Indiscernibility of Identicals. You can see that another way of putting this principle is that any two things that are quantitatively identical are totally qualitatively identical.

Note that this is to be distinguished from another principle: the Principle of the Identity of Indiscernibles. This one says:

- If A and B have all the same properties, then they are (quantitatively) identical.

In other words, if two things are completely qualitatively identical, they are the same thing—the "two" things are actually one thing. Is this principle true?

Our penny example, above, does not prove it false. Those pennies are not quantitatively identical, but neither are they utterly qualitatively identical. Even though they look just alike, a microscope could, we have no doubt, reveal small differences. And even if it didn't, it's clear u..at they have other differences in characteristics: for example, they're located in different places. Imagine two pennies that had precisely the same physical characteristics *and* were located in exactly the same place: that is to say, both of them occupied precisely the same small cylindrical area of space. Could they still be two *different* pennies—that is, quantitatively distinct? Would it make any sense to say that there were actually two pennies there? Or would this be just nonsense? (Try this experiment on your bank: bring in a roll of fifty pennies, and tell them that, through the miracle of philosophy, you have managed to cram two pennies that are completely qualitatively identical into each space of one; so they owe you one dollar for the roll. If they believe you, let me know.)

The second principle, the Identity of Indiscernibles, may be true. But the first principle, of the Indiscernibility of Identicals, seems undeniable and uncontroversial. Suppose that '*A*' and '*B*' are just two names for the same thing: then how could there be some characteristic that *A* has but *B* does not?

Well, consider this example. Think of me at age two (call that person Bobby) and me right now (call that person Robert). 'Bobby' and 'Robert' are just different names for the same person—me—right? So Bobby and Robert are quantitatively identical. But notice that Bobby is two years old and Robert isn't. Bobby is a cute little kid and Robert certainly isn't. Robert is a professor of philosophy and Bobby isn't. There are many differences between Bobby and Robert. Do you think that this shows that the Principle of the Indiscernibility of Identicals is wrong? Some philosophers have found that principle so obviously true that they would want to hold on to it no matter what. Suppose we agree that the principle is correct; what follows about Bobby and Robert?

> If that principle is correct, we would have to admit that Bobby and Robert are not qualitatively identical: that they are, strictly speaking, distinct things: Bobby and Robert are *literally* two different people. My parents, unbeknownst to them, actually had *two* sons (actually, many more than two). This sort of thinking is certainly bizarre.

In order to save the Principle of Indiscernibility of Identicals we would have to think of the universe in a drastically different way: it makes change impossible. Do you see why?

> For something to change, it has to have some characteristic at one time, and not have that characteristic at another. But the principle insists that it's impossible for *A* and *B* to be identical if *A* has a characteristic that *B* does not. So nothing changes.

It would seem, then, that if we want to hold on to this principle, we can think of something lasting through a period of time only if it changes in absolutely no way at all—not even in location. This certainly restricts the number of things that last. Except for these few unchanging things, the universe is populated by a huge number of different things, each lasting only an instant, replacing each other instantaneously. This is quite bizarre.

But worse still: the supposition that some things endure through a period of time by remaining utterly unchanged is also wrong. Even if a penny undergoes absolutely no physical change at all from one second to the next, it nevertheless changes in some respect: it becomes one second older. If the penny is one thousand seconds old now, in one second it won't be one thousand seconds old. Thus, by the principle, not even a physically unchanging penny can endure. It gets replaced by another one with a different characteristic (that is, a different age).

This principle, then, seems to imply the hugely surprising consequence that nothing endures. The reality we are aware of is not a world in which things last from one time till another; it is rather a world in which things exist only for an instant and then disappear, replaced by something else usually rather similar.

When you get a conclusion as bizarre as this, it's a good idea to try to find something that has gone wrong in your assumptions, or in your reasoning.

Try.

The Same Lump

Descartes invites us to consider a lump of beeswax. It is hard, cold, round, white; it smells like flowers and makes a sound when you hit it. Put it next to the fire and everything changes; soon it is soft, hot, and transparent, shaped like a puddle, not a sphere. The smell disappears and it makes no sound when hit. It even increases somewhat in volume. But we are sure that this puddle is *the same thing* as the earlier lump. Descartes reasons that *something* must remain the same from one time to the other; he called this something "physical substance." Note that we don't perceive physical substance; all we perceive are the changing characteristics that attach to the bit of substance—the colours, temperatures, and so on. How, then, do we know that it's there? Descartes answers: "It is my mind alone which perceives it."

This is not an answer that many people find satisfying. If you can't sense this something, how do you know when it's there? For all we know, maybe this something has also left when we put the wax next to the fire, and we now have a different thing. It must be by means of our senses that we determine that *this* is the same thing as *that*.

FOR FURTHER READING: René Descartes, *Meditations on First Philosophy*, meditation 2.

If you don't think Descartes is right, than why is this puddle the same thing as that lump? Here's one possible answer:

> The earlier lump and the later puddle are *spatio-temporally continuous*. Imagine that we place the lump next to the fire at noon, and observe what happens until 1:00. At every instant there is something there. Even if it moves somewhat, it describes a continuous path: at one instant, it is right next to where it was just before. That is to say: it is not the case that at one instant it's in one place, and at the next there's nothing there, but something at another location far away. Imagine marking a point in space at the centre of that thing at every instant. Either that centre doesn't move, in which case there will be only one point drawn at the end of the time, or else it does; but if it moves, it is a continuous motion, so you'll get a line.
>
> When we get something that follows a spatio-temporally continuous path like this, we tend to think of it as one thing that lasts, rather than as a succession of different things. Imagine that instead there was spatial discontinuity: the lump disappeared at one place, and a lump simultaneously appeared a foot away. Then we might want to say that the lump disappeared and a *different* lump appeared elsewhere. Or imagine that there was a temporal discontinuity: the lump disappeared at one place, then there was a few seconds when there was no lump there, and then a lump exactly like the one that disappeared appeared in exactly that spot. Again we might want to say that the lump disappeared, then later a *different* lump appeared in that place.

> *Don LePan interestingly speculates that the medieval mind may have thought differently about cases that we count as continuing identity. He considers the Anglo-Saxon phrase "Forst sceal freosan" [Frost shall freeze]. What can that mean? Perhaps they reasoned: Water is not frozen, so therefore water cannot freeze. What happens when the temperature falls is that one entity (frost) is created to take the place of another (water) that vanishes.*[1]

The Identity of My University

But the conditions for the continuing existence of the same thing through time do not always include spatio-temporal continuity. Consider the history of the university I work at. Several years after it was founded, it ran out of money and ceased to exist. A few years later, a generous benefactor donated a lot of money and it started up again, at

---

1   *The Cognitive Revolution in Western Culture*, vol. 1, *The Birth of Expectation* (London: Macmillan, 1989), pp. 64-65.

the same location. Was the university that started up after this time-lapse *the same university* as the one that earlier existed at that location?

> It seems clear that the answer is yes. We want to say that it was the same university starting up again, not a different one at the same place. Thus the university was temporally discontinuous.

A few years later, the university grew too large for its building downtown and moved to new, roomier quarters. What happened (we can suppose) is that one night at midnight the university instantaneously popped out of existence downtown, and simultaneously a university popped into existence uptown. Is the university located uptown the same university as the one that had existed downtown?

> Again we're tempted to say yes: it's the same university, which has merely moved to another location. Note, however, that this move involves a spatial discontinuity. When moving, the university did not follow a spatially continuous path. It did not "travel" from one point to the other. Robie Street runs between the former campus and the new campus, but there was no time at which the university was crossing Robie Street.

SOME QUESTIONS TO THINK ABOUT: If you accept these answers, you must admit that universities, at least, can be spatially and temporally discontinuous. Is this possible for other sorts of things? Suppose the chair you're sitting on disappeared, and simultaneously a chair exactly like it reappeared on the other side of the room. Could you count the object that reappeared as the same chair? Or suppose it disappeared, and then a few minutes later a chair exactly like it reappeared in exactly the same place; could this be the same chair? If you insist that these must be different chairs in both cases, then you appear not to allow spatial or temporal discontinuity in ordinary physical objects like chairs. Is there a special *sort* of things that can have spatial or temporal discontinuities? Try to think of examples other than universities that can.

The Disappearing Boat

Sally is leaving for Tibet for a ten-year stay, so she lends her boat to George, after getting him to promise to make any repairs necessary and to give it back to her when she returns.

Soon after getting the boat, George notices a rotten plank in the hull. He rips out the rotten plank, throws it into his garage, and replaces it with a new one. But a week later, he discovers that the rudder is broken. He removes it, throws it into his garage, and installs a new one. Next week the carburettor breaks; George replaces it, keeping the old carburettor. Soon something else needs replacement, and then something else. George, true to his word, has all these jobs done.

Ten years of continuous repairs on Sally's boat have passed, and shortly before Sally's return George has replaced every last bit of Sally's boat. She returns from Tibet. George proudly returns the boat in beautiful working order, but Sally is upset. "That's not my boat!" she complains. "It's all different!" George explains how he's had to replace every bit of it over the ten years. But Sally still claims that this is not her boat, because not even one atom of this boat was part of the boat she lent George. She admits that this boat is better than the one she lent George (which was disintegrating badly); but she explains that she is sentimentally attached to her old boat, and she wants *her* boat back, not this new one.

George has an idea. Every old, rotten piece he took off the boat has been thrown into his garage. He takes all those pieces out and assembles them into a boat—a rotten boat indeed—and presents it to Sally. "That's my boat!" she exclaims. "But it's a complete wreck! And you promised to keep it repaired!"

Which boat is really Sally's?

SOME QUESTIONS TO THINK ABOUT: If the old wreck is really hers, then why didn't George keep it repaired? Why did he spend all that time and money repairing a boat that was not hers? But if the new one is really hers, why isn't she pleased to have it back? And isn't it odd that the boat she lent George and this boat share not even one atom of matter? And what about that old wreck, which contains almost exactly the same material as the one Sally left? When did the boat that George kept repairing stop being Sally's? Did the pile of junk in the garage turn into Sally's boat at exactly that time?

FOR FURTHER READING: This is a version of the classical philosophical puzzle known as the Ship of Theseus, presented by Hobbes, *De Corpore* 2, 11. Hobbes got the story from Plutarch's life of Theseus. Even in Plutarch's day (c. first century A.D.) the story, as Plutarch mentions, "afforded an example to the philosophers concerning the identity of things that are changed by addition" (sections 22-23).

> *Douglas Adams reports visiting the Gold Pavilion Temple in Kyoto, Japan, and being surprised at how well it had stood up over the six centuries since it was built. He was told that it hadn't stood up well at all—in fact, it had burned down twice in this century. "So this isn't the original building?" he asked his Japanese guide. "But yes, of course it is," the guide insisted, while reporting, nevertheless, that the build-*

ing had burnt down to the ground several times, and each time it was rebuilt with completely new materials. "So how can it be the same building?" Adams asked. "It is always the same building," the guide replied.

Adams says that he found this point of view surprising but perfectly rational. The idea of the building, its intention, and its design remain the same. Only the materials change. "To be overly concerned with the original materials, which are merely sentimental souvenirs of the past, is to fail to see the living building itself."[2]

3. The Identity of Animals and People

Rover and Clover

Shocking experiments have been performed in the biological laboratory of the terrifying Dr. Frank Northrup Stein. In one experiment, Dr. Stein drastically altered the genetic structure of all the chromosomes in the body of a live dog, so that the result was nothing like a dog's genetic structure. In the process, all Rover's cells were kept alive, but were disassembled into a formless pile that Dr. Stein calls "Clover."

Dr. Stein's associate, the insidious Dr. F.M. Chu, was away on vacation while this experiment was being performed. When he returned, he asked Dr. Stein where Rover was. "That disgusting mess over there is Rover," replied Stein, pointing at the pile of cells. "I've renamed him Clover."

Having examined Clover, Dr. Chu said, "That's not Rover. Rover was a dog, but Clover isn't. Clover doesn't have the bodily organization of a dog, or its genetic structure."

"Clover is too Rover," insisted Stein. "I've just made some changes in him. When we administered growth hormone to Fido and made him grow to twice his size in a few weeks, what resulted was still Fido, though he was a lot larger. And how about Spot? After we administered potassium felinate to him for a month, he turned into something that looked exactly like a cat, but it was still old Spot. All we did was to change Fido's and Spot's characteristics; even if you wouldn't guess by looking at them, they were still Fido and Spot."

"No, you're wrong, Frank," said Chu. "When you make some kinds of changes to the material that makes something up, sometimes the original thing doesn't exist any more. Remember when you got so mad

2   Douglas Adams and Mark Carwardine, *Last Chance to See* (London: Pan, 1991), p. 141.

at Dr. Karloff that you chopped up Greta, his Mercedes? That was a drastic reorganization of the materials that made up Greta, and the pile of rusty metal that's still out there in the parking lot isn't a car. So you can't say that that pile of metal is Greta. Greta hasn't just been changed—it's been destroyed. It doesn't exist any longer. If you just drilled some holes in Greta, or painted it purple, it would still be a car. Then Greta would still exist, with changes. If you make changes to an *X* so that what's left isn't an *X* any more, the original *X* has been destroyed, not just altered."

"But, look, Chu," Stein replied, "I didn't destroy Rover. You know all that trouble we got into last year with the Animal Liberation Front after our Great Parakeet Massacre? Well, I'm being careful now. Nothing died during my Rover experiment. Clover is pretty weird, but he's alive. My techniques for altering genetic structure don't kill the animal. I can keep it alive even when it's a formless pile of cells. Rover didn't die, and Clover is alive. I've just renamed him. I can't have destroyed Rover if Rover didn't die."

But Chu wasn't convinced. "Rover doesn't exist any more, so he's been destroyed. I guess that what your experiment has really shown is that there are other ways of destroying a dog besides killing it."

Who is right?

FOR FURTHER READING: This example is adapted from Marjorie Price, "Identity through Time," *Journal of Philosophy* 74 (April 1977), pp. 201-217. Price argues that Rover is Clover. This conclusion is disputed by Baruch A. Brody in Chapter 4 of *Identity and Essence* (Princeton: Princeton University Press, 1980).

Getting Someone Else's Body

Suppose that a number of lineworkers employed by an electric company have in the course of their duties had live wires fall on them. Their protective clothing keeps them from being fatally electrocuted, but they do sometimes suffer total amnesia. To protect their workers from this disaster, the company buys a new machine: a craniorecorder. This machine consists of a little metal hat connected by wires to a huge computer. The hat gets strapped on your head, and the computer reads out and records all the patterns set up in your brain. The machine can also reprogram brains in accordance with the stored information. Each morning each worker's brain contents are recorded; if they suffer amnesia, their old memories are restored by the machine.

One day, a live wire falls on Harry and Hortense, and both of them suffer amnesia. Each is attached to the craniorecorder for memory restoration, but the technician sets the machine wrongly: Hortense's memories go into Harry's body and Harry's into Hortense's body. When the two wake up, they are deeply surprised to look in the mirror and see bodies of the opposite sex from the one they're used to. The craniorecorder technician tries to get them back into the machine to set things right, but both refuse. Harry, it turns out, has always yearned to be an expert swimmer; Hortense used to be a champion swimmer, and her body is perfectly trained for this. Similarly, Harry's body is that of a trained boxer, and Hortense has always wanted to be able to box. Besides, they both get kinky pleasure out of inhabiting the body of the opposite sex.

Are you convinced by this fable that what has taken place is a body transplant: that Harry has now been given Hortense's body? Consider that physical item that was Hortense's body before the accident. Is it now inhabited by Harry? Or should we say it's still Hortense, but it has been mistakenly programmed with Harry's memories and personality? Whoever is now in that body thinks that he/she is Harry, but is that person correct? To which body should Harry's paycheque be issued?

If you are convinced that memories make the person, and that Harry now inhabits Hortense's body, consider this amended fable: imagine that one morning Arnold, Mildred, and Francine have their brain patterns recorded, but the craniorecorder technician hates all these people, and so maliciously reprograms Mildred's *and* Francine's brain with Arnold's patterns, and reprograms Arnold's brain with Mildred's patterns. Then he erases all the recordings. On awakening, Mildred's former body and Francine's former body both claim to be Arnold. Both have equal claim to be Arnold. Should we say that they are both Arnold? But doesn't that make them the same person—namely Arnold? What happens when one body skips lunch while the other one eats: is Arnold then both hungry and not hungry? Should Arnold's two new bodies split Arnold's paycheque? Are they both married to Arnold's wife? What happened to Francine? Should the technician be charged with Francine's murder?

FOR FURTHER READING: The theory that memories make for personal identity was perhaps first stated by John Locke in chapter 27 of his *Essay Concerning Human Understanding*, 2nd. ed. (1694). Since then many philosophers have endorsed, modified, or at least discussed this view. For several views on this theory see John Perry, ed., *Personal Identity* (Berkeley: University of California Press, 1975).

> *It is said that medieval popes granted some of their bishops*
> *the gift of bilocation—the ability to be in two different places*
> *at the same time.*[3]

Keeping Your Own Body

If you are convinced that we should say that Harry is transplanted into Hortense's body, consider the following.

Suppose Harry is told, one day, that a live wire will fall on him tomorrow. He's understandably horrified; a terribly painful thing is about to happen to him. Now, suppose additional information is supplied: he will, in addition to the pain, suffer total amnesia as a result. Now his horror grows: not only pain, but amnesia! But there is more information: Hortense's memories will be implanted in the brain of his current body. Still more anguish! Harry doesn't want to get this whole pile of fake memories. He'd rather have no memories at all than get all those bogus memories. But this is not the end of the story: in addition, Harry is told, his old memories will be stuck into Hortense's body. This makes things even worse. Harry cries: "They're *my* memories! I'm really fond of many of them. I don't even like Hortense! I don't want her to get them!"

This might seem to be a reasonable attitude to have. But note that Harry is identifying his future self as the one that will occupy his body. If the interpretation we gave to the fable above is correct, Harry is wrong. Do you think he's wrong?

FOR FURTHER READING: See Bernard Williams, "The Self and the Future," for a discussion of a similar case. This article first appeared in *The Philosophical Review* 79, 2 (April 1970). It's reprinted in John Perry, ed., *Personal Identity* (Berkeley: University of California Press, 1975), pp. 179-198.

3 Mentioned in passing at the beginning of an article on something completely different, by Brendan Gill in the book review column of *The New Yorker*, 30 December, 1991, p. 92.

What it Takes to Be in Heaven

Most religions don't believe people take their bodies to heaven.

> *In Christian lore the Virgin Mary is an exception. According to the Doctrine of the Bodily Assumption of the Virgin, when she died her body was taken to heaven along with her soul. In certain paintings you can see her flying up into the air like a guided missile.*

When ordinary humans die, however, their bodies remain on Earth, turning rapidly into something unpleasant.

Without a body your existence would be rather different. It's hard to see how you could continue to ice skate, play the piano, or read the newspaper in heaven. At least in its more sophisticated versions, Christianity generally holds that our activities in heaven would be of a more rarefied form, involving such things as enjoyment of the full consciousness of God's presence. For this sort of thing, presumably, you wouldn't need a body.

The problem here is: on what grounds could it be said that *you* were in heaven? If something exists in heaven, why think that it's *you*?

We found it plausible to identify the same thing through time, in the case of Descartes's lump of wax, by means of spatio-temporal continuity. But this doesn't seem to work when somebody "goes" to heaven. Although heaven was considered to be a place, at least by early Christians and by children in Sunday school, more sophisticated Christians nowadays think differently. And even if it were a place, how could we trace the path of a non-material soul through space as it went there, to make sure that we're still dealing with the same person? But maybe persons resemble universities rather than lumps of wax: their continued existence does not require spatio-temporal continuity.

On one view, as we've seen, what makes somebody the *same person* as one identified earlier is that the later person remembers experiences the earlier one had. If this is the criterion for personal identity through time, then in order for that person to be *you* in heaven, that person must remember your experiences on earth. At least according to our current scientific views, memory is stored in the physical brain. It's difficult to see how memories can be carried to heaven when you leave your brain behind. But, of course, science doesn't know everything. This is another one of those religious mysteries about which science must be mute.

But even supposing that the memories physically encoded in your present brain could somehow be transferred into your heavenly person, there is a further difficulty: would you even have a *mind* in heaven, capable of retrieving those stored memories and of thinking about your past? Could you do any sort of mental activity in heaven? Could you even enjoy the full consciousness of God's presence? Science tells us that any sort of mental activity depends on a working brain; once again, we have a religious mystery beyond our ken.

However, not everyone shares the view that memory continuity is what constitutes the continued existence of a person. In some religious belief, the immortal soul isn't a mind, but something else: it's the thing that makes a person the same person from moment to moment and that continues after bodily death. So that will be *you* in heaven, though you will have neither mind nor body. This view is very much like Descartes's account of what explains the continuing identity of the lump of wax, and is equally hard to understand or apply.

It's dangerous to claim that you believe in something about which you have so little understanding. The danger is that your thoughts are so incoherent and mysterious that you don't really believe anything at all. In all of this, we must be very careful that we are not merely talking nonsense.

> *"I can't explain* myself, *I'm afraid, sir,"* said Alice, *"because I'm not myself, you see."*
> *"I don't see,"* said the Caterpillar.[4]

Into the Mainstream of Philosophy

Philosophers have noted that certain words in our language—'here', 'now', and 'I', for example—function peculiarly, in that they work by, as it were, pointing at something, not by naming or describing it. That's why they vary systematically in what is indicated in ways that other bits of the language do not. The name 'Fred Schmidlap' for example, refers to the same guy no matter who says it or when, but 'I' refers to a large number of people; which one it is depends on who utters the word. Problems result from this difference when we try to explain what somebody knows in terms of the sentence that expresses that person's belief. There's a definite external fact that I know about when I believe the belief that is expressed by the sentence, "Fred Schmidlap is at Sturdley's Pub." But what do I know when I know what's expressed by the sentence, "I am here now"? This problem is revealed when we consider what's communicated—if anything—by saying that sentence to some-

4   Lewis Carroll, *Alice's Adventures in Wonderland.* In *The Annotated Alice*, p. 67.

body else. Notice that what *you* know (if anything) might be quite a different matter from what you tell somebody else when you say this.

I am, unfortunately, unaware of any appropriate introductory readings you might consult to pursue these puzzling matters. The stout of heart might attempt to read Simon Blackburn's *Spreading the Word* (Oxford: Clarendon Press, 1984). He gets into these matters at the end of a book that goes quite deeply into issues in the philosophy of language.

Appropriate readings giving more puzzles, and considering several proposed solutions, concerning matters of identity are easier to come by. I strongly recommend John Perry's *A Dialogue on Personal Identity and Immortality* (Indianapolis, Hackett, 1978); this is an easy and informal discussion, in dialogue form, about many of the issues discussed in this chapter. Perry's anthology, *Personal Identity* (Berkeley: University of California Press, 1975) contains a wide selection of articles by many philosophers dealing with personal identity, at an appropriate level.

CHAPTER XIV

WHY SHOULD I BE MORAL?

1. The Student and the Match

In everyday life, we often act morally merely out of habit. Acting morally often has its costs, however, and sometimes we are tempted to act in our self-interest instead. I posed this question to some students I once had in a class: "Suppose somebody asked you for a match. It doesn't cost you very much to give it to her, but it costs you something. Should you do it?" My students replied that they thought they should. "Why?" I asked. Here are some replies. Do you agree with them?

> "Some day I might need a favour from her. If I gave her that match, she'd be more likely to help me out when I needed it. If I didn't, she'd feel less kindly toward me, and wouldn't help me out later.

"Well," I continued, "suppose you'll never run into that person again. Should you help her then?"

> "Yeah, but how can you be sure you'll never see her again? Maybe you will, right?"

They refused to let me raise the question the way I wanted to. Teaching philosophy is sometimes a difficult thing. I said, "Look, suppose you're absolutely sure, for some reason, that you'll really never see her again. Maybe you're in an airport in a distant city about to leave, and you're sure you'll never go back to that city again. That's possible, isn't it? What would you do then?"

They saw the problem. There was a widespread look of puzzlement. One replied:

> "I never exactly realized this before, but now that you put the matter that way, I can see that there's no reason to give her that match. I wouldn't do it."

Further discussion did not succeed in convincing this student to give away that match. I think I may have succeeded in turning a perfectly nice person into a nasty creep. Another triumph for philosophical education!

A QUESTION TO THINK ABOUT: Why, after all, should you be moral?

The Ring of Gyges

Plato raises the problem we have just noticed by telling another imaginary tale, known as the fable of the ring of Gyges. Glaucon, a character in Plato's *Republic*, tells the story: Gyges discovers a magic ring that turns the wearer invisible. Even the most firmly just of men, Glaucon argues, would act immorally if he possessed such a ring:

> No man would keep his hands off what was not his own when he could safely take what he liked out of the market, or go into houses and lie with any one at his pleasure, or kill or release from prison whom he would.... Then the actions of the just would be as the actions of the unjust; they would both come at last to the same point. And this we may truly affirm to be a great proof that a man is just, not willingly or because he thinks that justice is any good to him individually, but of necessity, for wherever any one thinks that he can safely be unjust, there he is unjust.

> *You might be interested to know what Gyges does with the aid of his ring. He arrives in court, makes himself invisible, seduces the queen, and with her help kills the king and takes over the kingdom. What's remarkable about this is the queen's behaviour: having been seduced by an invisible man, she conspires with him, presumably while he is still invisible, to kill her husband and to give this invisible man the kingdom.*

FOR FURTHER READING: Plato tells this story in *Republic*, Book 2: 360 (Translated by B. Jowett, in *The Dialogues of Plato*, vol. 1, [New York: Random House, 1892].) Plato argues (through his spokesman in the book, Socrates) that ultimately it's not to one's advantage to act immorally, even if one can get away with it.

When God Tells You to Do Evil

Some people think that the source of moral truth is God's will. Many philosophers (including believers) have argued that this is wrong—that to say that something is good because God desires it has things backwards. It's not good because God desires it: God desires it because it's good. So it's still an open question what makes something good.

Here's a picturesque way of putting this argument. Suppose suddenly one day angelic forms appear among the clouds, playing trumpets. The sky splits down the middle; lightning and thunder ensue. You hear a huge, deep voice. "This is God speaking," the voice says. "I have a message for you. You've been trying to be a good person, but you have it all wrong. My will is for you to murder, cheat, lie, steal, torture kittens, and throw your empty beer cans on your professor's lawn. Go and do it!"

No matter what fireworks accompanied this event, and no matter how huge and deep the voice was, you wouldn't believe that it was God. Why not? Because what the voice told you to do was so clearly wrong. It can't be God, because God wouldn't tell you to do bad things.

Why didn't you decide, instead, that you were wrong about your morality? The story appears to show that, rather than reasoning that something is good if God says it, you *first* have an idea of what's good, *then* you judge on this basis whether something represents the will of God.

2. The Prisoner's Dilemma

A Deal for the Prisoners

Suppose you and an accomplice have committed a crime. The police have evidence sufficient only to give each of you a two-year sentence, but they want to get at least one of you in jail for longer. If one of you confessed, giving evidence against the other, they could do this. So they put you in separate cells so you can't communicate, and come talk to you in your cell. They offer you this deal: if both of you keep silent, you yourself will get two years; but if you confess and your accomplice doesn't, then you'll get only one year. If you confess and he does too, then you'll get three years. If you stay silent and he talks, then you'll get four years. This is all very confusing, so you construct the following table to clarify things:

	HE CONFESSES	HE DOESN'T CONFESS
I CONFESS	I get 3 yrs in jail	I get 1 yr in jail
I DON'T CONFESS	I get 4 yrs in jail	I get 2 yrs in jail

The table shows the consequences for you, given your action and that of your accomplice.

The police also say that the same deal is being offered to your accomplice. You're only interested in minimizing your own sentence; you don't care how long your accomplice stays in jail. What should you do?

> You don't know whether your accomplice will confess or not. Suppose he does. Then you'll get three years if you confess and four if you keep silent. So if he confesses, you're better off confessing too.
> Now, suppose he doesn't confess. Then you'll get one year if you confess and two years if you keep silent. So if he doesn't confess, you'll be better off if you confess. Whatever he does, you're better off if you confess. So you confess.

Your accomplice, in his cell, was given the same deal, and he draws the same table to clarify his thinking. He reasons exactly as you do, and comes to the same conclusion. He confesses too.

So both of you get sentenced to three years in jail. But something has gone wrong here. Can you see what?

> If neither of you confessed, both of you would get a two-year sentence, and each of you would be better off.

This is a somewhat paradoxical situation: each of you has reasoned correctly about what would best serve your own self-interest. But this has resulted in a fairly poor outcome for both of you. If both of you had kept silent, both of you would have been better off. But given the situation, how could either of you have arranged this?

> You might have made a deal with your accomplice that neither of you would confess. Suppose you were not isolated in separate cells, but were together and could communicate. So you promise each other that you will cooperate by keeping silent.

But then the police take you out of your joint cell and ask you what you want to do. Notice that the table above *still* describes your situation: even if he keeps his part of the deal and stays silent, you're better off if you confess. Why keep your promise? You'd be ahead if you didn't. And when the police ask him, he realises the same thing. You're right back in the same mess.

It's often thought that this situation represents, in miniature and simplified form, a problem that is of central importance in ethics and political theory. Consider, for example, the ethical question: is it wrong to tell a lie? It seems that there are many particular circumstances in which it would be to my advantage to lie to others, whether or not they choose to tell me the truth, and in their advantage to lie to me. Nevertheless, if we all told the truth, we would all be better off in the long run, because we could come to trust each other's words: we could rely on each other in ways that would bring us the benefits of social cooperation. Thus lying is analogous to confessing in the prisoner's dilemma. If we could make a deal to pick the "cooperative" solution (by telling the truth in this case and keeping silent in the prisoner's dilemma), then we'd all be better off. But the deal would have to stick; there's always the temptation to "defect" from this cooperative arrangement, for one's own self-interest.

SOME QUESTIONS TO THINK ABOUT: In real life, what mechanisms do we use to arrive at such social "deals"? How do we get them (by and large) to stick?

Might this line of thought provide an answer to Glaucon?

The Tragedy of the Commons

Suppose that our city has a publicly owned grassy area of land in its centre. We all like having this grassy expanse in the middle of the concrete jungle. There are sidewalks built through the grassy commons, but when we're in a hurry we can get across the commons a lot faster by walking across the grass. You're just about to cut across the grass, and I stop you to try to convince you not to. Here is a transcript of our conversation.

ME: Don't do that!

YOU: Why not?

ME: We all like that grass there, and walking across it will kill it.

YOU: I like that grass as much as you do. But it takes a lot of walking across grass to kill it. If I walk across the grass right now, the resulting damage will be absolutely unnoticeable. It wouldn't even make a difference if I walked across every time I was in a hurry. Grass is stronger than that.

ME: Well, that's true. But what if everybody reasoned as you do? Then everyone would walk across the grass, and it would be dead, and we'd all be much worse off.

YOU: Look, I agree that if everybody walked across the grass, then the grass would certainly be dead. But then it would hardly matter what I did, would it? Anyway, we're just talking about *me*. I don't want *everyone* to walk across the grass, but what I do won't *make* everyone else do it.

Is there something wrong with this reasoning?

The Tragedy of the Commons is that if this line of reasoning is correct for you (as it seems to be), then it is correct for everyone else in town.

As a result everyone reasons this way, and walks across the grass; and it dies.

A QUESTION TO THINK ABOUT: Do you see why the Tragedy of the Commons has the general form of the Prisoner's Dilemma?

Coca-Cola Morality

"What if everyone did that?" This is the question that is often supposed to be the key to moral reasoning. You can see now why the question is relevant. We can all solve our prisoner's dilemmas, and prevent outcomes like the Tragedy of the Commons, by acting in a way such that we'd all be better off if everyone acted that way, and by refraining from actions that would have bad results if everyone did them.

But this sort of moral thought seems sometimes to result in some pretty foolish conclusions. Consider, for example, a trivial, perfectly ordinary, and morally innocent action like going to the corner store to buy a can of Coke on a Tuesday evening. What would happen if *everybody* descended on that corner store to buy Coke at exactly that time?

The result would certainly be disaster. Mobs of people would be trying to get into that little store. The crush would be enormous; that whole part of town would be immobilized. There would be pushing and shoving, things would get broken, and riots might break out. The store would quickly run out of Coke, and almost everyone would have to fight their way home through the mob, Cokeless.

The conclusion that your innocent action is immoral is obviously stupid. What has gone wrong with the reasoning here?

The answer we're tempted to give is that everyone is *not* going to descend on the store, so there's nothing to fear.

But what if everyone reasoned that way?

Why We Should Hire a Dictator

In his book *Leviathan*, published in 1651, Thomas Hobbes considered the problem for which the Prisoner's Dilemma provides a miniature model. He imagined a "state of nature" in which humanity might have existed prior to the development of society. In this anarchic state, each person seeks his or her own well-being; the result is constant conflict, in which we compete for benefits and attempt to dominate others: a "war, where every man is enemy to every man." In this uncooperative state, our lives are, in Hobbes's famous phrase, "solitary, poor, nasty, brutish, and short."

The solution to this problem, Hobbes argued, is a deal: a "contract" for cooperation. To ensure that nobody defects, we create the position of "sovereign"—a ruler with absolute power to enforce this contract and to punish all defectors. This dictator deprives us all of our personal liberty and restrains each person's natural tendency to seek power over others and to grab their goods. Thus we have the origin and the justification of the sovereign state.

This removes the Prisoner's Dilemma by changing the results of the participants' choices. Consider the Tragedy of the Commons: when you walk across the grass, you get punished by the police. This makes walking across the grass—the "defection" option—much less attractive than the "cooperative" one, no matter what other people do.

Hobbes argued that the only sort of state in which the war of each against all can be prevented, and in which it will be in our self-interest to pick the cooperative solution, is one ruled by a despotic tyrant with complete power. The problems with this arrangement are, of course, that our own freedoms are drastically reduced, and that we might be unable to prevent the sovereign from acting in ways not conducive to everyone's welfare—for example, if the sovereign decides to use that absolute power for his/her *own* benefit. The modern liberal state is designed to be responsive to the will of the governed and to guarantee individual rights. The question is, however, whether the arrangements in the liberal state will work to solve our Prisoner's Dilemma. In a modern liberal state, people can take advantage of this limitation on governmental sovereignty, by using their individual freedom and their power over the sovereign to defect from the contract.

FOR FURTHER READING: Thomas Hobbes, *Leviathan*, Chapter 13.

3. The Paradox of Deterrence

Bombing the Russians

Here is a situation that's related to the Prisoner's Dilemma. It's known as the Paradox of Deterrence.

Suppose you're the president of the United States; it's 1960, and the Cold War is in full swing. The Soviet Union has developed the atomic bomb, and they are expansionist and belligerent. You are afraid that they might make a "first strike," attacking the U.S. with their atomic bombs. In order to prevent this, you threaten them with massive nuclear retaliation. (This is familiar Cold War reasoning.)

During the Cold War, there was widespread feeling that this policy was immoral. But can you see how it could be argued that this policy is morally justified?

> You don't *want* to bomb the Soviet Union. But you think that unless you threaten them with retaliation, there's a good chance they'll bomb you; and let's suppose you're right. You suppose that this threat probably will prevent anyone from bombing anyone; and after all, that's what we want.

This reasoning, of course, is a matter of some debate, but notice that it may have been correct during the Cold War. During those years, neither side bombed the other. It's highly unusual in history to have two powerful enemies who manage not to go to war over such a long period.

Now, imagine that for some bizarre reason, the Soviets have just bombed Pittsburgh. Should you order the massive nuclear retaliation you threatened them with, and destroy Leningrad in retaliation?

> Bombing Leningrad is wrong. You would bring about nothing but needless destruction, suffering, and death if you destroyed Leningrad. The Soviets (you have reason to think) just wanted to destroy Pittsburgh, and won't be tempted to bomb more of your cities, so you won't prevent future harm to the U.S. by retaliating. Your choices are, then, either suffer the destruction of Pittsburgh without retaliation, or cause a large amount of useless destruction, in addition, to Leningrad. Clearly it would be immoral to do the second thing.

Nevertheless, it *was* moral to threaten such massive retaliation, since only by that threat did you stand a good chance of preventing the Soviet attack. It was the best bet, but it failed.

There is a paradox here. Massive retaliation is wrong, and you know it. To intend to retaliate is thus evil. But *having* that evil intention was good, since it stood a very good chance of preventing anyone from bombing anyone. The paradox is that having the intention to do something evil is a good thing.

And there is a further paradox. Now that they have bombed Pittsburgh, the threat has failed. It would be immoral to carry your threat through, and you don't. But the Soviets knew in advance that you were a good guy—that you were threatening retaliation only to prevent them from bombing. They knew that after they bombed Pittsburgh you would go through the reasoning above, and you wouldn't retaliate. No wonder your threat of retaliation didn't work. They knew you wouldn't do it.

How could you have made a threat that would work—one they would take seriously?

> One way you could have done it is by constructing a "doomsday machine" (somewhat like the one in the movie "Dr. Strangelove.") This machine detects nuclear explosions anywhere in the United States and reacts by automatically launching a devastating attack on the Soviet Union. The beauty of this machine is that, once installed, it can't be turned off by anyone, no matter what. Now, once this machine is turned

on, you telephone Khrushchev and tell him what you've done. *That's* deterrence. He would know then that if he attacked, there would be automatic retaliation. He'd realise that if he bombed Pittsburgh, you'd see that the threat had failed. You'd wish at that point that you were able to turn the machine off; but you couldn't.

The interesting thing about the story now is that it seems that the only way you can make a really effective deterring threat is to set things up so that later on you'll be unable to prevent carrying out the threat, despite the fact that you'll know that carrying it out will be immoral.

FOR FURTHER READING: Several paradoxes of deterrence are discussed by Gregory S. Kavka in "Some Paradoxes of Deterrence," *The Journal of Philosophy* 75, 6 (June 1978).

When It's Sane to be Crazy

If you don't have a doomsday machine, it seems that it's to your advantage to make the Soviets think that you're immoral. If they think you're moral, then they won't expect you will retaliate uselessly, so your threat won't work.

Suppose that you did your best to convince them that you really were crazy enough to retaliate uselessly. If you acted in sensible, morally justifiable ways in general, they'd realize you were only pretending.

The best thing to do is really to make yourself unreasonable and immoral. That sort of person, after all, often has the bargaining advantage when dealing with sensible, moral people. Eating a lot of LSD might transform you into the kind of person best able to act in your best interest. (Of course then, having gone crazy, you might not want what's in your best interest.)

> *Joseph Heller, the author of* Catch-22, *studied philosophy when in university, and it shows. The book's hero, Yossarian, a U.S. flier during World War II, wants out of the war. He acts bizarrely, contrary to the rules for military behaviour, and people keep accusing him of being crazy. He pleads with the army psychiatrist to discharge him from the army on grounds of insanity. The psychiatrist agrees that crazy people get sent home, but he won't send Yossarian home because Yossarian wants to go home; this eminently sane desire shows he's not crazy at all. The only people who can get sent home on grounds of insanity are people who want to stay in the war.*
>
> *Yossarian has refused to fly any more missions. Clevinger had stared at him with apoplectic rage and indignation*

and, clawing at the table with both hands, had shouted,
"You're crazy!"...
  "They're trying to kill me," Yossarian told him calmly.
  "No one's trying to kill you," Clevinger cried.
  "Then why are they shooting at me?" Yossarian asked.
  "They're shooting at everyone," Clevinger answered.
"They're trying to kill everyone."
  "And what difference does that make?"[1]

At the end of the book, Yossarian decides he's had enough
and announces that he's going to desert to Sweden.
  Major Danby replied indulgently with a superior smile,
"But Yossarian, suppose everyone felt that way."
  "Then I'd certainly be a damned fool to feel any other
way, wouldn't I?"[2]

3. More Dilemmas

The Chicken's Dilemma

The game called "chicken," the classical version of which was played
by 1950s male teenagers with hormone problems, is something like a
Prisoner's Dilemma.

Here's how you play chicken. On a deserted country road, you and
another driver race your cars toward each other. If neither swerves off
to the side, there is a head-on collision, and both you and the other
driver die. If you swerve and the other guy doesn't, however, this shows
that you're chicken, and (because machismo is very important to you)
you suffer a devastating humiliation. If the other guy swerves too, that's
not so bad: both of you survive, and neither is humiliated by the macho
of the other. No big deal. What you really want to happen, however, is
that you keep going while the other guy swerves.

This is the table listing the possible "payoffs" for you, given your
actions listed down the left, and given the actions of the other player
listed across the top:

	HE KEEPS GOING	HE SWERVES
I KEEP GOING	I die (4)	I win—big macho status (1)
I SWERVE	I lose—bad humiliation (3)	No big deal (2)

1 *Catch-22* (New York: Dell, 1961), p. 17.
2 Ibid., p. 455.

The numbers in parentheses give the value of that payoff to you, with 1 indicating your number-one preference, and so on down.

Note that the order of value of the outcomes is not exactly the same as it was in the Prisoner's Dilemma case discussed above. If you felt that death was better than dishonour, and gave the lower-left outcome a value of 4, and the upper-left outcome a value of 3, then it would be a Prisoner's Dilemma.

What is the best chicken strategy for you?

> It's not clear. You can swerve, hoping that the other guy will too. If you play chicken often, however, and get the reputation of a swerver, your opponents will always keep going.

But this suggests a better strategy for playing chicken: convince the other guy you're crazy and will keep going no matter what. If he's got any sense, then *he* will swerve. But how to convince the guy that you're that insane? After all, if he's smart he'll realise that giving the appearance of insanity is a good strategy for chicken players, so it's likely that you're not crazy at all—you're just smart.

It's even better if you really are crazy. Then you'll show your insanity in all sorts of ways, and he'll definitely be convinced. The advantages of insanity are the same here as in the case discussed above of relations with the Russians.

You might think that chicken is a game of deception, and that you'd be at a big disadvantage if your opponent could read your mind and know in advance exactly what you were going to do. But strangely, this is not the case. Can you see why?

> A mind-reading player would be at a big *disadvantage*—he'd lose every time, if you figured out the right strategy. If your opponent is a mind-reader, you should decide in advance that you'll keep going every time. Your opponent will read your mind. Because he's not suicidal, he'll swerve every time. You're a macho hero, and he's a humiliated chicken.

FOR FURTHER READING: This and other game-theoretical aspects of chicken are discussed by William Poundstone in *Labyrinths of Reason* (New York: Doubleday, 1988), pp. 240-41.

Beating the Computer

The following story is known as Newcomb's problem. It involves playing a game against an opponent who can predict what you do.

Suppose you are faced with the following choice. Box A contains either a cheque for one million dollars or nothing (you don't know which). Box B contains a check for one thousand dollars. You can take the contents of box A alone, or the contents of both boxes. A very smart computer has been fed information about you; if it predicted you'll take both boxes, it has already put nothing in box A; but if it predicted you'll take only A, it has already put one million dollars in there. The computer has almost always been right in predicting other people in the past.

Here is a table summarizing the situation:

	COMPUTER PREDICTS YOU'LL TAKE ONLY A & PUTS $1 MILLION IN A	COMPUTER PREDICTS YOU'LL TAKE BOTH BOXES & PUTS $0 IN A
YOU JUST TAKE A	You get $1,000,000	You get $0
YOU TAKE BOTH BOXES	You get $1,001,000	You get $1,000

What should you do? You will probably come up with one of these two conflicting answers:

(1) The computer has *already* put either one million dollars or zero dollars in A. What's in there won't change depending on your choice. If you take just A, you'll get whatever's in there; if you take both, you'll get that plus the thousand in B. Take both boxes.

(2) The computer has almost certainly predicted you correctly; so if you pick both boxes, it probably has put nothing in A, and you'll get only one thousand dollars. If you pick only A, again the computer has almost certainly predicted this, so you'll probably get one million dollars. Pick only A.

Is (1) or (2) the better strategy?

The odd thing about this problem is that people seem to divide into dogmatic one-boxers and militant two-boxers. There's really no consensus about who is right. Each faction has a perfectly good argument, which it keeps repeating louder and louder to the other side, to no avail.

A QUESTION TO THINK ABOUT: Which strategy do you think is right? Try to construct an argument to convince the opposition of your view.

FOR FURTHER READING: The first appearance of this problem (also known as Newcomb's Paradox) in print seems to have been in Robert Nozick, "Newcomb's Problem and Two Principles of Choice," in Nicholas Rescher, ed., *Essays in Honor of Carl G. Hempel* (Dordrecht: Reidel, 1969). (Nozick says that it was invented, but not published, by Dr. William Newcomb of the Livermore Radiation Laboratories in California.) Newcomb's problem is discussed in many places, including Richard C. Jeffrey's *The Logic of Decision*, 2nd ed. (Chicago: University of Chicago Press, 1983).

Into the Mainstream of Philosophy

The question, "Why should I be moral?" is one that has interested philosophers since philosophy began. It's one that deserves some thought, and that you can think about, and perhaps come up with some answers to, even if you have studied little philosophy.

David Hume, the eighteenth-century Scottish philosopher, discussed this problem in ways you might consider. He argued that morality is an unusual phenomenon. We all believe some moral "truths," but we are at a loss about how to prove what we believe. It seems to be impossible to justify these beliefs by means of pointing out facts about the world: no matter how many facts we adduce, the moral principles don't seem to follow. This position can be summed up by the slogan: "You can't derive an *ought* from an *is*." Do you think that Hume is right? As a way of considering this, you might begin with some moral principle you think is correct, for example, that torturing innocent children is wrong. Now imagine trying to convince someone who didn't believe it of the truth of this principle. You have at your disposal all the facts about the world you could want. Imagine the debate you might have with this moral sceptic. She's willing to grant the truth of any factual matter you like, and she's rational enough to accept the truth of any logical consequences of these facts. Could you convince her of the moral principle? (There really are people like this, with what's called psychopathic or sociopathic personalities. They may be intelligent and well informed, but they just can't be convinced that something is wrong.)

Hume argued that facts alone don't imply morals. He thought that in addition one has to have certain feelings—importantly, certain sympathies with others. Given this sympathy, people can be reasoned with morally, but without it, we're at a loss. Hume hoped that these feelings of sympathy were widespread. But what if someone just doesn't have them?

Much of this chapter concerns the sort of reasoning embodied in the Prisoner's Dilemma and in the Tragedy of the Commons. This sort of story has become important in much contemporary thought attempting to provide an answer to the question, "Why should I be moral?" Philosophers argue that considerations of this sort would lead someone who started without any Humean sympathy for others, but merely with selfish desires, to recognize the truth of some moral principles. The idea is that someone who is merely selfish could be led to see that in the long run his/her own interests would best be served by making a deal with others in such a way that his/her own interests are, to some extent, also served. The rules of morality, according to this view, represent these deals with others: by agreeing to them, we each serve our own initial selfish interests the best.

Often this sort of line of reasoning is best pursued by imagining a bunch of people in a Hobbesian "state of nature"; rational and selfish interests alone will eventually result in their adopting some sort of rules of morality. Try to imagine a story in which such a state of nature would result in a society governed by morality. Do you think this would actually happen?

Readings in which philosophers attempt to answer the question, "Why should I be moral?" are not hard to find. Most introductory philosophy anthologies will provide at least something along these lines. Another suitable place to start is Plato's *Republic*. The tradition that sees morality as the rational answer to the Prisoner's Dilemma is, however, on the whole too recent to be found among classical readings.

CHAPTER XV

RIGHT AND WRONG

1. Justice and Distribution

Why You Should Give Away Your Shoes

Wouldn't it be a better world if it weren't the case that some people lived in comparative luxury while others suffered as a consequence? Wouldn't you think that someone was morally lacking if that person knew of a way to right this inequality, yet didn't?

Here's a small way you can make the world a better place. You (I suppose) own several pairs of shoes. There are many people in the world right now who own no pairs of shoes, and suffer as a result. So you should give your shoes to them.

It doesn't follow that you should give away *all* your shoes. If you gave them all away, then your positions would be reversed—you would be the one who was suffering. How many pairs should you give away?

Suppose you own five pairs of shoes; number them arbitrarily 1 through 5. Now consider pair number 5. How much benefit does this pair give to you? Not very much. Certainly that pair would do a whole lot more good to someone who has no shoes at all. If you gave that person pair number 5, your well-being would be reduced by a little bit, while the well-being of the recipient would be increased by a whole lot. Giving that pair away would increase the sum of well-being in the world. You would lose a little, and the other person would gain a lot.

Okay, you should give away pair number 5. Now you are left with four pairs. How about pair number 4? Giving away that pair would diminish your well-being, perhaps by a greater amount than giving away pair number 5. Nevertheless, the well-being of another shoeless person would be increased by much more than your well-being would be decreased. You should give away pair number 4 too.

Of course, the same line of reasoning applies to pairs number 3 and 2. But giving away your last pair wouldn't increase the sum of well-being in the world, because the increase resulting from a shoeless person's getting them would be balanced by your becoming shoeless. In fact, if that person is somewhat used to going around shoeless and you aren't, perhaps you would suffer more than that person by being shoeless. So (you'll be happy to hear) it's not morally required that you give away your last pair of shoes.

What we have here is an example of what economists call the "marginal decrease of utility." This is a fancy way of saying that something would be worth a whole lot less to someone who has a lot of them than to someone who has few or none. Thus your fifth pair of shoes would be worth a lot more to a shoeless person than to you. One's first pair of shoes always is much more valuable than one's second, which is in turn more valuable than the third, and so on.

So you should give away all your shoes except one pair. Now consider the other things you own more than one of. You should also give away all of them except one to people who have none. In fact, if anyone in the world has less than you do of any good thing, you should give them some of your possessions until the two of you own equal quantities.

Almost nobody follows this moral advice. Some people give something to those who have less, for example, by giving to charities, but remember what our reasoning tells us to do: give your goods away until there is *nobody in the world* who is worse off than you are. Do you know of anybody who does this? Perhaps even Mother Theresa doesn't go this far.

Do you now feel like you're evil for not obeying this moral requirement? Well, you have company in your evil ways. By this criterion almost everyone in the world is, to some extent or other, evil.

Perhaps by now you've had the thought: something has gone wrong with this moral reasoning. Perhaps this is so. Reasoning that comes to the conclusion that almost everyone in the world is evil certainly merits a second (and third) look, in the next two items.

Your Shoes as Your Property

"But those shoes are *mine*—I own them," you might want to argue. "They're my property. I have the right to hang on to my own property."

Philosophers have frequently held that the right to own property is a central, fundamental human right. The idea is basic to the social philosophy of John Locke, for example, who held that the rights to life, liberty, and *property* followed from our very nature—that it's God's will, and is "writ in the hearts of all mankind." He wrote in his *Essays on the Law of Nature* that it is a self-evident truth that all people are endowed by their creator with these inalienable rights.

*Locke's idea was clearly a strong influence on Thomas Jef-
ferson when he wrote the U.S. Declaration of Independence.
Jefferson, however, changed the list of inalienable rights to
life, liberty, and the pursuit of happiness. Why did Jefferson
make this change? The right to property has certainly been
central to the U.S. political philosophy, from the founding
fathers on.*

Even Locke, however, didn't think that the right to property entitled
you to own whatever you could get. He thought that you have to earn
what you get by your labour (so stealing something doesn't give you
property rights over it.) He also thought that you don't have property
rights over things you earn in cases when this appropriation wouldn't
leave enough, and as good, for others.

SOME QUESTIONS TO THINK ABOUT: How did you get those shoes?
Were they paid for by your parents? In that case, you didn't earn them.
Does that show that you don't have the right to own them?

But suppose you earned the money to pay for them. By refusing to
allow shoeless people to use them, are you depriving them of
"enough"? By refusing to share them with people who have only terrible shoes, are you depriving them of "as good"?

Do you think that these considerations show that there's something
wrong with Locke's views on the right to property?

Other philosophers have not found the right to property writ in their
hearts. The nineteenth-century French thinker Proudhon, for example,
wrote a book called *What is Property?* and answered his question by
saying that property is theft. *Do* we have the right to property under any
conditions? Is it fair that one person have more of the goods of life than
another?

Your Shoes and Your "Families"

"I agree that I would be immoral if I owned six pairs of shoes, and my
brother or my children or my parents owned none, and I didn't give them
something. Maybe I even have some obligation to do something for
people far away, for example, in the poverty-stricken areas of Africa; but
I only have a very limited obligation to them. I don't have to give until
they're no worse off than I am. The reason is that they're not *my* family,
or *my* group."

It may seem reasonable to think that your obligations to help others
decrease as their "distance" from you increases. This would certainly
explain a good deal about how people actually feel. Most people are
willing to sacrifice a great deal for their immediate family. Many people would do something for their neighbours in need. Some people

sometimes respond to the need of others of their own nationality: for example, those of Greek descent in North America tend to be the ones who respond most strongly with aid when there's an earthquake in Greece.

But is the idea that one's obligations to others decreases as their "distance" increases correct? Why is failure to respond to your own child's need worse than failure to respond to the need of some child half-way around the world? Does your child deserve help more than that other child?

> This idea seems, from a certain point of view, to be morally objectionable. Looking out for your own family, or ethnic group, or race, at the expense of others is a normal and universal phenomenon, perhaps an inevitable one. But it does seem a bit selfish or racist; maybe it's the sort of thing we should try to avoid.

SOME QUESTIONS TO THINK ABOUT: To think morally and act fairly, shouldn't we take a disinterested view, trying to ignore our own particular position? Shouldn't we try to think of every human—not just those nearer to us—as having an equal claim on what's of value?

2. Rights and Wrongs

Rights vs. Utility

The idea that the basic principle of ethics is that one ought to do what maximizes the total of well-being or happiness in the world has a certain plausibility. It is the core of the moral theory called *utilitarianism*. Jeremy Bentham, a central figure among utilitarians, gave that theory its slogan when he wrote what he took to be a "sacred truth": that "the greatest happiness of the greatest number is the foundation of morals and legislation." But, as we have seen, this principle leads to some peculiar results. It seems to advocate that you give away almost all your shoes. (Another case in which this sort of thinking leads to bizarre results will be encountered in Chapter XVI, in "Ten-To-One Dilemmas.")

Some philosophers have thought that these and many other examples of the peculiar consequences of utilitarianism show that the theory is wrong. They argue that in addition to (perhaps even instead of) thinking about what promotes happiness, we ought to think about inviolable *rights*. As we've seen, a right to property might justify our keeping our shoes, at the expense of an increase in total happiness.

Bentham, of course, didn't think very highly of the notion of rights (he called them "nonsense upon stilts"), and other philosophers have had trouble figuring out what rights might be. Are there any such things? If you have a right to something, that seems to mean that that thing can't be taken away from you, no matter what consequences there are to the general welfare. It's pretty hard to think of anything we'd be willing to grant a right to, on this strict definition. We're all willing to grant that under some circumstances considerations of the general welfare justify taking away someone's property, when that's necessary for the general good. People's land and houses are expropriated (with compensation, of course) in order to build a national park, or a highway, or a dam that would benefit a large number of people. We don't even have an absolute unalienable right to life: under certain extreme circumstances—when disaster would otherwise result—police are allowed to kill people.

SOME QUESTIONS TO THINK ABOUT: Where do rights come from? How can we find out what rights people have? Locke argued that reason alone can reveal what basic rights everyone has, but it's not at all clear that this is so. A few years ago, the Canadian Rugby Team was prohibited by the government from playing a match against the South African team, as part of the general sanctions against the apartheid policies of that country. I heard a member of that team on the radio complaining that this ban was unjust because it violated their "right to play." I had never heard of *that* right before. Is there such a thing? How can we find out? Does Lockean pure reason tell you whether this right exists?

FOR FURTHER READING: Bentham's thoughts are found in *The Works of Jeremy Bentham*, vol. 10 (New York: Russell & Russell, 1962), p. 142.

Opening Pandora's Box

Pandora, according to ancient Greek mythology, was a woman created by Zeus, the most beautiful woman ever created, but also foolish. She opened a jar (or box) in which all the Spites that plague humanity had been imprisoned: Old Age, Labour, Sickness, Insanity, Vice, and Passion. The Spites flew out in a cloud, stung Pandora all over her body, and then proceeded to attack the rest of the human race. However, hope, a Spite who had also been imprisoned in the jar, discouraged afflicted humanity from mass suicide.

"Pandora" has been taken (perhaps ironically) as the title of a Halifax, Nova Scotia, feminist newspaper around which a controversy concerning rights has been raging. A man wrote to this newspaper to argue with an article they had previously published. The newspaper refused to publish his letter on the grounds that their policy is to publish only contributions by women. The man complained to the Nova Scotia Human Rights Commission, claiming sexual discrimination against him.

Pandora's lawyer argued that the newspaper is justified in its "women only" policy because it offers a place for women to air their views unafraid of being slammed by men. This is necessary given the male dominance of public debate throughout history. The opposition in this case agrees that the systematic exclusion of women in the past was a bad thing; it argues, however, that this was bad because everyone has the right to free public speech. Denial of this right to women in the past was wrong, but so is its denial to men in the current instance.

The case for *Pandora* illustrates what some feminists think is wrong with morality based on rights. Granting everyone the right to something means nothing when one group is oppressed by another with the result that the oppressed group is unable to take advantage of the benefits conferred by that right. Thus the principles of fairness that are behind rights-based ethics, and that underlie Lockean liberal social theory, aren't the ones that should be used to determine public policy. Fairness allows for continuing oppression of groups like women. It is unfair, they agree, that a women's newspaper should be allowed to practice sexual discrimination, while a general or man's newspaper should not. But given the current structure of society, they argue, fairness is a bad thing.

Similar arguments are showing up frequently in public debate. You can find the same sorts of consideration, for example, being raised in debates about preferential hiring and about the right to read pornographic literature.

But the philosophical feminists who argue against a morality based on rights do not advocate thinking in terms of maximizing the sum-total of good as an alternative. They might agree that sexual discrimination by *Pandora* (or denial of fair treatment in certain cases of hiring, or denial of the right to read what you want) might not lead to the greatest total satisfaction in society. They argue that neither rights-morality nor morality based on happiness-maximization is able to cope with the kind of systematic oppression they find in today's society and they seek a third kind of theory for moral thought.

The Nova Scotia Human Rights Commission has ruled that *Pandora* may refuse to print what's written by a man on the grounds that it was written by a man. But they probably wouldn't allow a men's magazine to discriminate against women. The difference is that women are a "designated group" who have been discriminated against in the past. This is why they're allowed to practice discrimination now.

SOME QUESTIONS TO THINK ABOUT: Do you think that the Human Rights Commission's decision was the right one? Note that it seems to indicate that women have the right not to be discriminated against, but men don't. Is this fair? Perhaps you think it is. If not, do you think that it's unfair but (under the circumstances) a good thing?

3. Getting What You Want

Past and Future Desires

What you basically want is to have a life in which, all told, you get what you want, right? Well, that's not so clear.

Suppose you are now eighty years old, and your doctor guesses that given your present state of health, you'll probably live for five or ten years more. Suppose further that for the past thirty years, you have had a very strong desire that there be a statue of Elvis in your back yard. You've never had the money to buy the statue, so your desire has been frustrated. Yesterday you won the lottery. For the first time you can afford the Elvis statue, but you discover that your interest in Elvis has completely disappeared, and you now think that having an Elvis statue would be foolish. Should you get the statue anyway?

If you put up that Elvis statue, you satisfy a strong desire that you had for thirty years. Of course, *now* you don't want that statue, so putting it up will go against your present (and, we can assume, future) desires. But this would mean only five or ten years or so of dissatisfied desire. Assuming that the kind of life you want is one in which, all told, your desire fulfilment is maximized you should put up that ugly statue.

The fact that this reasoning is foolish shows that there's something wrong with the principle that what we really want is a life in which desire satisfaction is maximized. We care about our present desires; our past desires are irrelevant.

But are our present desires the only thing that's relevant? How about our future desires?

Consider the following case. You're now twenty years old, and expect to live to a ripe old age. Your parents urge you to take a business degree, arguing reasonably that this is the best way to assure you a good income in the future. But you are young and idealistic, and you don't care about income: you want to join a group of ecology terrorists instead. Your parents argue that you feel that way only because you're young. They predict that in a few years, you'll change your mind; your aversion to business, indifference to money, and ecology fanaticism will all fade away, and you'll wish that you had taken that business degree. You sadly agree with them in their prediction of your future desires: you know that that's what happens to almost everyone.

Now, if it's rational to count future desires as well as present ones in what you do, the right thing to do is to enroll in that business course. Even though you don't now want to do it, you know that it will maximize your desire fulfillment, counting both your present and future desires. All told, your life will contain a far greater quantity of fulfilled desires if you take that degree. Is this the rational way to think? Don't be too quick in answering Yes. Remember that saving whales, not making money, is what you're now really interested in. Why should you balance these interests with what your future self will be interested in?

The Genie's Cousin

Sometimes, of course, getting what you want is difficult or impossible. Here's a solution to this problem: start wanting only those things you can easily get.

Suppose, for example, that Marvin is a connoisseur of fine wines. He's not very rich, however, and he's often dissatisfied at not being able to buy the vintages he craves. He devotes much of his salary to buying fine wines, and sacrifices other things he wants. The wines he buys aren't as good as the ones he wants, and he can't get enough of the very good ones. How can Marvin solve his problem? It would be solved, of course, if he could get enough money to buy as much of the finest wine as he wants, but this seems impossible. Here's a solution that does seem possible; what do you think of it?

> He should kill his desire for expensive wine—change his desires and tastes so that he enjoys low-cost, inferior wine.

But is this sort of alteration of desires and tastes really possible?

> Yes, it is. It does take time and effort to alter your tastes and desires, but it can be done. You can get yourself to like all sorts of things. One way to do it is by practice: if Marvin started drinking only Chateau Plonque, that miserable but cheap rotgut, in pleasurable surroundings, telling himself how delicious it was, after a long while he very well might get to like it—even to prefer it to the expensive stuff.

This sort of solution is widely applicable to the problem of not getting what you want. Matilda is in love with Matthew, but Matthew won't give her the time of day. Max is attracted to Matilda, but Matilda doesn't care for him. She only has eyes for Matthew. She has a problem, but she can solve it by ignoring Matthew and marrying Max. This will hurt for a while, but given practice and self-discipline, she can get herself, sooner or later, to love Max and to be indifferent to Matthew. It can be done. There are techniques by which one can alter one's own desires.

There are even better known and more effective techniques for altering people's desires. The advertising industry is wholly devoted to the alteration of desires. Perhaps this gives us a method whereby a government can give its citizens what they want. Giving them what they *already* want is often difficult or impossible, but changing their desires, so that they want what can be given them, is possible. It's clear that governments often apply this strategy. Your own government probably spends a lot of money on advertising for this purpose.

SOME QUESTIONS TO THINK ABOUT: There is something wrong in this line of reasoning, isn't there? What is it?

Let's put the problem in more picturesque terms. I know the genie who lives in a lamp and will grant three wishes—change three things to make them the way you want them to be. I know you'd like to meet this genie; unfortunately I've lost his address. But I can get you in touch with his cousin Fred, who is also a genie who can make the world match your desires. Fred does this not by changing the world, but by changing your desires. If something isn't the way you want it to be, Fred will change what you want. Are you eager to avail yourself of Fred's services? Why not?

Electronic Pleasure

A while back some psychologists claimed to have discovered the "pleasure centre" in rats' brains.[1] A tiny electric wire was inserted in this area of a rat's brain. The rat was given a little lever in its cage; when the rat pressed the lever, a mild current was sent through the wire, stimulating that part of its brain. The interesting thing was that the rat seemed to *love* this brain stimulation. Having discovered the effect, it soon was pressing the lever at a tremendous rate. It did not stop even to eat from the food bin right next to the lever. It would die of hunger rather than stop stimulating that area of its brain. We might think this stimulation was so pleasurable that the rat preferred it to anything.

Now, these psychologists claim that humans have a similar area of their brains, and they speculate that with the aid of a little wire painlessly inserted into that area of your brain, you might be able to give

1 James Olds, "Pleasure Centers in the Brain," *Scientific American* 195, 4 (October 1956) pp. 105-116.

yourself that overwhelmingly desirable pleasure. It's hard to imagine what that would feel like, but you might find it so wonderful that you would prefer it to anything else. Do you want yourself hooked up?

> Maybe you're afraid that you would get stuck to the push-button sending stimulation to your brain, like the rat, and be unable to eat. You would die after a short (but immensely pleasurable) life.

If this prospect doesn't appeal, then suppose we make getting wired a little more attractive by guaranteeing that you will be kept fed and otherwise taken care of. Now do you want to get hooked up?

Consider the consequences: you might like that stimulation so much that you might lose your job, give up your studies, never see friends, family, and loved ones ever again—you might, in short, abandon everything that now means something to you. But remember: this sensation is so fantastically wonderful that it makes absolutely all of this loss worthwhile. What do you say?

A QUESTION TO THINK ABOUT: Maybe you think that there's more to life than getting what you really want. What? Why?

4. Relationships With Other People

I'm Gonna Buy a Plastic Doll That I Can Call My Own

The following story assumes that the reader is a man, and manifests other sexist attitudes as well. It's worth considering anyway; part of the question it raises is exactly why you might find it offensive.

The Acme Robot Company, let us imagine, has perfected its mechanical female robots to the point that you can order one to fit your own specifications, and a carton will arrive from the factory containing Shirley, the girlfriend of your dreams (batteries not included). All of Shirley's characteristics will be perfect, as far as you are concerned: she will be mentally and physically exactly the woman you've always wanted.

Many men are not attracted by the idea of buying Shirley, though they would be very interested in meeting a real woman with her specifications. To justify this attitude toward Shirley, we need to find relevant differences between her and real women. What are these?

> It's hard to explain why Shirley's differences are relevant. She is made out of plastic and electronic components, not flesh and blood; but so what? Her plastic covering feels just like the skin you love to touch, so how can the fact that it's plastic make any difference? As far as *your contact* with her is concerned, she's indistinguishable from a real woman covered with real skin. Inside her is a computer, not a liver, pan-

creas, etc.; but again, why does this make any difference? You can't feel these insides, and they make absolutely no difference to any of your actual encounters with her.

Don't think of Shirley acting stiffly and mechanically like those robots in bad science fiction movies. She's much better made. She acts smoothly and naturally and is capable of showing the full range of emotions. Remember, she is indistinguishable from ordinary humans.

"Aha!" you say. "She *shows* the full range of emotions, but she doesn't *feel* them. After all, she's a machine. I want a girlfriend who really feels things, not one who merely acts like she does."

Well, what makes you think she doesn't really feel them? Does the fact that she is manufactured out of plastic and transistors show that it's impossible for her to feel things? (We ran into this question in Chapter XII.)

"But," you continue, "another difference between Shirley and real humans is her past. Real humans were born of woman, and had infancies and childhoods. Shirley can speak convincingly of her mother and her childhood, but this is all fake, programmed into her by the folks at Acme because they thought I might enjoy discussing her childhood with her. She was actually 'born' only six months ago in the factory."

But why does this make a difference? Again, she is now indistinguishable, for all practical purposes, from a real woman. If you didn't know her real construction and provenance, you would be completely fooled into thinking she's real, because she's such a good imitation.

"But I know that she's an imitation," you object, "so I wouldn't be able to have a good relationship with her."

But isn't this an unfortunate prejudice on your part—one you'd be much better off without?

"I just don't like imitations," you insist. "I always buy genuine leather shoes rather than those imitation-leather plastic ones."

Why do you insist on genuine leather? Because leather feels better, lasts longer, and so on? But suppose they developed an imitation leather that felt *exactly* like real leather, wore in *exactly* the same way, and was, in sum, indistinguishable from the real thing. The only difference between this perfect imitation and real leather was where the imitation came from (a plastics factory, not an animal) and its chemical constitution. But these have nothing to do with your actual relationship with your shoes, do they? If you still prefer real leather to this perfect imitation, you have some explaining to do. It seems that you're being irrational.

"I'm willing to grant that my preference for real over perfect imitation leather is unjustifiable, but it's different when we're talking about *people*. There's something special about a relationship with people. It's not merely a matter of the nature of the contact with them."

Maybe there is something to this. But it certainly needs more explanation. A good explanation might reveal something important about how we feel (or ought to feel) about other people.

Replaceable People in Literature

Similar concerns to those raised in the problem of the mechanical girlfriend come up occasionally in literature. One instance of this occurs (extraneously to the main point of the story) in a corner of the Book of Job, in the Bible.

God (as a result of a dare from Satan) deprives Job of everything he values: his sheep, oxen, camels, servants, and so on. God even kills off his seven sons and three daughters. Job is understandably miserable and puzzled, but he does not lose his trust in God. In the end he is given "twice as much as he had before,"[2] plus seven sons and three daughters—presumably *brand new* sons and daughters, but really good ones. Happy ending! But we are a bit taken aback by the idea that his replacement children could really set things right.

Another instance: Meursault, the hero of Camus's *The Stranger*, is a peculiar man. He is sensual, well meaning, truthful, but he lacks the complexity and the depth of commitment and relationship that we think characterize the normally developed adult. His friend Marie asks him if he'll marry her.

> I said I didn't mind; if she was keen on it, we'd get married.
> Then she asked me again if I loved her. I replied, much as before, that her question meant nothing or next to nothing— but I supposed I didn't.... Then she asked:
> "Suppose another girl had asked you to marry her—I mean, a girl you liked in the same way as you like me—would you have said "Yes" to her, too?"
> "Naturally."[3]

Perhaps Marie is asking Meursault the right question. Love of another person—we suppose—is not simply a matter of valuing the characteristics of another person. If it were, we would love anyone just as

---

2   *Job* 42: 10.
3   *The Outsider*, trans. Stuart Gilbert (London: Hamish Hamilton, 1946), p. 50.

much who had comparable characteristics, and we would be happy if a loved one were replaced by someone else just as good.

5. Disease As An Ethical Category

It might appear that whether someone is ill or not is a question for a physician, not a philosopher, to answer. But consider the following argument, from a paper arguing that public funding should not be used to pay for medical treatment for infertility.[4] The author agreed that infertility is a physical abnormality that medicine can often do something to fix, but he argued that infertility is not a disease. Having one's own genetic children is something that people sometimes *want* very much, but they don't *need* it. Society sometimes puts a negative value on childlessness, but public funding should be limited to curing disease, to providing for people's medical needs, not their wants, especially if those wants are a result of society's norms.

Maybe the author's conclusion—that public funding shouldn't be used to pay for medical infertility treatment—is right. But we can raise questions about a lot of steps in his argument.

What counts as a *disease* anyway?

A medical student I discussed this question with argued that infertility isn't a disease because infertility is not a state of morbidity.

But what's morbidity? My dictionary tells me that a morbid state is a state relating to disease. We're back to the starting point.

Diseases are things that have gone wrong with your body. But infertility is something gone wrong with one's body. Lots of people count going bald as something going badly wrong with their bodies. But baldness doesn't seem to be a disease. So what is a disease?

The article mentioned above suggests that diseases are things that go wrong with your body in a way that deprives you of what you *need*. If what you're deprived of is merely what you want, then it's not a disease.

But now we can ask: what's the difference between a need and a want? A want, we're tempted to say, is merely a subjective desire; but a need is...a need is...what?

Does the fact that someone's desire is socially inculcated make that desire less important? Almost all our desires depend to a large extent on influences from our society.

4   Thomas A. Shannon, "In Vitro Fertilization: Ethical Issues" in *Embryos, Ethics, and Women's Rights: Exploring the New Reproductive Technologies*, Elaine Hoffman Baruch et. al., eds. (New York: Harrington Park Press, 1988).

Maybe the author of that paper is making distinctions that don't make much sense. Maybe what we really should say is that anything counts as a disease if it's a physical state of the sort (perhaps) treatable by medicine, and if it runs counter to the desires of the person who has it. The question remains whether society should pay for treatment of infertility, or of baldness for that matter. But this question can be solved by considering how desperate people are to have their condition fixed. Maybe if bald people really thought that their state was worse than having cancer, it would be right to divert public funds from cancer treatment to hair-transplants.

However you want to answer these questions, you can see by now that they're the sort of questions you take to your family philosopher, not to your family doctor.

6. Killing Bambi's Mother

A few years ago a colleague of mine was teaching an introductory ethics class, and wanted to start with an example of a clearly immoral action. "Imagine that someone just went out on the street and killed a passer-by at random," he suggested.

The students by then were philosophically sophisticated enough to question conventional reactions. "What's so bad about that?" they asked. "What if the passer-by were a nasty criminal, and everyone would be better off if he were dead?" "What if that person wanted to commit suicide anyway?" "What's so bad about death?" "Suppose you hated that person and could get away with murder without being punished?" And so on.

These are all questions that deserve an answer, but my colleague wanted to start first with a clear example that seemed unquestionably wrong to everyone. "Well, suppose that the passer-by wanted to live, and wasn't a criminal? How about if the passer-by were a helpless and innocent child?" More questions and objections. Finally he had an inspiration: the hunter who killed Bambi's mother in the Disney film. *Everyone* agreed that *there* was an action that was despicable.

Those cute Disney animals, with their big brown eyes, tug at our heartstrings. Real animals—when they're cute enough, anyway—affect most of us in the same way. Think of the widespread reaction a few years ago when Brigette Bardot held those adorable baby seals up to TV cameras (big brown eyes again), and then we saw them clubbed by seal hunters. Suppose as part of your job you had to exterminate unwanted kittens in an animal shelter. Could you do it?

What's interesting is how strong these reactions are. Even if we know that those kittens must be destroyed, and that it will be done painlessly, it's extremely difficult to get used to the idea.

SOME QUESTIONS TO THINK ABOUT: What is it about certain animals (cartoon or real) that rouses these reactions? It's not at all clear that cuteness has any deep relevance to the morality of treatment of animals. It has to be just as immoral to squash a cute kitten as it is to squash a really ugly (but harmless) rat. Nobody has any trouble swatting flies: is it because they're not even a little cute? Imagine that flies just happened to look like tiny teddy bears. How would you feel then?

FOR FURTHER READING: The Mark III Beast is a mechanical contraption that looks like a beetle. It runs around the floor looking for an electrical outlet to "feed" on. It "purrs" while eating, or when held. It makes shrill little noises when attacked. It feels comfortably warm to the touch. It's enormously difficult to "kill." This amusing story is told in *The Soul of Anna Klane* by Terrell Miedaner (New York: Coward, McCann & Geoghegan, 1977), reprinted, with philosophical commentary, in *The Mind's I* by Douglas R. Hofstadter and Daniel C. Dennett (New York: Basic Books, 1981).

Into the Mainstream of Philosophy

In Chapter XIV we were worrying about a very general issue in ethics, about whether a justification could be given for any sort of moral thinking or acting. In the present chapter, by contrast, we have been assuming that ethics is somehow in general justified; here we have been searching, indirectly, for general principles of morality that could be used in deciding specific moral issues.

These two issues are connected. If moral rules exist to solve the Prisoner's Dilemma, then they are ways of regulating and restraining our already existing selfish desires, with the aim of coordinating our actions in order to maximize everyone's satisfaction of these desires. This suggests a test for the validity of our general moral rules: would acting in accord with such a general rule maximize everyone's desire satisfaction? This test, roughly speaking, is the one proposed by philosophers who advocate the major substantive ethical theory called utilitarianism. John Stewart Mill and Jeremy Bentham are two nineteenth-century English philosophers whose names are most closely associated with utilitarianism; their views are roughly summarized by the slogan that what's good is what produces the greatest happiness for the greatest number of people. Here we might understand "happiness" as desire satisfaction.

Any utilitarian must reply to several sorts of objection. For one thing, it seems implausible that we are all morally required to look out for everyone's happiness. The example concerned with giving away your shoes raises questions about this. The interesting thing about this example is that it does seem initially plausible that maximization of satisfaction is the criterion of morally right action: the view is widespread that we should, for example, act to eliminate poverty, in order to eliminate the rather unequal degree of satisfaction people experience around the world. But the consequence of thinking that way seems to be that we are all acting dreadfully immorally. Is this possible?

Many philosophers have objected to utilitarianism on the grounds that the maximization of the distribution of satisfaction to everyone would necessitate depriving many people of what they have a right to have. As we have seen, however, it's not at all clear how we could decide what rights people have, especially when granting them rights seems often to interfere with our desire to maximize and equalize desire satisfaction. How could it be proven that someone has a right to something? What is the basis of the existence of rights anyway?

A second sort of general objection utilitarians must face is that it seems clear to most of us that the point of morality can't be the satisfaction of just any desire. It can't be true that we'd all be morally perfect once things were set up so that we all get what we want to the greatest degree, because certain things people happen to want just seem wrong. Suppose that someone's deepest desires were satisfied by providing that person with a plastic companion. The feeling remains that something very important would be missing in that person's life with Shirley, even if he feels fully satisfied. Maybe there's more to the morally good life than merely getting what you want. But what? And why?

You won't have trouble finding lots of articles in anthologies in which philosophers argue for very different views on what the basic principles of morality and the good life are.

CHAPTER XVI

LAW, ACTION, AND RESPONSIBILITY:

Ethics and the Philosophy of Law

1. Problems For Judges

The Messier Contract

Mark Messier, a hockey player for the New York Rangers, holds a contract with the team with an unusual provision. It says that if he is chosen Most Valuable Player in the National Hockey League, then his salary will be raised, if necessary, to make him among the five top-paid players in the league for the remainder of his contract.

Here's a scenario that would make for difficulties. Suppose that five other players (call them LaMer, LaPerrier, LaRose, LaFleur, and Gretsky) each hold contracts specifying that if they score over one hundred points in a season, then their salary will immediately be raised, if necessary, to make each of them among the five top-paid players in the League. Imagine that they each succeed in topping one hundred points during the 1992 season, and at that point their salaries are raised. At the end of the season, here are their salaries:

LaMer	$10 million
LaPerrier	$9 million
LaRose	$8 million
LaFleur	$7 million
Gretsky	$6 million

Messier is chosen Most Valuable Player at the end of the season, when he's making a mere $5 million. He goes to the team owner, contract in hand, demanding a raise to put him in the top five. The owner agrees to raise his salary to $6.5 million. But then Gretsky finds out that he's no longer in the top five, and goes to the owner of his team. His salary is accordingly raised to $6.8 million. But then Messier goes back to his owner demanding and getting an additional raise. But then Gretsky does the same. Pretty soon, both are making more than LaFleur; so he demands additional money. And so on.

Soon the team owners notice that this leapfrogging has no end. All six players, with their six respective team-owners, appear before a judge whose job it is to sort out this mess.

Let's listen in to the debate in court.

Judge: Here's a solution. Let's go back to the time the problem came up. When Messier was chosen MVP, the salaries of the other five of you were above his. Suppose that Messier's salary is raised to $6 million, tied with Gretsky's salary. Then only four players would be making more than Messier, so his salary would be among the top five. Only four players would be making more than Gretsky, so his salary would also be among the top five. It's solved!

Messier: Wait a minute. If Gretsky and I both made $6 million, and if the four others made higher salaries, both of us would be among the top *six*, not among the top five. There would be no top five salaries.

Judge: Hmm. Okay. Well, in that case, it appears that it's impossible for all six of you to get salaries among the top five in the league. Contracts specifying that someone do the impossible are invalid. So I think that all six of your contracts are invalid. Go back and negotiate valid contracts.

Messier: Hang on again. I signed my contract before any of these other guys. When I signed it there was nothing wrong with it. Then LaMer signed his, and there was nothing wrong with his either. Then LaPerrier, LaRose, and LaFleur each signed perfectly acceptable contracts. Gretsky signed his contract last; it was only then that a potential problem arose. Gretsky's contract is invalid.

Judge: I guess that's right.

Gretsky: Hold on. None of us signed contracts that were impossible to fulfill when we signed them. When each of us topped one hundred points, we got raises, and there was nothing impossible about our all being in the top five. The problem came up later, at the end of the season, when that damned Messier was chosen MVP. Only at that point did problems arise. So Messier's contract is the one that's invalid.

Judge: Well, Okay.

Messier: Not so fast. No team owner has a contract that specifies an impossible action. When I won MVP my owner had to raise my salary, and he could. Then Gretsky wasn't any longer in the top five, so his owner had to raise his salary, and that wasn't impossible either. As salaries go up, one of the owners has to raise somebody's salary, but in no case does an owner have to do something that's impossible. The poor guys are just stuck with having to pay leapfrogging salaries.

Judge: That's true.

Owners: [In unison] But! But! But!

What should the judge do?

What Do Judges Do?

A continuing question in the philosophy of law is what the job of judges is supposed to be. What you learned in civics class is that laws are *made* by legislators, and it's the judge's duty only to *interpret* these laws. But here's a plausible story that casts doubt on this.

Imagine that years ago, when house trailers were first produced, Billy-Bob towed one of them into town, bought an empty plot of land, parked his trailer on his land, and moved into it. A few months later, Billy-Bob's mail contained a bill for city taxes. The amount of the bill was based on an assessor's judgement of the value of the land plus the value of the trailer. Billy-Bob complained to the city: he was taxable for the land, he agreed, but not for the trailer on it. Houses, not trailers, were taxable by the city. But the city assessment office insisted that he was living in his trailer, so it was a house. The matter went to court.

Trial judges have to decide on three sorts of matters: what the facts are, which laws are relevant, and how the facts fit the laws. The facts in this case were no problem; Billy-Bob's lawyer and the city's lawyer agreed readily about what these were. There was also no disagreement that only one law was relevant: the city bylaw that stated simply that the tax assessment was to be based on the value of the land plus the value of any houses on that land. The only matter under contention for the judge to make a decision on was whether Billy-Bob's trailer was a house. We imagine the following arguments made by the two lawyers:

City's Lawyer: It's a house. The word 'house' means "1.a. A structure serving as a dwelling for one or several families. b. A place of abode; residence. c. Something that serves as an abode."[1] It's a structure, and it serves as a dwelling for Billy-Bob's family. It's Billy-Bob's abode and residence. It's something that serves as an abode.

Billy-Bob's Lawyer: Gimmie that dictionary! The word 'trailer' means "A furnished van drawn by a truck or automobile and used as a house or office when parked."[2]

City's Lawyer: Aha! 'Used as a house'!

Billy-Bob's Lawyer: If my learned colleague would just hang on for a damned minute. *Using* something as a house doesn't make it a house. I refer to the case of *Arkansas v. Smedley*. Smedley was charged with owning a gun without a permit, and he argued that since he used it only as a paperweight it was a paperweight, not a gun. Smedley lost.

On what basis can the judge make a decision? Clearly there's some "interpretation" of the law necessary here. But what is "interpretation"?

There's no problem in understanding the wording of the law. It's nice and clear.

One basis on which hard judicial decisions are sometimes made is by consideration of precedents in decisions about similar cases. But house trailers were brand new. There weren't any similar cases.

Sometimes it's thought that one thing judges do when they "interpret" laws is figure out what intention the lawmakers must have had when they created the law. Even if this mind-reading trick is a sensible way of "interpreting" some laws, it wasn't useful in this case. The law had been made years before, when house trailers weren't even imagined: the legislators couldn't have had any intentions about them at all.

What the judges sometimes do is consider what the morally right decision is. But that didn't help in this case. On which side did justice lie? Neither side was trying to cheat the other. Neither was acting out of malice. Neither would have been *unfairly* victimized by a decision for the other side.

There didn't seem to be any good basis for a decision one way or the other. Maybe what would influence the judge's decision was the fact that Billy-Bob was a nice guy, or the fact that the city was running short on money. Such considerations don't appear to provide a good basis for a decision, but a decision had to be made.

1 He was reading from *The American Heritage Dictionary of the English Language* (New York: American Heritage, 1969), p. 638.
2 Ibid., p. 1361.

Whichever way the decision went, a precedent would have been set: the law would afterwards be taken to read, in effect, that houses and installed trailers (or houses but not installed trailers) are taxable. This judge made the law.

2. Problems About Actions

Why You Don't Drive When You're Drunk

Following is another philosophically interesting legal argument—this time, an actual case.

LaFontaine, after hours of heavy drinking, crawls out of the tavern utterly soused. Somehow he manages, mostly by random motion, to get in his car and start the motor. While he is slumped over the wheel almost unconscious, his foot presses the accelerator and his car lurches forward, crashing into a building with such force that the building is knocked off its foundation. The police arrive, extract LaFontaine from the wreckage, and (unsurprisingly) arrest him for dangerous driving.

The surprise is that, at his trial, LaFontaine pleads not guilty. His lawyer does not contest the fact that LaFontaine was drunk. Just the reverse: he bases his defence on the fact that he was drunk as a skunk.

This is the substance of the lawyer's argument: suppose someone is turning the dials on his stereo set, trying to tune in the radio. Unknown to him, the stereo is wired to his car in such a way that turning the dials results in the car's moving forward and backward. That person isn't *driving his car* because 'driving' is the name of an *intentional action*. This person isn't driving because he doesn't intend that his car move, and he's unaware that his actions result in that movement. Now, LaFontaine, it's clear, was so drunk that he had no idea what he was doing. He didn't even know that he was in his car. He had no intentions about moving his car. His actions—unbeknownst to him—resulted in his car's motion, but he wasn't *driving* it. LaFontaine might be charged with public drunkenness, and he might be sued by the owner of the building for unintentionally damaging it. But he's not guilty of dangerous driving. Dangerous, yes. Driving, no. Do you agree with LaFontaine's lawyer?

> LaFontaine didn't win his case, but his lawyer's argument is strangely persuasive. Many of the activities mentioned in laws are intentional actions—things that people *do*. Necessary conditions of *doing* something are that you're aware of your bodily movements and that you intend the consequences.
>
> This sort of distinction applies as well in ordinary moral thinking. If *C* tells *D* something that's false, but *C* doesn't want to deceive *D* and

believes that what he said was true, then *C* hasn't *told a lie*, and we don't blame *C* for what he did. If *C* is so drunk that he hasn't any idea what he's saying, he isn't *lying* when he says something that's false.

The Lucky Murderer

Your whole gang is out to kill Vito. You slip some poison in Vito's granola, and he eats it. An hour later, the police, having been tipped off by the extermination company where you bought the poison, arrest you and charge you with murder. At the same time Vito is rushed to the hospital, where his stomach is pumped, but it's too late—Vito is already showing the signs of fatal poisoning. As Vito lies in his hospital, near death, a fellow member of your gang, wanting to make sure Vito won't recover, slips into the hospital and shoots him in the head, killing him immediately. But now the police have to reduce their charge against you: you are charged only with attempted murder.

You were lucky. Had your pal not shot Vito, he would have died, and you would have been convicted of first-degree murder, which carries a much greater penalty than mere attempted murder. The puzzle here is that what your pal did had nothing to do with you. It seems that what crime you commit, and what your punishment is to be, should be a matter only of *what you do*, not of things that happen or don't happen afterwards. But it seems in this case that "what you did"—murder or merely attempted murder—depends on things that happen afterwards, and that are totally out of your control.

This puzzle does not merely apply to artificial, imaginary, or unlikely events. Think of all the things people do in real life for which they are praised or blamed. The praise or blame, and the extent of praise or blame, depends on what sort of action it was. And what sort of action it was depends on circumstances and consequences very often utterly out of the control of the doer. An unlucky speeding driver may kill a pedestrian, for example; whether this happens or not depends on whether any pedestrians happen to be around when the speeder is careering down the road. And, of course, this is a matter over which the driver has no control. The very same behaviour on the driver's part will be punished very differently if it constitutes mere speeding than if it involves killing a pedestrian. But this difference is merely a matter of good or bad luck for the driver.

A QUESTION TO THINK ABOUT: Is it fair to decide which act was committed, and to adjust the amount of punishment meted out accordingly, on the basis of circumstances utterly beyond the agent's control?

Now suppose your pal didn't get into the hospital, and Vito dies of the dose of poison you gave him. You have committed murder, but when? Suppose you put poison in his granola on Tuesday, he ate it on Wednesday, and he died on Thursday. Did the murder take place only on Tuesday? Or did it last from Tuesday through Thursday? This decision might have important consequences. Suppose your state legislature, meeting on Wednesday, votes to institute the death penalty for murders. Retroactive legislation isn't allowed, so murders that took place before Wednesday don't carry the death penalty. Is it clear that the murder you are charged with took place entirely before Wednesday? If "part" of it took place on Thursday, perhaps you face the death penalty.

Actions might be seen to be spread out not only in time, but also in space. Suppose you shot Vito instead, and that you were standing in New York at the time, near the border with Connecticut, and Vito was standing a few feet away from you, in Connecticut. Did the murder take place in New York or in Connecticut? This again might have important consequences. Suppose, for example, that New York has the death penalty for convicted murderers and Connecticut does not. It's tempting to think that the murder took place where you were, in New York. But now let's move you a few feet east, so that your outstretched arm, with the pistol in hand, is across the border in Connecticut while the rest of you is in New York. The hand that pulled the trigger, the gun, the path of the bullet, and Vito were all in Connecticut. But did the murder take place where you (all except for your arm) were—in New York?

3. Cans and Can'ts

Can Pierre Keep His Promise?

Pierre has promised you that he'll show up at noon in his car to drive you to the airport. Noon comes and goes: no Pierre. It turns out that he remembered his promise, but nevertheless he just sat in his room watching TV. Is Pierre to blame for his failure to keep his promise?

> Clearly he is. He could have kept his promise, but he didn't. It's his fault that he didn't show up to drive you. He's morally responsible for his failure.

But suppose it turns out that Pierre's crazy landlord has locked Pierre's room from the outside, and he can't get out. There's no phone in his room, so there's no way for him to warn you that he can't get there. All he can do is to sit there until someone comes by who can let him out. Now is he to blame?

> This additional information absolves Pierre from blame. We wouldn't
> say that Pierre *ought* to have shown up, because he *couldn't* have.

The only things one ought to do are those things one can do. Philosophers express this general moral principle by the slogan "Ought implies can."

 This seems clear and correct. But let's think about things a bit more deeply. What does it mean to say that someone *can* or *can't* do something?

> Perhaps we might say: the things you can't do are the things you try
> your best to do, but don't succeed. We imagine Pierre trying to get out
> of his room: he pushes on his door, turning the handle one way and the
> other. He bangs and yells, trying to attract the attention of someone who
> might be able to let him out. *This* is a case in which Pierre *can't* get out
> of his room.

 But this won't do as an account of 'can't', because we would agree that Pierre can't get out of the room even if he doesn't actually perform all these frantic attempts. Suppose Pierre hears the door lock, and he knows that now there's no way to get out, so he doesn't even try. He just turns on the TV and settles down for what might be a long wait. It's clear that in this situation Pierre can't get out, even though he doesn't even try to. Can you think of a better account of what it is not to be able to do something?

> Perhaps a better answer is: to say that Pierre can't get out of the room
> is to say that *if* Pierre tried his best to get out, he *wouldn't* get out. Nothing that Pierre might have done would get him out of the room. This
> means that it can be true that Pierre can't get out of the room, even
> though he doesn't actually try.

 But even this won't do. Suppose that Pierre's crazy landlord has installed a hidden button on the lock, which will unlock the door from the inside. The landlord hasn't told Pierre about this, and Pierre has no way of knowing about it. Now there is something Pierre might have done to get him out of his room: he might have pushed the button which that have unlocked the door. It's within Pierre's physical power to push the button. So should we still say that Pierre can't get out of the room?

A QUESTION TO THINK ABOUT: Maybe after some thought about this you might come up with a better account of what it means to say that one *can* or *can't* do something. But this question turns out to be surprisingly complicated and difficult.

The Incapable Golfer

Despite the difficulties of *can* and *can't* we have just noticed, at least one thing seems clear: whenever someone *does* something, it then follows that that is the sort of thing the person can do. If we see Matilda driving her car, that proves that Matilda can drive. Of course, this doesn't prove that she'll still be able to drive at any time in the future, because relevant circumstances might someday change. We see Matilda driving on Tuesday, but she suffers a paralysing stroke on Wednesday, and on Thursday she can't drive. Nonetheless, we have proof that on Tuesday she could drive.

By now you will hardly be surprised to find out that even this very clear principle might be mistaken. Consider this example:

Myrtle is a skilled golfer. She hits an ordinary shot off the tee; the ball travels down the fairway and finally rolls to a stop. Call the exact spot where the ball stops Spot *S*. What Myrtle did was to hit a golf ball from the tee exactly to Spot *S*. Does it follow that Myrtle *can* hit a golf ball from the tee exactly to Spot *S*? Suppose that we interrupt Myrtle's game right after this shot and ask her to repeat it—to hit another ball from the tee exactly to Spot *S*. Being a good golfer, she hits balls that wind up in the general vicinity of that spot, but after many tries, unsurprisingly, no ball has rolled exactly to Spot *S*. This seems to show that Myrtle can't hit a golf ball exactly to Spot *S*. But nothing relevant has changed since the time she actually did do so. It seems that even at the time she did it, she couldn't do it. No golfer, after all, has *that* much ability.

The principle we were considering claimed that the fact that someone actually does something proves that they can do it. But this example apparently shows that the principle is wrong.

No Absolution for Pierre

We have been considering, in the last two items, difficulties in explaining exactly what 'can' and 'can't' involve. Recall that all this was prompted by moral considerations, by the idea that Pierre isn't to blame for something he didn't do when he couldn't do it.

Let's now put aside the complications of 'can' and 'can't' and examine directly the notion that one isn't to blame for something one didn't do when one couldn't do it.

Let's change the Pierre example slightly. Suppose Pierre, as before, has promised to drive you to the airport but sits in his room watching TV instead. As before, Pierre's door is locked, and there's no way he can get out of his room. Pierre's not to blame, right?

Well, not necessarily. Suppose (and here we change the story a bit) that Pierre doesn't know that his door is locked. Why doesn't Pierre try to get out? He's feeling lazy, and he doesn't feel like driving you to the airport. He remembers his promise, and he knows that you're counting on him. "To hell with that!" Pierre thinks. "I'll just stay here and watch TV instead."

Pierre can't get out of his room, but now he is to blame. He's responsible for not having done something he nevertheless couldn't have done.

4. Acting and Refraining

Two Ways to Kill Granny

It's often taken to be a principle of moral reasoning that *doing* something is morally different from merely *refraining from acting*, even if the doing and the refraining have the same outcome. In ordinary circumstances, for example, merely doing nothing and thereby failing to save someone's life isn't, of course, a very nice thing, but it's supposed not to be as bad as actually killing the person, despite the fact that the refraining from acting (not saving the life) and the action (killing) have the same outcome: the person's death. Are you convinced that this is right? Then consider this:

Suppose evil Ian hates his grandmother and wishes she were dead. While she is taking her bath, Ian decides to enter the bathroom and hold Granny under water till she dies. Now compare these two scenarios:

1. Ian enters the bathroom and holds Granny under water, and she dies.

2. Ian enters the bathroom. By coincidence, just at that moment Granny slips on the soap, hits her head on the side of the tub, and falls unconscious. Ian notices that the water will soon rise above her head and drown her; all he has to do to save her life is to turn off the water. But he refrains from doing this; he does nothing, and she dies.

Scenarios 1 and 2 are designed to be as alike as possible, except for the difference that in 1 Ian's *action* results in death, whereas in 2 Ian's *refraining* has that outcome. But many people think that Ian would be judged to be equally at fault in both scenarios. Maybe there isn't a real moral difference between acting and refraining after all.

Moral Technology

The supposed moral difference between acting and refraining has led to the invention of a bizarre bit of medico-ethical technology.

There is a general rule of medical ethics that depends on this supposed moral difference. When someone is near death from an incurable terminal disease, modern medicine sometimes is able to prolong that person's life for a while by using elaborate life-support systems. But when that period would be full of unrelievable suffering for that person, and when death is only postponed a bit, not prevented, often everyone—the person him/herself, family and friends, the medical personnel involved, and experts on medical ethics—agree that it is better that the life not be prolonged.

The best solution, under the circumstances, is to refrain from attaching the person to the life-support systems. This would merely be refraining from prolonging life and would widely be found ethically acceptable. But suppose that the person was already attached to those systems when the decision not to prolong life was made. In order to end that person's life now, someone would have to switch off the life-support, but this would be *doing something* that results in death, not merely refraining from doing something. The acting/refraining principle we have been discussing would count *this* as morally forbidden. It is murder.

This is where ethics-tech comes to the rescue. A simple addition to the life-support system puts a timer on it, designed to shut it off after, say, twenty-four hours. If a button is pushed before this time runs out an additional twenty-four hours is added to the timer and the machine stays on for one more day. Pushing this button once every day can keep the machine on indefinitely, if that's what's desired.

You can see how this "solves" the ethical problem. If it is decided that prolonging the life would be a bad idea, nobody has to *do* anything. All that we have to do is to *refrain* from pushing the button; the timer would run out, all by itself, with the desired result.

There's a danger in using this adapted machine: in other cases it is of course important that the machine stay on, and what if someone forgets to push the button? But this danger is outweighed, in the eyes of some people who take the acting/refraining distinction seriously, by the moral advantage this adapted machine sometimes gives us.

But there's something very bizarre about this ethical "solution." The object, everyone agrees, is to provide an earlier, more humane end to the unfortunate patient's life. Can it reasonably be supposed that using a machine that stops all by itself, as opposed to one which has to be shut off, makes the difference between a humane, morally praiseworthy procedure and a morally hideous, utterly forbidden murder? An ethics that tells us that the addition of this timer makes that difference is clearly an ethics run amok.

Here we have another reason to doubt that the acting/refraining distinction is a morally important one.

Ten-to-One Dilemmas

Here are a couple of additional cases to try out your moral intuitions out on.

Imagine you're standing on a railroad line at a point where the track splits into two. There's a manually operable switch at that point, which can send a train coming down the track onto one or the other of the branches at the fork. A short way past the fork, some children are playing on the tracks. Ten of them are playing on the north fork and one on the south. You notice that the switch is now set to send a train down the north fork, and a high-speed train is approaching. There's no time to warn the children to get off the tracks. If the train continues, it will kill ten children. But you do have time to throw the switch, sending the train down the south track, where one child will be killed. Should you throw the switch? Here are two possible answers:

> 1. A horrible tragedy will result whatever you do, of course. But there would be a worse tragedy—the death of ten children—if you don't throw the switch. If you do, only one death will result. It seems that you should throw the switch.

> 2. But the acting/refraining distinction gives a different answer. If you throw the switch, you are *acting*. If you just stand there and do nothing, you are *refraining*. Your action will save ten lives, but you will knowingly bring about the death of that child on the south track. This is murder, and forbidden.

Perhaps by now, having been convinced by all these examples, you doubt that the acting/refraining distinction is a morally relevant one. Maybe you think it's clear that the right thing to do is to throw the switch, sacrificing one child's life to save ten.

Well, if that's what you think, here's one final example designed to confuse you.

Suppose you are the physician in charge of the transplant division at a big hospital. Ten children are under your care. All of them are dying from various organ failures, and all of them can be saved only by organ transplants. One needs a heart transplant, two need kidney transplants, three need liver transplants, and four need lung transplants. None of these organs is available, and none will become available until after all ten have died. All you need is one healthy dead body, out of which you can extract a heart, two kidneys, and the liver and lungs (which can be cut up into pieces to provide all the transplant material needed to save the lives of your patients). (This is, of course, science fiction. Transplant recipients have to be carefully matched to donors, and it's unlikely that one donor could provide organs for all ten patients. Other features also make this story currently impossible. But ignore all this.)

While you're pondering your problem, you idly glance out the window. There, playing on the sidewalk outside the hospital, is a healthy-looking little girl the same size as your patients. You run outside, grab the child, and carry her to the operating room, where you cut her up to provide the parts necessary for your patients. Ten children are saved; one dies.

Everyone would agree that, at the very least, you should be locked up in some unpleasant prison for a good long time as a result. But what's of interest here is the moral reasoning that condemns this. In particular, if you accepted the conclusion that you ought to throw the railroad switch in the example just above, you should consider what makes that case different from this one. In both cases, there are ten children who will die if you do nothing, and in both cases the life of one innocent child, who would live if you did nothing, is sacrificed to save the ten. What, if anything, is the difference?

How to Assault a Police Officer by Doing Nothing

Here's another interesting actual legal case with an ingenious defense. This one raises questions about acting and refraining.

Fagan is parking his car on a city street, and a constable is guiding him into the space. Without knowing he's doing it, Fagan brings his car to a halt with one of its tires resting squarely on top of the constable's foot. The constable points out that the car is on his foot. Fagan responds with an offensive remark and tells the constable he can wait. Finally, after repeated requests, he moves his car.

Later Fagan is arrested and charged with assaulting a police officer in the execution of his duty. He pleads not guilty, on the following grounds. An assault is defined in law as an action (of a certain sort) accompanied by a malicious intent. When Fagan's car rolled onto the constable's foot this may be construed as his action, since he was in control of his car, but there was, as yet, no assault, because he did not know that the foot was there. He had no intention to stop his car on the foot, so assault, which presumes intent, had not yet been committed. A moment later Fagan became aware that his tire was on the constable's foot and developed the malicious intention to leave it there. But leaving the car there is not doing anything—it's not an *action*, so it can't be an assault.

Fagan's defense did not work. In finding him guilty of assault, a judge gave this (perhaps not entirely convincing) reasoning: Fagan's action was an ongoing one, beginning with his rolling his car onto the foot, and continuing through the time when he refused to get it off. The malicious intention developed during this extended action, so the requirements for assault were satisfied.

FOR FURTHER READING: The Canadian case of *Fagan* v. *Commission of Metropolitan Police* [1969] 1 Q.B. 439, is described and analysed in *An Introduction to Criminal Law* by Graham Parker (Agincourt, Ont.: Methuen Publications, 1977).

Into the Mainstream of Philosophy

Laws often exist to prevent immoral action, but it's clear that the fact that something is immoral is not sufficient grounds for saying that there ought to be a law against it. Suppose you were prime minister of a country, and had the power to influence Parliament to make any law you wanted. One thing that's always been a minor annoyance to you is that some people show up late for appointments with you. It's not controversial whether this sort of thing is immoral—everyone agrees that showing up late is wrong. It's obvious, however, that it would be stupid to make lateness illegal, punishable by law. In this case, the reason is that it's such a trivial matter. But there are other, much less trivial wrongs that should also not be a matter of law. For example, some parents bring up their children to have very low self-respect, with disastrous psychological consequences on those children for the rest of their lives. I don't think you'd want to create a law against this either. What principles are there for which wrong things should be prevented by law, and which should not?

Another sort of issue dealt with in philosophy of law is the nature of the actual (or the proper) function of judges and juries. Do they *make* the law or merely *interpret* it? If the latter, what exactly is *interpretation*? This issue is raised in the example above concerning the house trailer. It's a philosophical question, not a factual one; it's not easily answerable even after we've observed the actual procedures followed by judges. You probably know enough about what actually goes on in courts to think about this question.

Several interesting philosophical questions arise not only in philosophy of law, but also when we consider ordinary matters of action and responsibility in everyday contexts. We have seen how questions arise concerning the time and place of an action. These questions might be important to answer not only in legal contexts. The notion of an *action* is philosophically interesting. Sometimes we describe actions in terms merely of intentional bodily movements. But sometimes action-descriptions include what happens outside the doer's body, as a result of the bodily motions. In the philosophical area called theory of action, philosophers consider questions about delimiting and counting such actions.

Another interesting, difficult, and often important family of questions concerns responsibility. It seems we're not always responsible for the unintended consequences of otherwise intentional actions. For example, if you intentionally hit a golf ball, and unintentionally hit a golfer in front of you on the head, you're (in a sense) not responsible for harming the other golfer. But things are not this simple. You might justly be blamed for the harm even if you didn't anticipate it (for example, if you should have made sure you wouldn't hit her, but you didn't.) Can you give a general account of what sort of bad results one is responsible for?

A related issue concerns what we can and can't do. You're not to blame for not doing something you can't do, but it's sometimes not clear what you can't do. It seems plausible to think of a person's actions as being caused, but if the causes of a person's actions actually took place, could that person have acted otherwise? This issue is one of the questions raised in conjunction with the general topic of freedom—it's the issue of free will. Do we actually have free will? What is free will supposed to be, anyway?

The acting/refraining distinction is another one considered in action theory. This issue has special relevance in ethics, since we're often supposed to be more to blame for the bad results of our actions than for similarly bad results of our refraining from acting. You might think about this issue by imagining and morally comparing pairs of circumstances that differ only along acting/refraining lines. One currently lively and important debate along these lines concerns euthanasia—mercy killing. It's widely thought that it's morally permissible to let someone die—to refrain from keeping him or her alive—in the terminal and horribly painful stages of a disease, but that it's morally impermissible to act to kill that person. If the acting/refraining distinction makes no sense, or is morally irrelevant, then we shouldn't make this distinction. What do you think about euthanasia?

You'll often find articles dealing with the issues raised in this chapters in introductory anthologies. And there are plenty of books available dealing with practical ethical problems in many areas; in these, you'll often find philosophical discussions of law, action, and responsibility.

CHAPTER XVII

JOKES AND OTHER AESTHETIC MATTERS

1. The Aesthetics Of Humour

The Joke I Didn't Get

Kenny was the humorist in my eighth-grade class. One day he told a number of us this joke:

> Two elephants are sitting in a bathtub. One of them says, "Pass the soap, Millicent." The other replies, "No soap—radio."

Kenny grinned nervously at the end of the joke. The listeners smiled politely and half-heartedly. We walked away, wondering what was supposed to be funny.

I puzzled over this event a long time. Years later I was able to figure out what had been going on, after I read the following description of a classical practical joke. You and a group of others who are in on the plot find an unwitting victim. You tell the victim that pointless "no soap—radio" story. At the end, you and your confederates, as you have pre-arranged, all pretend to collapse into helpless laughter, watching the victim who, embarrassed by not getting it and not wanting to appear to be the only one who didn't, pretends to crack up too.

But Kenny didn't do it right: he had no confederates. Nobody laughed. What must have happened was that Kenny himself had previously been the victim of this practical joke. Thinking that the "no soap" story must be hilarious, even though he didn't get it, he told it to us. The joke continued to be on him.

It's interesting that the tradition for playing this practical joke includes telling exactly that "no soap—radio" story, when any pointless story would do. The reason for this is, I suppose, that it's very difficult to come up with a genuinely pointless and unfunny story—more difficult than thinking up a funny one. The "no soap—radio" story is actually a very artful and clever creation: it's a story with all the form and rhythm of a joke, but utterly lacking the funny content. Whether or not you approve of practical joking, you have to admire the skill involved in the creation of this one.

There are two questions suggested here. One is: what, really, is joke form? Everyone who has heard jokes told badly knows that to be funny, jokes need to have exactly the right structure and need to be told exactly right. This one has the form exactly right, and Kenny was a master of joke execution. But form and execution aren't sufficient to make something funny. The second, and more difficult question, is: why is some content funny?

Prison Humour

Here's a joke about jokes that illustrates these questions.

A man is spending the first day of his sentence in prison. He is at lunch in the huge prison dining hall; all the inmates are quietly eating. Suddenly one inmate shouts out, "Sixty-three!" and everyone laughs. A few minutes later, another inmate yells, "Three hundred and four!" and everyone laughs again.

The new arrival is puzzled. "What's going on?" he asks the man sitting next to him.

His neighbour replies: "We've all been together so long that we've heard each others' jokes over and over again, and we have all the jokes memorized. To save effort, we've given each joke a number, so all we have to do to tell one of these jokes is to give its number."

"Hey, that's a good idea," says the new arrival. "I think I'll try telling one." He shouts, "Ninety-seven!" Silence. Nobody even smiles. "What did I do wrong?" he asks his neighbour.

The neighbour replies: "Well, some people just don't know how to tell a joke."

Laughter is the Best Medicine

Immanuel Kant is among the most ponderous of philosophical writers, but even his writing contains a few jokes (presented in connection with his theorizing on humour). This is one:

> The heir of a rich relative wants to arrange for him a very solemn funeral service, but complains that things are not quite working out: for (he says) the more money I give my mourners to look grieved, the more cheerful they look.

Another Kantian joke is the story of

the grief of some merchant who, during his return trip from India to Europe, with all his fortune in merchandise, was forced by a heavy storm to throw everything overboard, and whose grief was such that it made his *wig* turn grey that very night. (Kant's—or his translator's—italics)

Kant remarks that the second joke "will make us laugh," and that the first "evokes ringing laughter in us." Whenever you read philosophy, you must ask yourself whether what the philosopher says is true.

Kant theorizes that "[l]aughter is an affect that arises if a tense expectation is transformed into nothing." He gives a physiological explanation of how laughter results, and consequently of why we enjoy humour:

For if we assume that all our thoughts are, in addition, in a harmonious connection with some agitation in the body's organs, then we can pretty well grasp how, as the mind suddenly shifts alternately from one position to another in order to contemplate its object, there might be a corresponding alternating tension and relaxation of the elastic parts of our intestines that is communicated to the diaphragm.... The lungs, meanwhile, rapidly and intermittently expel air, and so give rise to an agitation that is conducive to our health. It is this agitation alone, and not what goes on in the mind, that is the actual cause of our gratification in a thought [by] which [we] basically present nothing.[1]

Kant is not the only one with theories about what makes something funny.

A 1990 issue of The Realist *carries a report of a conference on popular culture at which a paper was given titled "The Illusion of Ontotheological Reality in the Three Stooges." They go on to say that none of the three stooges graduated from high school, but that Moe's daughter, who spoke at the conference, reported that her father frequently expressed his concern about the ensemble's ability to create the illusion of ontotheological reality.[2]*

(No, I don't know what "ontotheological reality" means either.)

1   Immanuel Kant, *Kritik der Urteilskraft*, section 54. Trans. as *Critique of Judgement* by Werner S. Pluhar (Indianapolis: Hackett, 1987).
2   Robert Myers, "Pop Goes the Culture!" in *The Realist*, 113 (Summer 1990), pp. 5-6.

2. What's So Good About Art?

I Loved That Movie! I Cried the Whole Time!

The theory of humour is tucked into a corner of that branch of philosophy called philosophical aesthetics. A more major concern of philosophical aesthetics is explaining why we like to experience art.

The experience of art is really quite peculiar. Some art is quite grotesque, brutal, ugly, or disturbing. Nevertheless people *want* to experience it—they *enjoy* it. How can that be? People who watch horror movies sometimes have intense feelings of terror. Other movies are effectively designed to reduce the whole audience to uncontrollable tears. Terror and sadness are not the sorts of emotions most of us enjoy. We'd go out of our way to avoid them. But we pay to have these emotions created by art. What's going on here?

One suggestion that has been made is that the sort of terror we feel at a horror movie isn't *real* terror. It's just in some ways similar to real terror. Similarly, the revulsion we feel at some particularly bloody movie scene isn't the same feeling as we'd get if we came across a real and horrible automobile accident. Is this right?

How Do You Like Them Apples?

The central questions in philosophical aesthetics are: What makes something a work of art? and What makes something a *good* work of art? (Sometimes these are taken to be the same question. When you say, "Now, that's *art*!" you probably mean, "Now that's a *good* work of art!")

> The first characteristic that probably comes to mind when you try to think of what makes art good is *beauty*. A good work of art is a beautiful one, right?

There are several reasons why this answer isn't very helpful. For one thing, this answer immediately raises a second question: what makes something beautiful? It seems that this depends on the kind of thing you're talking about. For some kinds of things, the answer is fairly clear. Suppse, for example, that you are presented with a bushel of apples and asked to sort out the most beautiful ones (just to look at, not to eat). What characteristics do you look for? The large and symmetrical ones are probably more beautiful than the small and lumpy ones. Bright colour and shine are probably also plusses. The ones that contain rotten bits or worm holes are out. A nice curved stem, perhaps with a single perfect leaf attached, helps.

But there are even problems with apples: you and I might sort the same bushel quite differently. You might put the ones that are uniformly red into the "most beautiful" pile, while I might want to put the ones that have some green parts on that pile. Who is right?

> We're tempted to say that there is no "correct" way to sort the apples—it depends on who is doing the sorting. You like the looks of the uniformly red ones and I like the two-tones, and that's all there is to say about it. Maybe we could even find someone who makes her "most beautiful" pile out of the small, dull-coloured, wormy, bruised ones. She just likes the way they look. Maybe beauty—even in apples—is only in the eye of the beholder.

But maybe not. People who put together those expensive fruit baskets for sale as gifts pick the most beautiful apples for their baskets—they're the pros at apple aesthetics. Other pros work in apple-packing houses grading the apples, partly on the basis of aesthetics, for sale in different categories at different prices; the more expensive ones are the more beautiful ones. These pros have know-how we ordinary apple eaters don't. They have trained apple-perceptions. So perhaps you should trust them to pick the ones that are genuinely beautiful, even if you can't see it.

On the other hand, maybe all they're doing is sorting out the apples that will appeal to most people. Maybe their expertise is not in recognizing genuine apple beauty: maybe it's just in recognizing which apples they can sell at the highest prices. They're pros in apple marketing, not in apple aesthetics.

A QUESTION TO THINK ABOUT: So does it really come down to just a matter of what you like, after all?

We've had some troubles deciding about the "objectivity" of judgement about the beauty of apples, and the same sort of considerations seem to transfer, more or less, to questions about the "objectivity" of judgement about art. It's sometimes thought that in art, too, it really does come down to just a matter of what you like, after all.

But the problem gets even more complicated when it comes to art. We imagined sorting out the beautiful apples from the rest, but *beauty*, it turns out, is almost never what's at issue when art is being evaluated by knowledgeable people. Read some book or movie reviews in the newspaper. Look at what's written by critics of music or architecture. Listen to what those pompous and mannered people say to one another in art galleries. 'Beauty' is a word that's almost never used. What is it they're looking for, in general? Maybe there *isn't* any one thing that's the general characteristic of good art.

Yummie Yummie?

Here's another problem. Apple critics look for characteristics that will appeal most to most people. But art critics don't. Merely in terms of general appeal, Beethoven's relatively obscure Second Symphony is beaten hands down by "Yummie Yummie Yummie (I've Got Love in My Tummy)," though you couldn't find a single music critic who thinks that "Yummie" is better than Beethoven's Second. For every person who really enjoys looking at Vermeer paintings, you might easily find several thousand who much prefer toreadors painted on black velvet.

Next time you're in an art museum or at a symphony concert, concentrate on the audience rather than on the art. Are they enjoying themselves, or are they suffering through a boring experience they think they ought to like but don't? Some people do show signs of enjoyment, but maybe they're the ones who have been brainwashed into thinking that there's something wonderful there.

Well, I think that Beethoven really, *objectively* beats "Yummie." Do you? If you do, just try convincing someone who disagrees. You might be able to bully or shame them into admitting you're right, or even into pretending to prefer Beethoven, but it's not at all obvious that there are rational considerations to be brought to bear to convince someone genuinely.

Into the Mainstream of Philosophy

There is such a field as philosophy of humour. (*Warning*: philosophers who think about this area sometimes write in a deadly serious manner, and give terrible jokes as examples.) What, after all, makes a joke funny? Kant suggests that a joke reverses our expectations and turns something sensible into nonsense. Perhaps he's right about some jokes, but you might test his hypothesis on things you think are funny. Do they all involve this reversal? And think about things that do involve such a reversal: are they therefore funny? (In the Greek tragedy, Oedipus's assumptions suffer a severe reversal when he discovers that a man he killed long ago was actually his father and that the woman he's now married to is actually his mother. The audience does not collapse in giggles as a result.) Even if Kant is right about some jokes, there's a question that remains: why do we enjoy humour? Do you really enjoy having your expectations overturned?

Other philosophers (Hobbes, for example) think that jokes are enjoyable to us because they allow us to affirm our supposed superiority to others by making fun of them. Again you might find that this applies to only some humour. To the extent that this theory is right, it would make joking a rather nasty matter.

Philosophical aesthetics studies some difficult questions. One thing philosophers try to do here is to explain what art is. When you stop to think about it, art seems like quite a peculiar thing. People spend a great deal of effort dabbing pigments on canvas or arranging a series of noises. What are they doing *that* for? Imagine yourself trying to explain art to an uncomprehending Martian.

Philosophical aesthetics and ethics can both be included in one field: value theory. In aesthetics we face the same sort of problems as we do in ethics. Are there any sorts of general principles that summarize why we value certain sorts of things? Is their value an objective matter, or does it exist only in the eye of the beholder?

CHAPTER XVIII

WISDOM AND DOUBT

In this book there have been many more questions than answers. Puzzle-books often contain, at the end, a section of answers, but you won't find that sort of section in here. That's not because there are no answers. In many cases, philosophers have found what they take to be answers to these questions, and in some cases I have hinted at what these answers are, or at least at the way one might begin thinking to arrive at them. But to understand these answers you must go a good deal farther and deeper than we have. That's what the serious study of philosophy is for. In many cases, however, there is no general agreement, and a lot of controversy, about what the answers are. Unanswered questions are what makes philosophy interesting.

Maybe you have been wondering why there are so many quite particularized problems in this book, and so little in the way of the generalized "wisdom" people expect to get from philosophy. It may be a little late to tell you this, but philosophers aren't in the business of constructing wise sayings. We leave that to the people who write bumper stickers. The first job of philosophy is to question what other people take as given. Philosophy is the doubting profession.

> *I am plagued by doubts. What if everything is an illusion and nothing exists? In that case, I definitely overpaid for my carpet.*[1]

---

1   Woody Allen, "Selections from the Allen Notebooks" in *Without Feathers* (New York: Warner Books, 1976), p. 10.

Printed in Canada